THE TABERNACLE

A Personal Journey

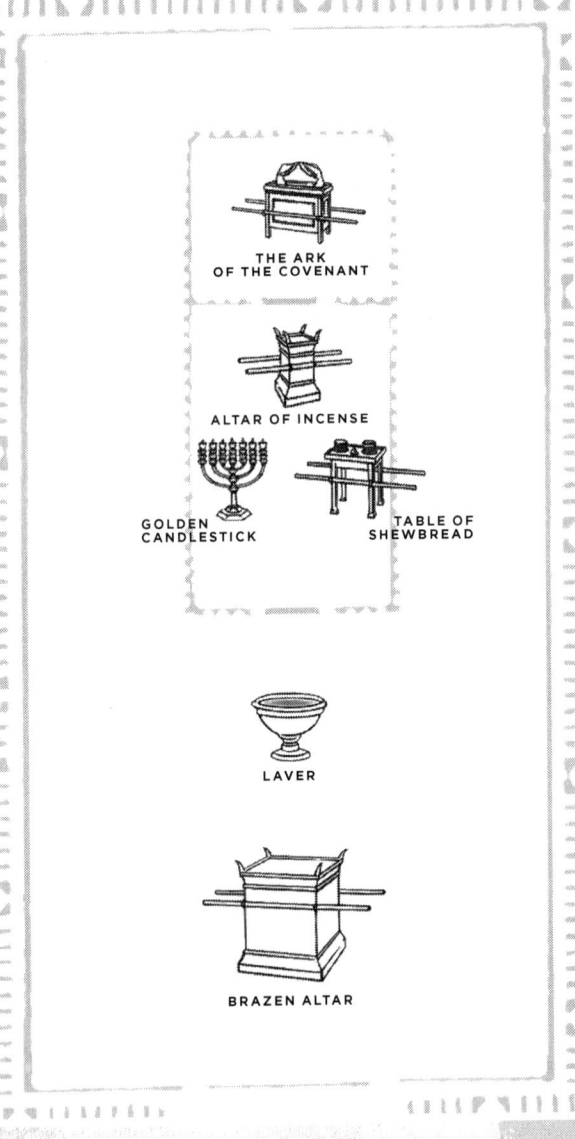

THE TABERNACLE

A Personal Journey

GINNY EMERY

The Tabernacle: A Personal Journey
© 2022 by Virginia B. Emery

All rights reserved. Reproduction of portions of the text (excluding scripture and quotations copyrighted by others) for study and devotion is welcome to extend the kingdom of God, but all copying or reprinting for commercial gain is forbidden by conscience and copyright law.

Unless otherwise noted, all scriptures are from The Holy Bible, Berean Study Bible, BSB Copyright ©2016, 2018, 2019 by Bible Hub. Used by Permission. All Rights Reserved Worldwide.

Scripture quotations marked AMP are taken from the Amplified ® Bible, Copyright © 1954 1958, 1962, 1964, 1965, 1987 by the Lockman Foundation. Used by Permission (www.Lockman.org).

Scripture quotations marked BLB are taken from The Holy Bible, Berean Literal Bible, Copyright ©2016, 2020 by Bible Hub. Used by Permission. All Rights Reserved Worldwide.

Scripture quotations marked CEV are taken from the CONTEMPORARY ENGLISH VERSION, Copyright © 1995 by the American Bible Society. Used by Permission.

Scripture quotations marked ESV are taken from The Holy Bible, English Standard Version® (ESV®), Copyright © 2001 by Crossway, a publishing ministry of Good News Publishers. Used by permission. All rights reserved.

Scripture quotations marked LSB are taken from the Literal Standard Version of the Holy Bible, Copyright © 2020 of Covenant Press and the Covenant Christian Coalition. Life Sentence Publishing, Inc. Used by permission of Life Sentence Publishing, Inc., Abbotsford, Wisconsin. All rights reserved.

Scripture quotations marked NASB are taken from are from the New American Standard Bible®, Copyright © 1960, 1962,1963,1968,1971,1973,1975, 1977, 1995 by the Lockman Foundation. Used by permission.

Scripture quotations marked (NIV) are taken from THE HOLY BIBLE, NEW INTERNATIONAL VERSION®, NIV® Copyright © 1973, 1978, 1984, 2011 by Biblica, Inc.™ Used by permission of Zondervan. All rights reserved worldwide.

Scripture quotations marked (NKJV) are taken from the New King James Version®. Copyright © 1982 by Thomas Nelson, Inc. Used by permission. All rights reserved.

Scripture quotations marked (Mof) are from the James Moffatt, A New Translation of the Bible, Containing the Old and New Testaments. New York: Doran, 1926. Revised edition, New York and London: Harper and Brothers, 1935. Reprinted, Grand Rapids: Kregel, 1995.

Public Domain Scriptures marked YLT are taken from the 1898 Youngs Literal Translation of the Holy Bible by J.N. Young. Scriptures marked WEB are taken from The World English Bible. Scriptures marked WNT are taken from the Weymouth New Testament by Richard Francis Weymouth.

Some Bible versions use initial capital letters for pronouns referring to divinity and capitalize the names LORD for the name Adonai and GOD for Jehovah or Yahweh, the Hebrew name for God.

I am grateful for permission to quote from James Goll, *The Lost Art of Intercession*, ©2007 by James Goll. All rights reserved. Used by permission of Destiny Image Publishers, Shippensburg PA 17257 and for permission to quote from Rex Andrews, *What the Bible Teaches about Mercy*, © by Zion Faith Homes. All rights reserved. Used by permission of Zion Faith Homes, Zion, Illinois.

To my knowledge, all other published quotations footnoted in the book are in the public domain.

Ginny Emery
Given Word: www.givenwordnow.com

Book Design: Peter Gloege
Cover & Interior Images: Dreamstime, iStock, ShutterStock

ISBN: 978-0-9676193-3-0 (paperback)
ISBN: 978-0-9676193-4-7 (eBook)

Printed in the United States of America

Dedicated to you, the reader

*May the Lord bless you and keep you.
May the Lord cause his face to shine upon you
and be gracious to you;
May the Lord lift up his countenance toward you
and give you peace. Numbers 6:24-26*

AUTHOR'S NOTE & ACKNOWLEDGMENTS

Around 1440 BC, in an unusual mountain top encounter, God told Moses exactly how to build a tabernacle. Moses followed God's directions exactly. Then, he wrote about it in the Pentateuch. His records survive in the Jewish Torah and the Christian Bible. About 3,500 years later, in 1980, glimpses of the beauty and significance of Moses's tabernacle moved off the pages of history and into my heart as I took a class on the tabernacle. I saved my class notes.

In January of 2020, I wanted those notes. I searched the basement and was delighted to find a yellow folder with every page. I needed them to share in an ecumenical Bible study with a group of elderly friends who were studying the Book of Hebrews. As we talked about the tabernacle and Moses's

> *testimony of those things which would be spoken of afterward.*
> *Hebrews 3:5 NKJV*

I happened to mention that the tabernacle pictured Jesus. My friends were surprised. They'd gone to church all their lives and had never heard a word about it. Eagerly interested to know more, they all wanted to interrupt our study of Hebrews and learn about Jesus and the tabernacle. To prepare for our next meeting, I entered my handwritten answer to a forty-year-old final exam question, "Discuss Christ in the Tabernacle" into the computer. As I typed, new thoughts, scriptures and personal illustrations began to flow. I added a personal introduction, and at our next meeting I read the first pages to my friends. Interest in the tabernacle continued to rise and our discussion was lively. The next week, I wrote more and revised my manuscript to answer their questions and clarify fuzzy spots. At meetings, Jesus felt near as the Holy Spirit opened our eyes to God's long-range planning. We saw that Moses's tabernacle was evidence of God's purposeful intervention in human history. Knowing that the Holy Spirit was teaching us, we all continued to want more, so I kept on writing and reading my essays to my friends.

Then covid-19 shut down our meetings. While sheltering-in-place, I wrote on, adding more insights, illustrations and personal comments. I used my class notes, began to read the Bible more closely and browsed on-line articles to answer questions and fill in gaps. After many revisions, I shared the manuscript with my pastor and others. Their feedback helped me finish the text you are reading.

One question asked by several early readers was, "How much is yours and how much is from your notes?" Although my fifty-six pages of scrawled large handwritten notes grew into a two-hundred-seventy-page manuscript, the original organization came from the class. I supplemented the framework in my notes with more facts, scriptures, imaginative recreations, personal illustrations and perspectives. Fresh (to me) insights came while writing. Again and again, the Holy Spirit taught me, led me and fed me.

Much information on the tabernacle is accepted as "common knowledge", but not all "common knowledge" is accurate. In reading about the tabernacle, I found sound Bible support for many prophetic comparisons between the tabernacle, Jesus and the church. However, tabernacle studies and preaching also include a long tradition of devotional suppositions.

Some stretch the imagination and ignore facts. But many of these inferences are fascinating possibilities, illustrations consistent with biblical truth but not supported by specific scriptures. To scholars in search of minute accuracy, not every illustration and parallel between Jesus and the tabernacle is credible. But I'm more poet than scholar; metaphors, parables and abstract fancies are more plausible to me than to concrete thinkers. I did my best to avoid error and to note all unsupported thoughts, trusting in my reader's discernment if any slipped through. As both writer and Christian, I feel very small and inadequate before the mystery of God's revelation to mankind. We see through a glass dimly—not only Jesus, but all of reality and all of the unity and harmony inherit in the things of God.

I'm grateful for suggestions from Tom Severson, Peter Payne, Dan Rak, Lorin Olsen and Kathleen Trock-Molhoek. Feedback from my Michigan Bible study friends, especially Margaret Hoeft, Sandy DeRosset and Lilli Miller encouraged me to keep revising and amplifying. Susan Luckhardt's listening ear influenced every page. Martha Wilson's supportive editing sustained me. And Kathryn Riss's editing and input on the final drafts helped me to clarify fuzzy thinking, correct significant mistakes and fill in omissions. When energy for the last lap lagged, God supported me with continuing prayer from Lila Bishop, the Elgin Vineyard Prayer Altar and my dear friend Kathleen.

Two readers noted my wide, shotgun approach (my word) and wanted me to focus on a particular target audience. I wanted to comply. But as a random thinker, I couldn't figure out how to do that without dumbing it down and losing my voice. The biblical record lays a foundation of historical truth. The allegorical-typological insights turn our thoughts to Jesus and reveal the unity, harmony and purpose of God's ways. Imaginative recreations enliven the text. And surprisingly, my friends wanted both the historical facts and my personal ramblings and experiences. They said my digressions brought the tabernacle truths to life. As a writer, many repetitions bothered me, but friends who are unfamiliar with the material repeatedly reassured me that the repetitions helped them learn. If the mixture bothers you, I hope you will skim through to find what the Holy Spirit might say that is just for you.

Everything about the tabernacle points toward Jesus. His life and death fulfilled much of the prophetic symbolism that God commanded Moses to build into it. Although Jesus's death did away with the need for a physical temple, his followers are continuing to fulfill the tabernacle symbolism directed by God. God does not change; thousands of years have not changed his heavenly specifications. As a result, believers have hungrily studied the tabernacle for centuries, seeking to uncover all the buried treasure in this portion of God's word. A rich cache of far more scholarly and complete discussions on the tabernacle's significance is available in books and on the internet. Apart from my own experiences and observations, I've added little that is new. So why am I publishing this?

First, I think God wants it published for others. Second, as I wrote about the tabernacle, I felt Jesus drawing near. That led me to hope that others will sense his loving reality as they read these pages. Third, scripture came to life as I wrote; I hope it will come alive to readers, too. Fourth, I need structure, but I'm tired of books about Christian methods—methods to pray, to evangelize, to heal and deliver others, methods to hear from God and so on. The tabernacle teaches God's method—God's pattern. Following it leads to Jesus. I like that! I want to share that insight. Learning that everything in the tabernacle prefigured Jesus and his Church is encouraging. Understanding what God wants gives me a goal. He wants all who live to know his ways and to move into the holy of holies, to see the glory of God on earth as it is in Heaven and know the fullness of God's mercy to us in Christ Jesus.

TABLE OF CONTENTS

INTRODUCTION 1
THE TABERNACLE'S IMPORTANCE: *A Neglected Truth* 5
CHRIST AND HIS WORK AS SEEN IN THE TABERNACLE 15
    The Tabernacle's Holiness 22
    The Tabernacle in the Camp 31
    The Tabernacle's Portability 36
    The Tabernacle's Layout from an Aerial Perspective 42
    The Tabernacle Materials and Colors: *An Overview* 45
    The Value of the Tabernacle 47
    Approaching the Tabernacle: *Praise* 48

THE COURT YARD 57
    The Tabernacle Fence and Curtains 57
    The Silver of Redemption 59
    The Tabernacle Doors 62
    The Pillars 63
    The Brass Pins 63
    The Veils 69
    Looking Around: *More Outer Court Thoughts* 72
    The Brazen Altar: *The Cross* 75
    The Fire 89
    The Laver 95
    The Water 95
    Getting Clean 97

THE TWO COURTS: *Thoughts on Inner & Outer Court Ministries* 111
    The Inner Court: *It's Structure* 139
    The Foundation 140
    The Walls 148
    The Tabernacle Coverings or Roof 149
    The Tachashim Skins: *The Outer Protective Humble Covering* 152
    The Rams' Skins Dyed Red: *Our Shepherd and Blood Sacrifice* 158
    The Goat Hair: *Our Scapegoat Substitute* 160

- Fine Twined Linen of Love: *Purity and Righteousness* 165
- The Inner Court: *The Lampstand* 166
- The Oil 173
- The Gold 181
- The Lampstand Itself 183
- The Light and Wicks 184
- Inner Court Memories 192
- The Inner Court: *The Table of Showbread* 195
- The Golden Altar of Incense 215
- The Horns of the Altar 238
- The Golden Crown 239
- The Inner Court: *A Few More Thoughts* 240

THE HOLY OF HOLIES 249
- The Veil of Cherubim 252

THE ARK OF THE COVENANT 271
- Inside the Ark 276
- The Manna 276
- Aaron's Rod that Budded 282
- The Stone Tablets 285
- The Mercy Seat 296
- Jesus is God's Mercy to Us 296
- Recognizing and Receiving God's Mercy 305

A WAVE OF WORSHIP: *Final Thoughts and Looking Forward* 313
- God's Timetable 319

AN AFTERWORD 337
APPENDIX 339
- 1: Why is the Brazen Altar That Important? 339
- 2: Inwardness 349
- 3: Spirit Baptism 350
- 4: Abiding 363
- 5: The Stone Tablets 366
- 6: Faith 368
- 7: Worship 370

INTRODUCTION

One warm morning in May 1967, when the blue sky was cloudless and green leaves were opening on the trees, I walked out of my familiar life into a different reality—one filled with peace, harmony, beauty and meaning. Everything from the music on the radio, my morning coffee, my children, and the Chicago Tribune's horse racing results fit into a seamless, beautiful, inter-connected, purposeful and ordered whole.

It was a one-time experience. I don't live inside of such harmony and insight. God's grace has steadied me through decades of ordinary hours, teaching me to find faith, beauty, peace and joy in the midst of stress, uncertainty, tough decisions, responsibilities, pain and fatigue. I am grateful for the Holy Spirit's comfort, support and guidance for an aging body through routine days.

But in studying the tabernacle in detail, my hours and days came alive in a new way as the Holy Spirit moved me into another powerful experience of seeing the harmony, beauty, meaning, purpose and order in God's ways. It was qualitatively different from my first experience. The first could not be shared. I hope the second experience, revealed in these tabernacle studies, will come alive for you as you read these pages.

I love it when the Lord breaks through humdrum circumstances with unexpected revelations of himself. He talks to us in countless ways: through dreams and visions, books, songs, words from others, relationships, nature, answered prayers and always, the Bible. Sometimes, he intervenes in our own lives, like the day he dissolved a friend's tumor as we prayed or the time he supernaturally changed an impossible situation to help a friend rise above intentional opposition and start a successful business. She did it with no finances at an age when most of us would retire. Another time, the Holy Spirit told my husband and me to buy a particular house in another state and reordered events to move us there.

Such breakthroughs let us know that God cares for us personally. When some of us first begin to believe in God, Jesus and the Holy Spirit all that we may see or care about is our own experience of their love, of getting our prayers answered and receiving the Holy Spirit's gifts. But, as we grow-up to know and love God for himself and not for what he does for us, the Holy Spirit opens our eyes to see that God's personal loving kindness and plans for us are part of his long-term, large-scale historical plans, plans that were recorded in scripture thousands of years ago.

That's only one reason why the tabernacle is relevant. Truth-seekers who begin to look at the Bible through the lenses of secular education and upbringing will automatically filter God's word through astigmatic eyes. They've been taught differently. We all need to be taught. We all see through distorted lenses at times. As the Holy Spirit teaches us, he opens our eyes, often with amazement, to discover that God's word is true. It may take paradigm shifts and a great deal of new information before minds steeped in relativism and materialism can accept how fully and consistently the Bible record of creation agrees with reliable scientific truth.[1] Only the Holy Spirit can open our eyes to God's spiritual truths.

---

[1] See any of astrophysicist Hugh Ross's books. A couple titles to check out are *Why the Universe is the Way it Is, Beyond the Cosmos* and *More than a Theory*. Since I first wrote this, Eric Metaxas published *Is Atheism Dead*, a well-documented easy-to-read summary of scientific, archeological and logical proofs that all point to God. Salem Books, 2021

Eventually, if we're teachable, I've read that the Holy Spirit will reveal the reality of Jesus to us on every page of scripture.

In recent centuries, as believers have watched Bible descriptions of the last days unfold before our eyes, God's word has alarmed many culturally influential unbelievers into flat-out dismissals and denials of scripture. Glimpsing the tabernacle truths about God's holiness and learning about the long-range loving kindness and mercy in God's plan has potential to disarm these denials in reasonable minds. God's truth, quickened by the Holy Spirit, sets free. It releases the supernatural courage our generation needs to face sin's realities, accept God's redemptive love and escape his judgments. We all need the Holy Spirit to rest on God's truth and open our eyes to what the historical fulfillment of God's Old Testament object lesson to Israel means for us today.

Truth encounters with God's word take humility, courage and honesty. It gets in our face, insistently asking us to confront our denials and think through the consequences of our own beliefs, values and choices.

The tabernacle is only one of many Old Testament prophecies about Jesus that reveal that God was, is and always will be in charge. It was impossible for human imagination or creativity to design and build the tabernacle. In detail after detail, God's directions to Moses specified specific, startlingly clear prophetic symbolism about his plan for Jesus's earthly life and gruesome death. This place of God's presence among the children of Israel is a unified, symbolic picture of Jesus that undeniably foreshadows God's well-thought-out plan for our redemption—his intent to set us free from slavery to the world, the flesh and the devil, to show us his glory, to win our worship, and reunite us with himself.

THE TABERNACLE'S IMPORTANCE:
A Neglected Truth

God's word is not dead. His truth, as recorded in scripture, is every bit as alive at this very moment as it was when first chiseled on tablets of stone and penned on scrolls of papyrus. The Old Testament was written for us.

> *For all that was written of old has been written for our instruction, so that we may always have hope through the power of endurance and the encouragement which the Scriptures afford. Romans 15:4 WEY*

> *Now these things happened to them as an example, and they were written for our instruction, upon whom the ends of the ages have come. 1 Corinthians 10:11 NASB 1977*

> *Every scripture is inspired by God and is useful for teaching, for convincing, for correction of error, and for instruction in right doing. 2 Timothy 3:16 WEY*

Surprisingly, God wrote more about the little tabernacle Moses built in the wilderness of the Sinai Peninsula than about creation, salvation, healing, Jesus's second coming or any other doctrine in the entire Bible (except, it seems to me, God's merciful loving kindness). It must be highly significant instruction from the Holy Spirit.

God's emphasis on tabernacle worship was part of a change in world view that God wanted to instill into Israel. He succeeded. Through Israel, God has blessed the world. Many of his values and perspectives have now become so thoroughly ingrained into western civilization we take them for granted.

One change was the view of time. Until Moses, our ancient ancestors in almost every tribe and nation viewed time as Buddhists and Hindus do today. They saw time as circular, repetitive, like a clock, like the seasons of springtime and fall, sowing and harvest, death and rebirth.

Israel's deliverance from slavery shot holes into that paradigm of time and shocked the surrounding nations. God's miraculous intervention to free the slaves from Egypt and his visit to the Sinai mountain-top were clearly unrepeatable one-time events. The Hebrew's God defied the pattern of cyclical thought. He was qualitatively different from the collection of fertility gods peopling the ancient world. The reality of God's presence in the cloud and fire hovering over the tabernacle in the middle of Israel's camp confirmed both God's uniqueness and the concept of linear time to Abraham's descendants. They knew that God had told Abraham that they would be enslaved and set free.

> *Your descendants will be strangers in a land that is not their own, and they will be enslaved and mistreated four hundred years. Genesis 15:13*

Israel's deliverance from Egypt and God's continued protective presence in their midst helped strengthen and establish the Hebraic view that historical time, while linear, is not measured by dates alone. Time is also measured by God-events: by divine, one-time markers in human history. For the Israelites, these God-events began with creation.

Human history started with Adam, who lived for an unspecified amount of time in a perfect garden. Then (as recorded in Genesis), history moved through a succession of God-encounters: Adam's expulsion from the Garden, his meeting with Cain and Abel, Seth's birth and Noah's ark. God's historical plan continued to unfold through Noah's son, Shem, right down through the generations to their own patriarch, Father Abraham.

When God amazingly met with Moses and the leaders of Israel, just as he had once met with Adam, Enoch, Noah and Abraham, he did not repeat himself. His intervention was purposeful and forward looking. Israel's history was not like the mythologies of other nations, where threads of divine truth and interventions in history were embellished in weavings of human imagination. The Hebrew world view was based on a clearer, cleaner, less humanly contaminated sequence of oral history. A comparison between the epic of Gilgamesh and the biblical narrative is one major example of this.[2] Hebrew history was based on an oral tradition of true stories about once living people whose life events were significant, sequential markers of God-encounters throughout the passage of what we call time.

Not only did God's view of time suggest a new, expanded paradigm, so did God's view of the sanctity of human life. Moses knew it. When Moses' said yes to God at the burning bush,[3] he shook off the last traces of Egyptian values and embraced the God of Abraham, Isaac and Jacob. He accepted God's call to pro-actively challenge the ancient world-system, the enslavement system of idolatry. And God won. The slaves were set free—at least physically. But, their adaptation to the prevailing spirit over Egyptian culture had mentally, emotionally and spiritually wrecked

---

2 https://www.compellingtruth.org/Gilgamesh-flood.html

3 You can read about it in Genesis 3

many of them. Their thinking had been shaped by centuries of slavery. They didn't want God; idolatrous Egyptian thinking still bound their souls. Like little children who haven't learned the difference between right and wrong, they needed teaching. They needed to learn God's rules and patterns of worship to help them grow-up into the responsibility of faith and freedom.

God responded by giving Moses laws and ordinances that were specifically designed to teach the Israelite children how to live together in health and harmony. He directed Moses to build the tabernacle for worship in a divinely-given pattern. Tabernacle worship showed a nation with an idolatrous slave-mentality how to live in freedom and avoid future enslavement. It protected them from being ambushed and subjugated by the lusts and cruelties of the idolatrous nations around them. It taught clear differences between right and wrong and provided for forgiveness, not retribution. It offered individual and community safety in repentance instead of harsh punishment for breaking God's laws. It showed them how to connect with God.

God had a plan for these Hebrew slaves: a plan to answer his promise to Abraham and bless the world. I wonder how much Moses knew. He surely knew that obeying God's laws would bring God's presence and protection and foster healthy, loving, community living. Did he ever imagine that the ten simple laws God gave Israel would prove so trustworthy and reliable that they would eventually change the moral outlooks and legal systems of billions of people?[4]

---

4 To support this, I recommend *The Book that Made Your World: How the Bible Created the Soul of Western Civilization* by Vishal Mangalwadi, Thomas Nelson, 2011. With the clear sight of an outsider, Mangalwadi, an Indian philosopher, describes how our political, social and economic vision arose from a biblical world view. How modern science, medicine, education and technology are the fruit of Judeo-Christian faith. And how biblical principles and compassion have birthed and nurtured our values of human dignity and human rights and driven our sense of social justice and freedom for all. He warns how the current rejection of Bible truth and changing worldviews based on individualism, immanence and humanism threaten the strength, order, unity, purpose and heart that built and sustained civilization as we've known it.

God's Ten Commandments and the pattern for tabernacle worship began a lasting change of mindset for western civilization. Tabernacle worship and feasts are profoundly concrete and natural. They conform to familiar cycles of planting and harvest, sunrise and sunset, and the phases of the moon. Tabernacle worship is also intensely spiritual. It pictures the possibility of meeting with God, of inviting one-time life-changing God-events and encounters for people and nations.[5] Finally, it is prophetically significant for world history, because the tabernacle symbolism looks ahead in a linear fashion toward a distant future when all worship will focus on Jesus's love.

The tabernacle was a step in God's progressive revelation of himself. It anticipates a day when Israel's redemptive story will culminate in God's final judgment for those who refuse his law of love. In that day, God will welcome all who have learned to love him and others into eternal glory.

Thus, the tabernacle incorporated the natural reasonability of the circular and then transcended it by inviting God into our lives. It was purposefully goal directed. It illuminates how we are to approach God today in preparation for the culmination of all things in Jesus Christ, who said,

> *Behold, I am coming quickly, and My reward is with Me, to give to everyone according to his work. I am the Alpha and the Omega, the Beginning and the End, the First and the Last. Revelation 22:12-13 NKJV*

Why else is the tabernacle important? It's a concrete visualization that's all about God's heavenly pattern for worship. It also pictures God's

---

[5] Please, please read the inspiring account of how William Wilberforce became the conscience of England and eventually changed our entire civilization's view of slavery in *Amazing Grace: William Wilberforce and the Heroic Campaign to End Slavery*, by Eric Metaxas, Harper, 2007.

eternal plan to redeem Adam's offspring from the curse of sin[6] and to win a holy bride for his Son.

The tabernacle shows us God's glory and symbolizes God's plan to bring us, Adam's wayward children, back home to himself, our heavenly Father. God's family is not a natural one, born of flesh in the image and likeness of humanity, but is a family born of the Spirit into the exact image and likeness of our Father God. It's clear that God knew all this. He provided for it before the beginning of time. The pattern of worship God gave to Moses

> *is a copy and shadow of what is in heaven. This is why Moses was warned when he was about to build the tabernacle: "See to it that you make everything according to the pattern shown you on the mountain." Hebrews 8:5*

As a copy of the tabernacle in heaven, the tabernacle in the wilderness teaches us that Jesus's death on the cross was planned before the beginning of time. Centuries before Jesus's life and death, he was prefigured in God's exact specifications for the tabernacle. The tabernacle symbolically illustrated God's holiness, justice and mercy to a people familiar with the servitude and domination in an unholy merciless culture where gods were expiated by animal and human sacrifice. Thus, the tabernacle testifies to God's omniscience. From his overarching view outside of time, God knew that Adam and all his family would rebel against his love. He deliberately chose to work through Israel's descendants to prepare the earth for Jesus, who came to bridge the distance between God's love and humankind.

This is so vital that I'm repeating myself. The tabernacle is concrete

---

6   Since the word sin and entire concept of sin are out of favor today, I want to clarify what I mean by *sin*. Because no other word can take its place, I use it often. To me, sin is all that is inconsistent with or falls short of God's holy loving character, nature and will. We're all sinners. See *Words to Know* at https://givenwordnow.com/downloads/

evidence that Jesus's death at Passover wasn't optional.[7] God's plan to save mankind from sin wasn't a last-ditch choice made after Adam sinned; it was foreordained in heaven. John described Jesus as

> *The Lamb slain from the foundation of the world.*
> *Revelation. 13:8b NKJV*

The tabernacle confirms the necessity of Jesus's blood sacrifice—the drops of blood on Gethsemane's ground when he died to his own will, the bloodshed in both Herod's and Pilate's precincts, the blood that must have marked the Via Delarosa as he carried the cross and the blood that spilled forth at Golgotha. All were prophetically pictured when

> *[Moses] sprinkled with blood the tabernacle and all the vessels used in worship. According to the law, in fact, nearly everything must be purified with blood, and without the shedding of blood there is no forgiveness. So, it was necessary for the copies of the heavenly things to be purified with these sacrifices, but the heavenly things themselves with better sacrifices than these.*
> *Hebrews 9: 21-23*

The tabernacle is also one of the earliest scriptural revelations about the throne room in heaven. Books about near-death experiences and visits to heaven make bestseller lists because so many of us want assurance that heaven is real and wonder what it's like. Often people who return to earth from near death experiences describe seeing Jesus or meeting

---

[7] Relativists find that the idea of sin and the need for Jesus's death to free them from a bondage they can't recognize or acknowledge is quite strange, perhaps off-putting. If you've read thus far and find yourself questioning my world view, I ask you to please keep an open mind and read on. Much in life is relative, but not all. While various faiths assert different world views and absolutes, the evidence of divine forethought in the tabernacle and the anecdotal evidence of my own personal spiritual journey might help you to understand a world view based on Christian absolutes. There is historical and personal evidence supporting the idea that because all of us sin, that is, fall short of the glory of God's holy love, Jesus's blood sacrifice for our sin was a necessity.

loved ones who have died, but very few mention the throne room. It's clear that their experiences were not the glory described by Isaiah, Daniel or John. We shouldn't be surprised. Jesus told us,

> *In My Father's house are many rooms [mansions]. If it were not so, would I have told you that I am going there to prepare a place for you? And if I go and prepare a place for you, I will come back and welcome you into My presence, so that you also may be where I am. John 14: 2-3*

Our places, our personal spaces in heaven are not quite the same as God's. A study of the tabernacle moves from the outer courts into the inner courts and ends up in the holy of holies, a room designed to typify God's throne. The Holy Spirit wants us to know about this holiest of all holy places and longs to give us a fuller experience of the glory of God that fills his temple. He wants us to understand the serious significance of God's filling a temple with himself.

Every temple in Jerusalem was built to be the place of God's presence: the first temple of King Solomon's (950-586 BC), the second temple, built by Zerubbabel and Nehemiah (517 BC), the future temple prophesied by Ezekiel and Herod's temple, which Jesus declared was to be a House of Prayer. (38 BC to 70 AD).[8]

Each temple also reveals a facet of Jesus's person, life or ministry. Because each temple pointed to Jesus, not one ever was or could have become an end in itself. All (except Ezekiel's, which is either symbolic or hasn't been built yet), have been destroyed. While Jesus lived, he was God's dwelling place on earth. But when Jesus foretold the destruction

---

8   Every temple except Ezekiel's has been destroyed. Bible scholars don't know if Ezekiel's Temple is symbolic, is totally spiritual or won't be built until Jesus' returns to earth in His second coming.

of Herod's corrupted temple[9] in Jerusalem, he knew that destroying the physical temple in Jerusalem didn't do away with the need for a temple on earth. By taking his blood to heaven on our behalf, Jesus made it possible for us to become God's temple, his habitation. Purified by his blood, we can become a very special dwelling place for his presence on earth.

> *According to the law, in fact, nearly everything must be purified with blood, and without the shedding of blood there is no forgiveness. So, it was necessary for the copies of the heavenly things [the tabernacle] to be purified with these sacrifices [of animals], but the heavenly things themselves with better sacrifices than these. For Christ did not enter a man-made copy of the true sanctuary, but He entered heaven itself, now to appear on our behalf in the presence of God. Hebrews 9: 22-24*

Jesus went before us as God's dwelling place on earth. The tabernacle and Jerusalem temples were God's Old Covenant dwelling place on the earth. Jesus was God's New Covenant dwelling place on earth. Today, as we turn toward Father God, as we choose to unite ourselves to Jesus, as we accept his holy love[10] for our brothers in sisters in Christ, and as we allow the Holy Spirit to have his way in our lives, we are not only God's family, we also become the living temple of the living God.

> *As God has said: "I will live with them and walk among them. I will be their God, and they shall be my people." Therefore, "Come out from among them and be separate, says the Lord. Do not touch what is unclean, and I will receive you. I will be a Father to you, And you shall be My sons and daughters, says the LORD Almighty." 2 Corinthians 6:15-18 NKJV*

---

9 This was fulfilled when the Roman army completely destroyed the temple in 70 AD,

10 For a rich introduction to holy love see *Holy Love: Finding and Becoming Holy Love* by Peter Payne. The booklet is available at https://givenwordnow.com/downloads/

THE ABERNACLE

> *Do you not know that you yourselves are God's temple, and that God's Spirit dwells in you? I Corinthians 3:16*

Thus, the tabernacle, a precursor of every temple and a type of Jesus's body, is full of prophetic insights for us as God's dwelling place on earth. Although Moses built the tabernacle and Solomon, Nehemiah and Herod built temples,

> *The Most High does not dwell in temples made with hands, as the prophet says: "Heaven is My throne, And earth is My footstool. What house will you build for Me? says the LORD, Or what is the place of My rest?" Acts 7:48, 49 NKJV*

God's people are his house, his temple, his own tent in the wilderness. As we live in him and he lives in us, we are to be the place of God's rest. Jesus said,

> *Come to Me, all you who are weary and burdened, and I will give you rest. Take My yoke upon you and learn from Me; for I am gentle and humble in heart, and you will find rest for your souls." Matthew 11:28-29*

and the writer of Hebrews taught that

> *There remains, then, a Sabbath rest for the people of God. For whoever enters God's rest also rests from his own work, just as God did from His. Hebrews 4: 9-10*

As we rest in God, God rests in us. We are to be his holy temple, his tabernacle and Jesus's body on earth. We are to carry God's presence and God's glory! That's important.

CHRIST AND HIS WORK AS SEEN IN THE TABERNACLE

Every aspect of the tabernacle in the wilderness speaks of Jesus Christ. As a pattern of heavenly truth, God left nothing to chance. The layout, design, dimensions, materials, construction details, colors—every tiny detail is meaningful. God planned the tabernacle to prepare the children of Israel and all believers through all time to see that Jesus, the Son of God, who was coexistent with the Father and slain from before the foundation of the world, is the sacrificial Passover lamb who died for our sins.

It matters that God directed only one tabernacle, one altar and one cross. The only place where man and God have fully met on earth was in Jesus Christ. Only in him will we find a place to meet fully with God today. When Jesus came, he was God's dwelling place on earth.

> *The Word became flesh, and made His dwelling [tabernacled] among us. We have seen His glory, the glory of the one and only Son from the Father, full of grace and truth. John 1:14*

The glory of God is a recurrent theme in discussing the tabernacle. God's glory is our goal, our motive and our purpose as believers. It's also our inheritance. And his glory is often misunderstood. For decades I pasted together random observations and thoughts with bits of Bible revelation and came up with my own semantic schema, my own ideas, about glory. I saw God's glory like a vision board with pictures that included the pure and shining gold of the holy of holies in the tabernacle and the glorified Christ in the Book of Revelation—a man with dazzling white hair, eyes like blazing fire, feet like highly polished bronze, and a voice that roared like the tumult of the sea or Niagara Falls. His face was blindingly brilliant, brighter than the shining noonday sun. (Revelation 1:14-16). I added the glory of his return to earth on magnificent clouds as well as large expressions of his natural-creation-glories like the Grand Canyon, Niagara Falls, volcanic eruptions, thunders and lightnings and the beauties of the earth. My pictures of glory included the wild activities of heaven, with flashes of light, cherubim and the continual calls of "Holy, Holy, Holy!" around a throne like jasper and carnelian. It sat on a sea of glass and was circled by a rainbow that gleamed and sparkled like the finest emerald. (Revelation 4: 2-3) To that, I added bits of supernatural revelation from Isaiah, Daniel and Ezekiel and bathed everything except the storms in glowing supernatural light, like the light in John's description of the New Jerusalem.

> *And the twelve gates were twelve pearls, with each gate consisting of a single pearl. The main street of the city was pure gold, as clear as glass. But I saw no temple in the city, because the Lord God Almighty and the Lamb are its temple. And the city has no need of sun or moon to shine on it, because the glory of God illuminates the city, and the Lamb is its lamp. By its light the nations will walk, and into it the kings of the earth will bring their glory. Revelation 21: 21-24*

That's all pretty glorious, isn't it? It's all true, but it doesn't say enough; it's incomplete. The Hebrew word for glory, *kabod,* means weight, splendor, copiousness, glory and honor. *Kabod* is all about reputation, what makes someone or something important. It's from a root that means heavy.[11] The Greek word for glory, *doxa*, is derived from words that mean radiance and suggest dignity, glory, honor, praise or worship.[12]

The English word for glory suggests super abundance.[13] That's Jesus! He's always more than enough. Because his humility was total and he did nothing without the Father, all that Jesus said or did was weighted with the glory of God.

The first time Jesus revealed his glory to his disciples, his eyes didn't blaze. He didn't call forth thunder and lightning or give his disciples visions of cherubim and emerald-like rainbows. It was at a wedding feast where the host had run out of wine. His mother went to Jesus and suggested he do something about it. Initially, Jesus put her off, saying, "It's not my time yet." Then, quietly, out sight of everyone but his disciples and a few servants, Jesus honored his mother's request and turned water into wine—lots and lots of wine—at least 120 gallons.[14]

> *On the third day a wedding took place at Cana in Galilee. Jesus's mother was there, and Jesus and His disciples had also been invited to the wedding. When the wine ran out, Jesus's mother said to him, "They have no more wine."*
>
> *"Woman, why does this concern us?" Jesus replied, "My hour has not yet come."*

---

[11] *Strong's Old Testament Hebrew Concordance*, No. 3519.

[12] *Strong's New Testament Greek Concordance*, No. 1391. The Greek word for glory, *doxa*, means an apparent or figurative dignity, glory, honor, praise or worship.

[13] In current American English the word *glory* suggests abundance and copiousness. English synonyms for glory include words such as copiousness, plentiful, ample, profuse, full, extensive, considerable, substantial, generous, lavish, fulsome, liberal, bountiful, overflowing, abounding, teeming, countless and innumerable. https://www.lexico.com/synonyms/copious

[14] The jars Jesus used to turn water into wine were those used for the Jewish rites of purification. At the last supper, before his death and resurrection, Jesus told his disciples that wine represented his blood, shed for them to cleanse them from sin.

His mother said to the servants, "Do whatever He tells you."

Now six stone water jars had been set there for the Jewish rites of purification. Each could hold from twenty to thirty gallons. Jesus told the servants, "Fill the jars with water."

So they filled them to the brim.

"Now draw some out," He said, "and take it to the master of the banquet."

They did so, and the master of the banquet tasted the water that had been turned into wine. He did not know where it was from, but the servants who had drawn the water knew. Then he called the bridegroom aside and said, "Everyone serves the fine wine first, and then the cheap wine after the guests are drunk. But you have saved the fine wine until now!"

Jesus performed this, the first of His signs, at Cana in Galilee. He thus revealed His glory, and His disciples believed in him. John 2: 1-11

John first saw Jesus's glory on earth as his young, beloved disciple. Decades later, as an elderly apostle writing the Book of Revelation, John described how he was lifted up to see glimpses of Jesus's heavenly glory, the glory John had once heard Jesus praying about shortly before his crucifixion, when he said,

And now, O Father, glorify me together with your self, with the glory which I had with you before the world was. John 17:5 NKJV

Jesus not only asked our Father to glorify him, he also asked God to give his glory to his disciples and to us. Jesus invites us to be with him and join him in his glory.

> *I am not asking on behalf of them [my disciples] alone, but also on behalf of those who will believe in Me through their message, that all of them may be one, as You, Father, are in Me, and I am in You. May they also be in Us, so that the world may believe that You sent Me.*
>
> *I have given them the glory You gave Me, so that they may be one as We are one—I in them and You in Me—that they may be perfectly united, so that the world may know that You sent Me and have loved them just as You have loved Me.*
>
> *Father, I want those You have given Me to be with Me where I am, that they may see the glory You gave Me because You loved Me before the foundation of the world. John 17: 20-24*

Day by day, Jesus wants to strengthen us with power from his glory. When his love lives and rules our hearts, and we abide in him, his glory will reside in us.

> *I ask that out of the riches of His glory He may strengthen you with power through His Spirit in your inner being, so that Christ may dwell in your hearts through faith. Then you, being rooted and grounded in love, will have power, together with all the saints, to comprehend the length and width and height and depth of the love of Christ, and to know this love that surpasses knowledge, that you may be filled with all the fullness of God. Ephesians 3:16-19*

When God told Moses how to build that little tent in the Sinai Peninsula, he was preparing the way for us to move into the glory of worshipping Jesus. Although the actual tabernacle, with all the furniture, rituals and animal sacrifices disappeared centuries ago, it prophetically symbolized God's progressive, historical revelation of eternal patterns for worshipping Jesus in Spirit and in truth.

> *Then I looked, and I heard the voices of many angels and living creatures and elders encircling the throne, and their number was myriads of myriads and thousands of thousands. In a loud voice they were saying:*
>
> *"Worthy is the Lamb who was slain,*
> *to receive power and riches*
> *and wisdom and strength and honor*
> *and glory and blessing!"*
>
> *And I heard every creature in heaven, and on earth, and under the earth, and in the sea, and all that is in them, saying:*
> *"To him who sits on the throne and to the Lamb*
> *be praise and honor and glory and power forever and ever!"*
> *And the four living creatures said, "Amen," and the elders fell down and worshiped. Revelation 5: 11-14*

I can't emphasize strongly enough that, as God's earthly dwelling place, the tabernacle was a type[15] of God's Son. It foreshadowed us, his worshipping family. As God's dwelling place on earth, the tabernacle was gloriously beautiful physically. When all the work on it was complete, God dwelt under the glory cloud that descended to fill it.

> *Then a cloud covered the tent of the congregation, and the glory of the Lord filled the tabernacle. And Moses was not able to enter into the tent of the congregation, because the cloud abode*

---

15 A type is a likeness, picture or representation of one thing or person by another. For example, Isaac, Joseph, David and Solomon are all types of Jesus. They represent him or facets of him. In different contexts, many words are interchangeable for *type*. They include foreshadow, prefigure, prophetic picture, represent, and illustrate. I use them all.

> *thereon, and the glory of the Lord filled the tabernacle. Exodus 40:34-35 KJV*

That very glory of our Creator's presence lived inside of Jesus. What a drawing power this compassionate, tender-hearted and humble man had as he went about healing the sick, delivering the demonized and preaching the good news of God's kingdom. After a leper openly told everyone of that Jesus had healed him,

> *Jesus could no longer enter a town in plain view, but He stayed out in solitary places. Yet people came to him from every quarter. Mark 1:45*

No wonder the priests were jealous of him.

> *It was out of envy that the chief priests had handed Jesus over. Mark 15:10*

Lord, please help us realize the truth of John's testimony when he wrote,

> *The Word became flesh and made His dwelling among us. We have seen His glory, the glory of the one and only Son from the Father, full of grace and truth. John 1:14*

At times (especially when I see believers acting and speaking without the humility, purity and the love of Jesus) it feels incredible to me that God entrusted Jesus's glory, the reputation of his name, to you and me. I don't know about you, but I'm not worthy. I make mistakes. I'm imperfect and falter in love. Lord, help your family on earth today. Help everyone who reads these words. We all need your power to turn away from our own ways and agree with yours. Teach us to live in humble, joyous, holy union with you. Give us your very own obedience of faith, hope and love in our relationship with you and with our Father in heaven.

> *But we have this treasure in earthen containers, so that the extraordinary greatness of the power will be of God and not from ourselves; 2 Corinthians 4:7 NASB*

Jesus's glory comes whenever the Holy Spirit helps us to do his will and to worship God in Spirit and truth. His presence always carries the weight of his glory. In his glory, he does what his love alone will do. When Jesus comes, people are healed, saved, delivered, encouraged, strengthened, taught, guided, comforted and fulfilled.

THE TABERNACLE'S HOLINESS

The tabernacle was holy. It was set apart. Holy, in Hebrew is *qodesh* or *kadosh*. It means to be set apart or separated to God. God is holy. He is set apart, distinct, of a completely other and different order than his entire creation. God is absolutely pure, clean and undefiled. People and things that are set apart from normal use for God's exclusive purposes are also holy. Every item in the tabernacle was described as holy—the rooms, the furniture, the utensils, the oil, the sacrifices, and the priests' holy garments.

A word picture for an adequate response to God's holiness is impossible. *Reverence* is the best word I can come up with. But what is *reverence*? Reflecting on words and phrases for reverence gives only a glimpse. Reverence for God contains deep respect, an untainted honor toward God and a profound carefulness in when he draws near. Reverence bends us low in totally sincere, worshipful regard before a greater presence than any other. True *reverence* springs naturally from a humbled heart. It's a flow of inexhaustible deference, loving obedience and a huge sense of awe.

Convincing reverence is rare. I've only seen it in a handful of believers. Each one had a personal history of experiencing God's heavenly glory and holiness. An unusual humility was written all over them. Humble reverence toward God is unmistakable and incredibly appealing. I recognize it, I've tasted of it, but I don't have it worked into my depths. It scares me, but I want it. Once, I saw a woman who knew God's glory power pick up a Bible that had accidently slipped onto the floor. A holy fear crossed her face; she bent down and dusted it off with great care. She handled it with unconscious grace and reverence. I instantly saw that that she knew God; she believed and reverenced his word in a way I'd never seen or thought possible for myself. Without a word spoken, I understood that I did not know the holy book or its author anywhere near as well as she did.

I wish I could share that holy moment with every reader. Like so many spiritual experiences, it's almost inexplicable. Being with her didn't set the standard discouragingly high or holy at all. It lifted me up. It was flavored with an awe that, in an earthly sense, reminds me of the joy of watching young Nureyev leap across the stage and land on his toes as gracefully light as a feather or listening to Renee Fleming sustain a high note to perfection or seeing a 10/10 skater or gymnast. It was an elevating sense of "Look what God can do inside a human being like me." Her humility and love brought a longing, a foretaste of heaven and a peaceful order. Comparisons were impossible and would have robbed the moment of God's presence. She was in her rightful place, I was in mine, Jesus loved us equally and my understanding of holiness was enlarged by that brief glimpse of her love and respect for God's word.

This concept of holiness, a separateness calling forth a reverence that's foreign to our modern, self-centered minds was built into the tabernacle.

It stood apart from the camp in a place all its own. A distance of one to three miles separated it from the tents of Israel. To approach it, the Israelites had to walk away from their own tents, their daily routines, positions and possessions. On reaching the tabernacle, they entered an area totally and exclusively dedicated to God. What does that suggest for us?

The space around the tabernacle reminds me that when Jesus wanted to find God's mind and pray, he often went to a space apart. He drew away from the crowds. He left all his close friends and family behind. That's God's design for us, too. Whether we're alone, in the midst of a great congregation, or with an intimate group of friends, when it's time to pray, to praise and to worship, the Holy Spirit wants us to turn away from distractions. He wants us to expect to see Jesus, to focus fully on him and not to look at each other.

Our unity with Jesus and other believers is not a clone-like, humanly orchestrated soulish agreement; it is always a unity in diversity. When Jesus draws near and we welcome the Holy Spirit, we don't forget about others, but in his presence we don't usually look around to see what they are doing. We look to Jesus. We might sit in silence, fall to our knees, stand to wave our arms, shout hallelujah, open our Bibles, speak what comes to say, or dissolve in tears. When we come together in unified worship, Jesus is our head. The Holy Spirit moves as he wills. We listen for him. There is an underlying order. At times, we will all be silent, at other times, some may pray, some will weep and others will laugh with joy. The Holy Spirit has joined entire congregations in harmonious spontaneous song or given groups a single voice in intercession. When our Lord orchestrates believers, the Holy Spirit himself becomes the form and structure of our meetings.[16] We follow his order, not vice versa; our

---

16 In sacramental worship the Holy Spirit can mysteriously fill, transcend and become the forms.

various gifts and individual differences are unified in him, not in any protocols, liturgical plans or outward uniformity. The Holy Spirit freely imparts a glorious humanly impossible agreement between his people and between heaven and earth.

The Father draws us to Jesus, Jesus calls us to love and adore his Father. The Holy Spirit facilitates our relationship with both the Father and the Son. Jesus longs to live in us with the same unity he enjoyed with our heavenly Father. He sent the Holy Spirit to teach us, guide us and strengthen us in the same obedience of faith and love that marked his own life.

We begin the journey toward this divine glory by choosing to leave our own tents. After Father God draws us to Jesus, our faith in Jesus plants a seed of the Holy Spirit within us. The Holy Spirit teaches us (if we want to learn) to yield to the grace of our Father and the Lord, Jesus Christ. As we lay down our own ways and choose Jesus, we begin to change. We find time and space for the Lord in the midst of our own busy lives. One of our first lessons from the Lord is to begin to learn to pray. As we talk with our Father and practice listening for his answers, he meets our needs. Often, as we worship him and wait on him in silence, our needs change, or we find that he has met them before we asked.

At times, the Holy Spirit may cry out through us like he did with Hannah, David, Jeremiah in the Book of Lamentations and Jesus at Gethsemane. The Spirit himself helps us to pour out the anguish in our hearts. But more often than we usually realize, the Holy Spirit wants our full attention on praising and worshipping Jesus. In worshipping him, we also worship our Father. As Jesus said,

> *Therefore, do not worry, saying, 'What shall we eat' or 'What shall we drink' or 'What shall we wear?' For the Gentiles strive after all these things, and your heavenly Father knows that*

you need them. But seek first the kingdom of God and His righteousness, and all these things will be added unto you. Matthew 6: 31-33

To digress a moment, what is the kingdom of God that we're to seek first? God's kingdom is not a specific geographical place or earth. His kingdom comes whenever and where ever he rules. God's kingdom comes wherever his love conquers hate, his forgiveness defeats vengeance, his truth destroys lies, or his compassion releases power to heal and restore the sick, broken and wounded. God's kingdom comes when divine comfort brings joy to those who mourn, when hope triumphs over despair, and when faith in God's most sovereign goodness replaces doubt and unbelief. I could go on. God's kingdom comes when light overcomes darkness, when building-up beats out destructive tearing-down, when peace prevails over violence and insanity flees before soundness of mind. It's law over lawless disorder and self-control over lust. God's kingdom breaks through whenever God replaces hate with love and overcomes death with faith in everlasting life. His kingdom comes into our hearts as we lay down our lives to let the Holy Spirit live in us. Jesus promised

Blessed are the poor in spirit, for theirs is the kingdom of heaven. Matthew 5:2 NASB

God's kingdom does not come to or through the proud or to the professional Christians who may act on their own to try to bring it in.[17] God's kingdom comes to the meek, the humble, to those whose self-life has been broken until they seek God for himself alone. His kingdom comes to those who are willing to wait like beggars before God, knowing

---

17 Despite occasional evidence to the contrary in men and women who, like King Saul, were anointed by God and, despite sin, continued to function in the office he gave them.

that they have nothing to give or offer of their own. His kingdom often comes in hidden ways through his tenderhearted hidden servants, men and women who seek no glory, credit, acknowledgment, affirmation or acceptance for themselves. And at times his kingdom breaks forth for all to see. Thousands were healed in Kathryn Kuhlman's meetings, yet I recall her honest beseeching voice over the radio repeatedly saying that without the Holy Spirit she was nothing. She could do nothing. In a tribute to her ministry, David Wilkinson wrote,

> *"Over and over again she cried:*
> *"Dear God, unless you anoint me and touch me I am nothing. I am worthless when the flesh gets in the way. You get all the glory or I cannot go out there and minister. I won't move without you."* [18]

God's kingdom breakthroughs come in many ways, but always Jesus is exalted. When Kathryn Kuhlman waited on the Holy Spirit and made Jesus real to people, God's kingdom came. Hundreds and hundreds of people were healed. People came to know Jesus. Thousands of lives were changed. God's kingdom breakthroughs often visibly follow repentance and intense intercession for revival. This happened in the Scottish Hebrides in 1949.[19] Sometimes, God's kingdom comes quietly, in humble, unseen acts of kindness or in faith for miracles and answers to prayer that few ever hear about. Sometimes, the Holy Spirit washes over us in waves of glory that are almost palpable. When that happens, it's not, like riding a roller coaster, an experience we walk away from, it's a life-transforming encounter. When the Holy Spirit helps us abandon ourselves to worshipping God, whether we wait in silence or our

---

[18] David Wilkerson from the Forward by to *Nothing is Impossible* with God by Kathryn Kuhlman, Bridge-Logos, Gainesville, FL, 1974, page ix

[19] https://annointing.files.wordpress.com

voices raise up in praise and worship, we sense the holiness of God filling the atmosphere around us. The very air we breathe is energized with his being.

For this, God wants our full attention. He wants us to walk away from all our distractions and appetites. We don't bring preoccupation with our cell phone-twitters and I-pad updates into worship, although we can worship with others via electronic media. And we can't expect to casually amble into God's arms munching on a bag of Tostitos, guzzling a diet Coke or sipping a gin and tonic. (Although, since God is God, he might surprise us. And since he's relational and loving, I'm sure that if communion bread and wine aren't available, he'd be glad to break a potato chip with us if we ate it in remembrance of him.) But, the principle behind tabernacle worship, the truth of it is, that God wants us to come apart to him. He doesn't want us to clutter prayer and worship with the paraphernalia of our daily lives. God asks us to give our anxious cares and distractions to him, to approach him intentionally, empty handed except for our sacrifices and offerings. As we move into his courts freely, by our own choice and in our own power, we enter a unique space, set aside and separate, holy as he is holy. The tabernacle courts are designed for us to center our full attention on God and acknowledge his rule.

Our time in God's courts strengthens God's indwelling life and our hold upon the truth that he is with us 24/7, even (paradoxically) in situations (like Jesus's crucifixion) where the evil one invades to attack and destroy and it might seem that God's not in charge. God does not leave us when we're occupied with challenges and everyday tasks. In every situation, his Spirit is alive inside of all who welcome him by faith.

In all circumstances, the Holy Spirit invites us to trust God and learn of Jesus. His kingdom will come, if we're willing to receive, to turn to him and agree with his Holy Spirit.

Although worship may lift us into realms of glory at times, God's Holy Spirit is intensely practical too. Last week, I sensed the Holy Spirit telling me to clean my desk and sort through files I'd not purged or reorganized for ten years. It was a huge job. I didn't think I could do it. He helped every step of the way. An orderly office might not seem like kingdom work, but it must have mattered to God. Nothing else was peaceful. He cleared my calendar; my friends weren't available for our weekly zoom call; other weekly interruptions were all canceled. Step by step I knew what to do and how to do it. Yes, it was work; I got tired. Yes, my back hurt, but his Spirit buoyed me repeatedly, with moments of praise, gratitude and joy for all that was done. As we follow Jesus and seek to rest in him, he is with us. Moment by moment, he brings stability and purpose through tedium, through uncertainty and trial and through hours of tremendous glory.

The tabernacle symbolism is all about moving us closer and closer to living in communion with God—full-time. It's about how the Holy Spirit transforms us from sinful creatures, existing apart from God, into cleansed saints whom the Lord welcomes as his own dear children. With great grace, his indwelling Holy Spirit helps us in practical matters like paying bills and washing the dishes as well as inviting us to stand before the Lord within the holy of holies, the place where we will fall on our faces and tremble with awe before the Creator of universes, the place where we're struck dumb with his unimaginable brilliance and power; the place of God's presence where, but for God's grace and mercy, life would be unsustainable for our human flesh.

Got it? With that in mind, we can begin to approach the tabernacle courts just as we are, reluctant and defensive, eager and glad or hurting and broken. It doesn't matter if we're indifferent, curious, unbelieving, sinful, needy, pouting, grumbling, weeping or filled with grateful joy. God

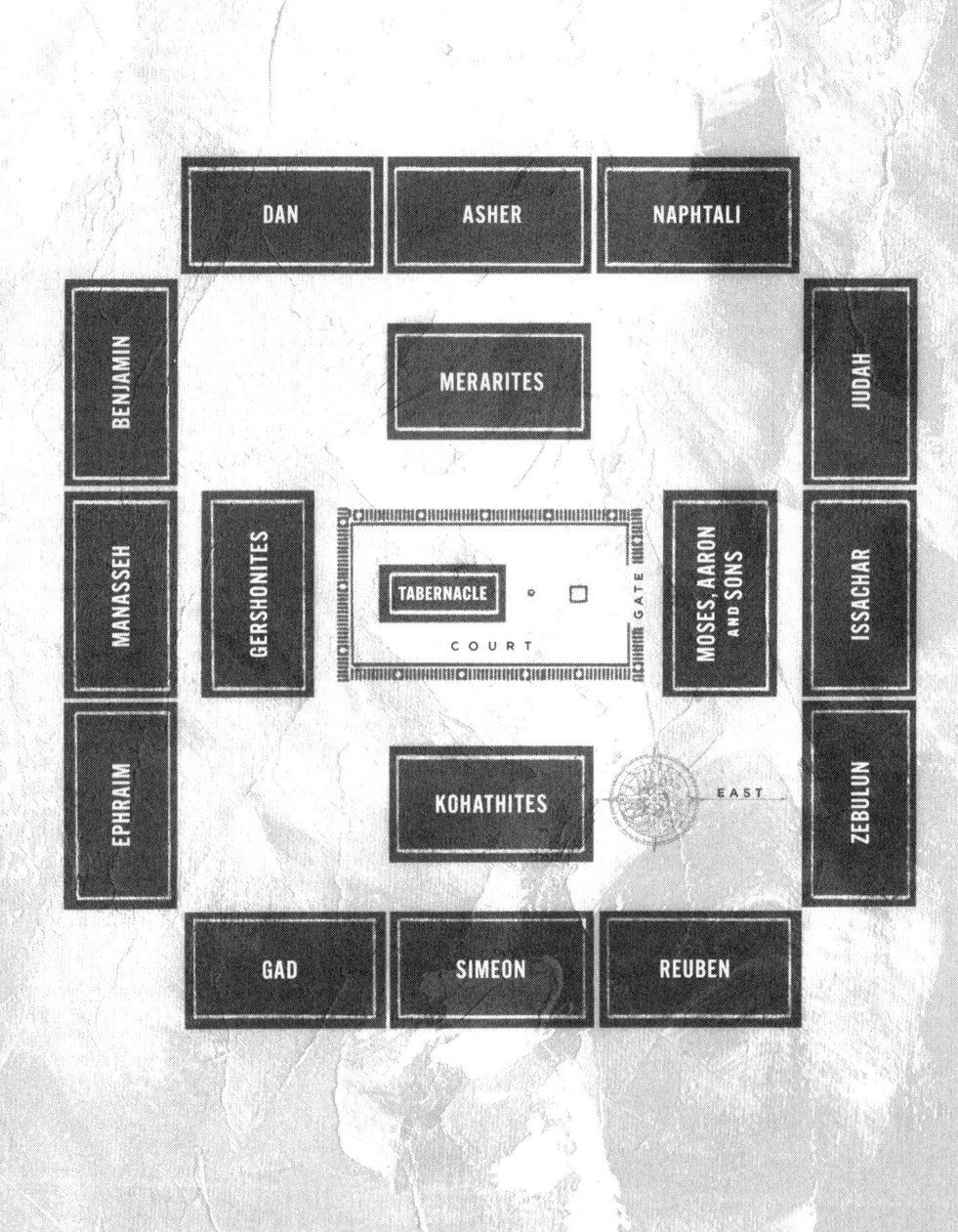

	DAN	ASHER	NAPHTALI	
BENJAMIN		MERARITES		JUDAH
MANASSEH	GERSHONITES	TABERNACLE / COURT / GATE	MOSES, AARON AND SONS	ISSACHAR
EPHRAIM		KOHATHITES		ZEBULUN
	GAD	SIMEON	REUBEN	

EAST

meets us where we are. But if we choose to enter, to stay in his courts and move closer to God, we've got to align ourselves with the pattern for change that he prophetically pictured in the tabernacle. Anticipating the joy being with Jesus, we will repeatedly

> *Enter His gates with thanksgiving and His courts with praise; give thanks to him and bless His name. Psalm 100:4*

God does not invite us into his courts to command us into dutiful servitude as slaves or to meet the obligations of servants. He invites us into loving relationship as his very own sons and daughters. With that in mind, let's begin to look more closely at the tabernacle itself.

THE TABERNACLE IN THE CAMP

The tabernacle, under the cloud of God's presence by day and his fire by night, was Israel's central hub of activity. Their camp was built around it. At a respectful distance away from the cloud and fire, the priests, Moses, Aaron and his sons and their cousins, the Levites, pitched their tents in a rectangular order closest to the outer court. Another distance away, extending out beyond the priests, the twelve tribes of Israel set up camp in their assigned places with three tribes on each side of the place of God's presence.

The tabernacle door faced East, toward the sunrise. Several interesting unfulfilled Scriptures suggest that at some time in future history Jesus, the Son of Righteousness, will return to earth or appear to us from the East.

> *But for you who fear My name, the sun of righteousness will rise with healing in its wings, and you will go out and leap like calves from the stall. Malachi 4:2 B*

And I saw the glory of the God of Israel coming from the east. His voice was like the roar of many waters, and the earth shone with His glory. Ezekiel 43:2

In talking to the disciples of his return, Jesus's own words suggest he may return from the East.

For just as the lightning comes from the east and flashes as far as the west, so will be the coming of the Son of Man. Matthew 24:27

Whenever the cloud of God's presence lifted from the tabernacle, Moses signaled the trumpets to sound and alert the tribes that it was time to break camp and follow the cloud. I had once thought that the tabernacle was taken down first, and the priests carrying the ark of the covenant led the Israelites through their wilderness journeys with the Levites carrying the tabernacle furniture, vessels, walls, foundation, coverings and curtains following behind the ark in a designated order. It's an appealing but highly inaccurate misconception.[20] God given details matter to God. The tribe of Judah led the way, not the ark.

In the middle of the camps, the Tent of Meeting is to travel with the camp of the Levites. They are to set out in the order they encamped, each in his own place under his standard. Numbers 2:17

At a trumpet sound, Judah and the tribes under his standard broke camp first and led the way. That makes sense, for we are to follow the cloud of God's presence with praise and Judah signifies praise. Following

---

20 Scripture alludes to the possibility that the tabernacle led the way in Numbers 10:33 where it says that ark traveled ahead of Moses and his brother-in-law Hobab, but that puts both the ark and Moses in the center of the traveling nation.

the tribes under Judah's standard came the Gershonites and the Merarites, the two Levitical tribes assigned to carry the tabernacle and the fence. After the Gershonites and Merarites came the three tribes following the standard of Reuben. Next came the tabernacle furniture, including the ark,

> *"The Kohathites set out, transporting the holy objects; the tabernacle was to be set up before their arrival." Numbers 10:21*

Then, at their trumpet signal, each of the remaining six tribes broke camp and followed the ark and the priests in their own assigned places.[21] As the central hub of the camp, it makes sense for the tabernacle and the ark to travel in the center of the moving families and armies.

When the cloud rested and a new camp was set up, the outer court fence and the tabernacle were set in the middle, in the center of the camp. The outer court had been fenced in and marked off and the tent of meeting was ready and waiting when the priests arrived with the ark and the tabernacle furniture. Moses and Aaron pitched their tents to the east, facing the tabernacle door. The Levite sons of Kohath, Gershon and Merari pitched their tents on the other three sides. Then, as the final tribes arrived from their journey, they too set up camp, three tribes on each side of the tabernacle in their designated places. At every stop on their forty-year journey through the wilderness, each tribe traveled in order and each tent was pitched to face the tabernacle, so that every single tent opened to look toward the place of God's presence.

> *So the Israelites did everything the LORD commanded Moses; they camped under their standards in this way and set out in the same way, each man with his clan and his family. Numbers 2:34*

---

21 Numbers 10: 14-28

The entire camp's layout represented a God-centered order. Similarly, we are to look to Jesus first, to establish our relationship with him before all others. He wants to be secured in the central place within our lives, with all our families, friends, activities and belongings ordered around him.

When we start to put Jesus first and honor him as our central hub, he often brings a new order to our lives. If we keep our eyes on Jesus, The Holy Spirit will anchor us in God's purposeful love if and when he rearranges our relationships, activities and circumstances to further his good plans for us.

The encampment of the twelve tribes of Israel around the tabernacle symbolizes Christ's work on the cross, for the tents were laid out in the shape of a cross. The four tribes closest to the tabernacle: Judah, Ruben, Ephraim and Dan set up their standards or ensigns in front of their tents.

Although not supported anywhere in scripture, the Jewish oral history and Talmudic[22] commentary about these tribal standards is intriguing. Judah's standard on the north is a lion; Dan's to the west is a flying eagle; Ephraim's to the south is an ox; and Reuben's on the east is a man. These were also the faces of the four beasts surrounding God's throne described in John's apocalypse.

> *And before the throne was something like a sea of glass, as clear as crystal. In the center, around the throne, were four living creatures, covered with eyes in front and back. The first living creature was like a lion, the second like a calf, the third had a face like a man, and the fourth was like an eagle in flight. And each of the four living creatures had six wings and was*

---

22 https://www.myscripturestudies.com/2008/08/four-ensigns.html

covered with eyes all around and within. Day and night they never stop saying:

Holy, Holy, Holy, is the Lord God Almighty,
who was and is and is to come! Revelation 4:6-8

Sir Isaac Newton picked up on this Talmudic description of the standards and agreed that the tribes were specifically placed around the tabernacle to represent the four beasts around the glory of the throne of God in heaven. Ezekiel identified these beasts as cherubim and says they were possessed of the spirit of God. They guarded the holiness of God, just as cherubim guarded the gate to Eden, the first biblical picture of a place of God's presence on earth. With eyes in every direction, the cherubim illustrate God's capacity to see everywhere all at once. In another intriguing Bible parallel, the cherubim's faces correspond to traditional descriptions of Jesus in the four gospels. The lion of the tribe of Judah foreshadows Jesus's kingship as described by Matthew. The ox of the Tribe of Ephraim pictures Jesus as a servant, as in Mark's Gospel. The man of the tribe of Ruben stands for Jesus's humanity, the perfect man, the Son of Man, as in Luke's Gospel. Finally, the eagle of the Tribe of Dan represents the Son of God as in John's Gospel. It is a short mental hop to see that Jesus, like the cherubim, not only guards access to God's throne but faith in him determines who can who approach it. For he said,[23]

I am the way, the truth and the life. No one comes unto the except through me. John 14:6

I am the gate for the sheep. John 10:7b

---

23 For more information, check out: J. A. Seiss, *The Apocalypse: Lectures on the Book of Revelation*, (Grand Rapids, MI: Zondervan Publishing House, 1966), 106 and also read https://www.biblestudytools.com/commentaries/revelation/related-topics/camp-of-israel.html

THE TABERNACLE'S PORTABILITY

The tabernacle was a small, temporary, portable structure, not at all like a building. It was designed to be taken down and reassembled to follow the cloud of God's presence. All the tabernacle furniture was small enough to transport. Carrying the ark was an honor reserved for Levites from the family of Kohath. Whenever Moses saw the cloud (representing the Holy Spirit and the presence of God) lift from the tabernacle, he knew God was moving. With this signal to pick up camp and follow the cloud, the Levites began to move into action. Moving the ark took great care. Since only Aaron, the high priest, was allowed to see God's manifest presence, and that only on the day of atonement, the ark itself had to be carefully covered over before the two priests, one in front and one behind, lifted the poles up onto their shoulders.

Putting clues from Exodus together, I can picture the priests carefully guarding their eyes as they uncoupled the veil that hung between the altar of incense and the ark. Once uncoupled, was the veil designed to naturally fall over the ark? Perhaps, holding the veil before their faces the designated priests carefully walked forward toward the ark to drape the shielding veil over the golden cherubim. Or, faces averted from the ark, did they walk backwards to fully drape the veil over the place of God's rest among the Israelites?

> *And he brought the ark into the tabernacle, hung up the veil of the covering, and partitioned off the ark of the Testimony, as the LORD had commanded Moses. Exodus 40:21 NKJV*

> *Put the ark of the testimony in it and screen off the ark with the veil. Exodus 40:3*

For the journey itself, the covered ark was permanently suspended on two gold-covered poles of acacia wood that fit through four golden rings. God directed that the ark itself should always be carried on the shoulders of men, by priests in their human strength. Similarly, Jesus carried God's presence in his physical body and we are to follow his example and carry God's presence in our human bodies.

When the Israelites were finally ready to leave the plains of Moab, cross over the Jordan River and enter the land of Canaan, God commanded the priests carrying the ark to touch the water first.

> *Now the Jordan overflows its banks throughout the harvest season. But as soon as the priests carrying the ark reached the Jordan and their feet touched the water's edge, the flowing water stood still. It backed up as far upstream as Adam . . . while the water flowing toward the Sea of the Arabah . . . was completely cut off. So the people crossed over opposite Jericho. The priests carrying the ark of the covenant of the LORD stood firm on dry ground in the middle of the Jordan, while all Israel crossed over the dry ground, until the entire nation had crossed the Jordan. Joshua 3:15-17*

Covered and hidden or open and perceived, God's presence will effectively do what God intends to be done as we follow his directions.

Soon after the Israelites had crossed the Jordan and encamped in Canaan, they began to follow God's instructions to

> *Drive out before you all the inhabitants of the land, destroy all their carved images and cast idols, and demolish all their high places. Numbers 33:52*

Their very first attempt to take the land was the battle of Jericho. The Lord appeared to Joshua, son of Nun, and set out the battle strategy. He told Joshua to summon the priests and say,

"Take up the ark of the covenant and have seven priests carry seven rams' horns in front of the ark of the LORD." And he told the people, "Advance and march around the city, with the armed troops going ahead of the ark of the LORD." Joshua 6:6-7

God wanted the Israelites to be sure of his presence, to trust his strategies and to know that as they stepped out in the obedience of faith, he would fight their battles for them. With the ark leading the way, the twelve tribes followed God's instructions and Jericho's high, fortified walls fell down.[24]

Quite practically, God's presence at Jericho illustrates the truth that if God tells us to go someplace and do something and we follow his directions, we can be confident that he will be with us. If we're not sure, it's wise to pray, to wait and to praise and seek him until his peace confirms our direction. But if we're heading some place or other, whether it's physical, mental, emotional or spiritual, and we sense that God is not going there with us, we'd better say no to the invitation, refuse the relationship, turn off the TV, change our thinking and surrender our feelings and decisions to him.

On one occasion, after settling in Canaan, the high priest's sons didn't listen to God and presumptuously took the ark to war. The Israelites lost the battle, the high priest's sons were killed and the ark was captured by the Philistines. The ark's portability and their priesthood did not give the priests a license to take it when and where they wanted.

The temporary and portable nature of the tabernacle and ark continued after the Israelites had moved into the promised land. During

---

24 This exciting story is in Joshua 6. Archeological evidence confirms the accuracy of the Bible account in minute detail. The forty-six foot walls fell down outwards, the city was burned, no booty was taken, and one portion of wall, suggesting Rahab's home was still intact. The Bible account is in Joshua 6, an article about the archeological finds is at https://israelmyglory.org/article/archaeology-confirms-the-walls-fell-flat/

the times of the Judges the tabernacle was set up at Shiloh, about thirty miles north of Jerusalem. At another time, the tent of meeting, with the bronze altar and laver was in one place and the ark in another. Although Nehemiah and Solomon built temples for the ark itself, the prophets sensed its transience. Stephen summed it up in the Book of Acts.

> *Our fathers had the tabernacle of the testimony with them in the wilderness. It was constructed exactly as God had directed Moses, according to the pattern he had seen. And our fathers who received it brought it in with Joshua when they dispossessed the nations God drove out before them. It remained until the time of David, who found favor in the sight of God and asked to provide a dwelling place for the God of Jacob. But it was Solomon who built the house for him. However, the Most High does not dwell in houses made by human hands. As the prophet says:*
>
>   *Heaven is My throne and the earth is My footstool.*
>   *What kind of house will you build for Me, says the Lord,*
>   *or where will My place of repose be?*
>   *Has not My hand made all these things?*
>   *Acts 7:44-50 quoting Isaiah 66:1-2a*

The tabernacle's portability is a concrete reminder that our earthly lives are temporary. We can fulfill God's invitation to carry his Holy Spirit in our mortal bodies for a short time. The choices we make here and now are determining our reward in heaven and our life for all of eternity. Jesus was keenly aware that his hours and days on earth were temporary too. He went to the cross with joy for the reward set before him.

THE TABERNACLE

Let us fix our eyes on Jesus, the author and perfecter of our faith, who for the joy set before him endured the cross, scorning its shame, and sat down at the right hand of the throne of God.
Hebrews 12:2

As we fix our eyes on Jesus, he wants to look into them, search our hearts and build a closer relationship with us. The church is his bride; we're part of his joy. He wants us! He wants to be near us, he wants to prepare us to be with him. Could it be that Jesus's strong desire for closer relationship with us is reflected in the tabernacle's size, placement and portability? All illustrate the tension between God's separateness and his availability to the people. Holiness requires separation from sin, yet Jesus welcomed relationship and closeness with God and with others. He is available to those in need.

The whole idea of a guiding relationship with the personal God whom Moses and Abraham had trusted and followed was new to the children of Israel when they crossed the Jordan and began to occupy the promised land. No nearby religion had a caring god who loved them and invited their love in return.

These Hebrew ex-slaves of the Exodus had grown up in an idolatrous culture. They were familiar with bribing and expiating natural gods, like pharaohs, frogs, lice and snakes. Their horizons had been confined by power, control, cruelty, legalism and forced obedience. Although their identity as Hebrews remained intact and they remembered stories about their fathers' God, they did not know him. They had no experience of a culture or community built on trust, freedom, truth and mutual responsibility. They had little concept of a two-way love relationship with the true God. Like victims with a slave mentality, they were fearful and mistrusting. Hearts and wills that had been hardened into rebelliousness by cruel masters automatically turned hard and rebellious toward Moses and God.

When God came to them on the mountaintop, the people were afraid. They kept their distance and told Moses to talk with him. When they rejected God and chose to turn back to their familiar idols and worshipped a golden calf, the law became essential. They were like children who didn't know (or care about) the difference between right and wrong, between liberty and license, between a living, loving Holy God and an inanimate idol. Many of them had been conditioned by generations of being ordered around. Steeped in Egyptian customs, they couldn't think beyond them. God's commandments began to educate them about his character, requirements and merciful loving kindness. To begin to teach them his ways, God entrusted Moses with the gigantic task of setting up an entirely new system of worship and human relationships—with the tabernacle at the center.

When the Hebrew children chose to worship a golden calf over the powerful living God of miracles who'd set them free from Egypt, God burned with anger. He wanted to forget about them and start over again with Moses's family. God said to Moses,

> *I have seen this people, and they are indeed a stiff-necked people. Now leave Me alone, so that My anger may burn against them and consume them. Then I will make you into a great nation. Exodus 32: 9-10*

But Moses interceded. He asked God to change his mind, Moses didn't want the Egyptians to get the wrong idea about God and God's promises to Abraham, Isaac and Jacob. Fully in tune with God's own longing for relationship, when Moses begged God to relent, God did. God then gave Moses ten simple laws, rules that would guarantee Israel's safe, respectful, healthy, peaceful and prosperous community living. These laws, called the Ten Commandments have become the basis of our legal system, our sense of individual responsibility and morality.

THE TABERNACLE

Then, following the principle of first the naturals and then the spirituals, God began to teach the Israelites his ways by telling Moses to build him a tabernacle. The tabernacle was an object lesson illustrating God's pattern of worship and a prophetic witness to his long-range plan. The construction work was organized to be a co-operative venture for the entire community. The Israelites willingly contributed the material needed. Both men and women wove the fabric and the men helped with the construction. God handpicked two artist-craftsmen to oversee the work. He gave them skill and filled them with his very own Spirit so that they could execute his design down to the tiniest detail.[25]

As long as the children of Israel camped around God's tabernacle and his presence, visible to them in his cloud by day and pillar of fire by night, continued above them in the center of their camp, God provided for them, protected them and guided them. Through his commandments and the daily visible indications of his reality in their midst, God began to teach these former slaves and their free-born children about his ways.

THE TABERNACLE'S LAYOUT
FROM AN AERIAL PERSPECTIVE

The tabernacle's layout prophetically illustrates God's long-range plan. Looking down on the tabernacle, God would see Christ's work in three crosses. The arrangement of the twelve tribes and their tents around the tabernacle formed the first cross, with the larger tribes on the north and south forming the vertical beam and the smaller tribes to east and west

---

[25] I find that fascinating. To make a huge generalization, throughout history many artist-craftsmen, like prophets, have been forerunners. Many artists are free spirits with wisdom and understanding that rises above cultural conformity and control. Many artists are pioneers; men and women with a willingness to explore new territory in their creations. Sadly, not all gifted forerunners get their inspiration from the Holy Spirit. The two artist-craftsmen God hand-picked to oversee the tabernacle work were the first men mentioned in the Bible who were filled with God's Holy Spirit.

forming the horizontal bar. The priests' placement around the tabernacle formed a second cross. The tabernacle furniture was placed to form a third cross: the brazen altar, the laver, the altar of incense and the ark covered by the mercy seat were in vertical alignment; the lampstand and table of showbread were opposite each other in horizontal alignment inside the tent of meeting.

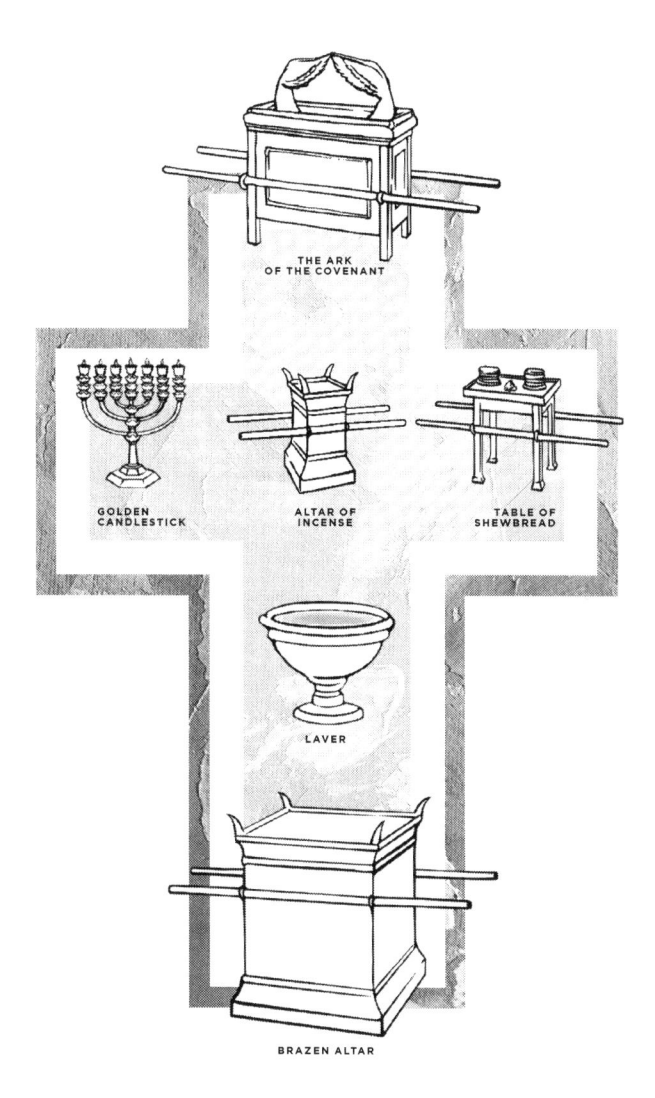

The layout of the tabernacle into distinct areas of outer court and inner court complements the dominant Christian view that humans are bipartite: that is, we're divided into two parts, body and soul. Others, who believe that we are tripartite,[26] made of body, soul and spirit, view the tabernacle as divided into three parts: outer court, inner court and holy of holies. In either view (dichotomy or trichotomy), the need for consecration and purity increases as you move closer to the presence of God in the holy of holies.

The symbolic imagery of the tabernacle furniture is compatible with either view. The outer court furniture was of brass, representing our humanity and God's judgment. The inner court furniture was of solid gold representing divinity and of wood that was covered with gold signifying our redeemed humanity. In the holy of holies every visible hard surface was also gold, pure gold to represent God's purity, his Spirit, his value and divine nature.

Although God's ways with us as individuals don't always seem to fit neatly into his own patterns and most generalizations have exceptions, most usually it's in the outer court, the place of sacrifice and cleansing, that we first present our bodies to the Lord.[27] We can enter "just as we are, without one plea, but that Christ's blood was shed for us."[28]

---

26 The tripartite view is supported by 1 Thessalonians 5:23: *Now may the God of peace himself sanctify you completely, and may your entire spirit, soul, and body be kept blameless at the coming of our Lord Jesus Christ.* And by Hebrews 4:12: *For the word of God is living and active. Sharper than any double-edged sword, it pierces even to dividing soul and spirit, joints and marrow.*

27 As soon as we enter God's courts, he begins to deal with us. The outer court is a place of repentance, of sacrifice for sin and for offering ourselves to the Lord. it is also a place of cleansing from the ungodly deeds of our bodies and souls. After our sin and is forgiven and washed away, the outer court becomes a place of thanksgiving, celebration and other offerings.

28 The words of "Just as I am without One Plea" were written by Charles Elliott and first published in 1668 hymnals.

Therefore, I urge you, brothers and sisters, in view of God's mercy, to offer your bodies as a living sacrifice, holy and pleasing to God—this is your true and proper worship. Romans 12:1 NIV

In the second area, the inner court, we meet God with our souls, that is, with our minds, wills, affections and emotions. The Holy Spirit sheds his light upon us. We eat his food; we smell his sweet incense; we know something of his presence. We worship him in prayer and in communion with others.

The third area, the holy of holies, was off-limits for all but the High Priest. Once a year, after careful consecration and preparation, he entered into the holiest of holy places to make atonement for the people. The holy of holies represents a powerful one-on-one spiritual encounter with God's glory. In the holy of holies, we maintain our own awareness, our own individuality and personalities. But somehow, quite mysteriously, by God's mercy to us in Christ Jesus, God becomes our "all in all" as we experience his manifest presence. In the holy of holies, while we're not "possessed" by God as we might be by a demonic personality or force, we are, in an inexplicable way, consumed by our realization of God's majesty and power. In God's manifest presence, all of our worship and prayers will be inspired and uttered by the Holy Spirit who dwells within us and by God, whose presence surrounds and fills us.

THE TABERNACLE MATERIALS AND COLORS: A BRIEF OVERVIEW

All the materials and colors used in the tabernacle speak of Jesus.

- *Blue speaks of heavenly places, of Jesus's origin, of his continual connection to his Father in heaven, and where he sits now.*

- *Purple speaks of his royalty.*

- *Scarlet speaks of the blood Jesus shed for us and of his earthly suffering and sacrifice.*

- *Gold illustrates his deity, his beauty and divine nature.*

- *Silver symbolizes his redemption.*

- *Bronze or brass represent God's judgment. God judged our sins on the cross; currently, God judges us by the standard of Jesus's love and his own word; at the last day Jesus will judge us all.*

- *The goat's hair represents Jesus's atonement: the scapegoat carried our sins away.*

- *The rams' skins represent Jesus as our ram, the head of the flock, the sire of lambs, and our sacrifice.*

- *The red dye of the rams' skins represents Jesus's blood, consecrated and devoted to God.*

- *The outer covering of tachashim skins, translated traditionally as badger skins, signifies God's protective covering over us.*

- *The acacia wood is interesting. Wood represents Jesus in his eternal humanity, but because it is a dry desert wood, like Jesus who was a root out of dry ground, it is incorruptible and impervious to rot. On earth, although fully human, Jesus was impervious to rot; he was free from sin.*

- *The gold covering over the wood and boards signifies the unity between the divine and human natures in Jesus Christ.*

- *Gold over wood illustrates that we "put on Christ." Only Jesus, who was and is both fully God and fully man, can bridge heaven and earth for us. In his earthly life, through his death and now in heaven, he was both man and God.*

- *The spices and incense represent Jesus's life of worship and prayers to the Father: they were a sweet-smelling savor to God.* [29]

THE VALUE OF THE TABERNACLE

Although, Moses clearly lists the exact weight of all the gold, silver and copper (called brass or bronze in most translations) used in the tabernacle (in Exodus 38:24-31), it is impossible to accurately estimate the value of the tabernacle today. Scholarly estimates of the weight of a shekel and a talent and the length of a cubit vary. No one knows the thickness of the gold leaf covering over the acacia wood. The value of gold, silver and precious stones fluctuates daily. One online estimate for the gold was slightly over $10,000,000.[30] By my calculations, based on a conservative estimate of a light weight for the gold[31] at today's live gold prices[32] the gold alone would be valued at $8,300,000. That's costly. My class notes from around 1980 give heavier weights and a gold value of over $63,000,000. This wide range of weights and values surely indicates human uncertainty and error. What is divinely certain and true is that the tabernacle's value is inestimable. Every grain of precious metal, every drop of oil, every thread of fine material and every moment of inspired

---

29 Recent research confirms that the ancient use of spices and incense may support health and promote healing and well-being.

30 https://tabernacleofmoses.wordpress.com/cost/

31 https://usgoldbureau.com

32 https://www.onegold.com/live-gold-price?

and skilled craftsmanship in weaving, sewing, embroidery, metal work, sculpture, furniture and design all speak of the inestimable value of Jesus Christ. It cost all of heaven's glory to redeem you and me. The very presence of God who once dwelt in the tabernacle is now available to all who believe. What a great treasure—one of immeasurable value. It's worth repeating that

> *God, who said, "Let light shine out of darkness," made His light shine in our hearts to give us the light of the knowledge of the glory of God in the face of Jesus Christ. Now we have this treasure in jars of clay to show us that this surpassingly great power is from God and not from us. 2 Corinthians 4:6-7*

APPROACHING THE TABERNACLE:
PRAISE

Imagine with me that we're walking through a tent city. Hundreds and hundreds of dark, goat hair tents surround us in every direction. We're headed toward the tabernacle. It sits in the very center of the camp, where a wide, spacious area is set apart for God. Looking ahead of us, across a long stretch of land, we see the courts of the Lord, a small area fenced in by white linen curtains. The curtains hang on silver rings from silver rods that glisten in the sun. The single door into the tabernacle courtyard is an opening in the curtains. To reach it, we must pass by the tents of Judah. As we approach the entry, Judah's camp is directly behind us to the East, facing the tabernacle door. All who travel to the tabernacle's door must walk before the three tribes who pitch their tents and travel behind the standard of Judah.

As we get closer to the tabernacle, we'll most likely sense an indefinable difference in the atmosphere. We might not understand it at first. It might be a longing for more of God, an eagerness, or an alertness in our spirits that he's nearby. Perhaps we pick up on a calming steadiness in the air. A desire to sing God's praise may rise in our heart; surges of gratitude may fill our soul. The vibrations of praise and worship surround us; they're coming from both the tabernacle ahead and from Judah's tents behind us.

Judah's name was identified with praise from the moment of his birth, when his mother, Leah, happily said,

> "This time I will praise the LORD. So she named him Judah." Genesis 29:35

When Judah's father, Israel (who was called Jacob until God changed his name), was dying, he called his sons together and said,

> "Gather around so that I can tell you what will happen to you in the days to come."

When he spoke God's prophetic words for Judah, he said,

> "Judah, your brothers shall praise you." Genesis 49: 1, 8

Centuries later, God's praises in the Psalms poured forth from King David, a descendant of Judah. Most important of all, Jesus comes from the tribe of Judah. One of his many names is the Lion of the Tribe of Judah. And Jesus is worthy of all praise. It's no coincidence that David wrote,

> Enter His gates with thanksgiving and His courts with praise! Give thanks to him; and bless His name. Psalm 100:4 and

> Yet You are holy, enthroned on the praises of Israel. Psalm 22:3

Praise is our approach to God. There is a mystery to praise that language can't express. Praising God turns us from ourselves and awakens us to God's life. It seems that our praises either bring God closer to us or pull us toward him. However it works, when we enthrone God on our praise, his majesty, his energies, and his divine purposes begin to charge the atmosphere. When he comes on the wings of our praise, he turns our hearts to worship. Eventually, if we continue to follow his Spirit's leading in worship, we'll find ourselves in his glory. Because we long for his glory, because we seek it and cry out for it, we often forget that one of the surest ways to reach the reviving realities of God's personality and the capacity to do his will is through praise.

As we walk before the tents of Judah, God begins to teach us about praising him. We might catch it before we understand it because praise is more likely caught than taught. Our trip's most likely been a dusty one. Possibly we're eager and joyful. Just as likely, we might be tired, broken and hurting. We're likely to have desert sand between our toes and maybe a bit of dirt and perspiration on our forehead. The offering we carry may be heavy, and we may feel too tired to praise God. Yet, praise for his goodness is in the air. He understands all about our dust and sweat, and he welcomes us to come as we are. God wants us to be totally honest with him. He's our good Father who, knowing all, still wants to hear our truth straight from us—all of it. He wants us to share our needs, difficulties and desires—our dirty spots and dreams. At times, we must pour out our hearts to God before we can even begin to think of praise.[33]

---

33 Under pressure, I've often "let it all hang out" in talking to God. So did King David. God invites us to be real with him, but our own soulish authenticity is not always prayer. Dumping without communicating with God and calling it prayer can be like wallowing in an emotional monologue without making contact with our listeners. That might turn God away just as quickly as it turns people away. In such "prayer" we can get stuck and end up unchanged or even more tightly wrapped up in our own highs and lows. Prayer is relational. It brings us to God; it's getting in touch with Him whatever our feelings might be. It is not a personal venting or an outpouring of emotion. It's not declaring or proclaiming what we want to happen or believe either. The Holy Spirit teaches us how to pray and God listens when we come to him through Jesus Christ and his heart for all men. Many mature believers guard against self-absorbed and subjective prayers by supplementing their personal prayers and communion with God with scriptures or the prayer book.

At other times, as we get closer to God's presence, all the loads we carry—our physical fatigue or pain, our inmost feelings and greatest concerns—will begin to fade and dissolve in God's holy love and the glory of his majesty. Either way, it's Jesus's nature to mercifully touch our spirits with the exact kind of love that he alone knows we need. We may cry; we may sing; we may kneel, dance, speak or simply look to him in silence. Whatever we do, God calls us to approach him in praise. He alone can meet our need; he alone can give us the supernatural directions, anointings, faith and peace we need. He alone can quiet our souls until all we want is him and his will. He alone teaches us how totally worthy he is of our praise.

God is patient and longsuffering. If we don't praise him, he will continue to teach us; he will woo us and give us opportunities to change. But if we repeatedly and willfully refuse to gratefully glorify him for whom he is, God's Holy Spirit will eventually withdraw, leaving us sometimes in the dryness of dead religion and control, sometimes in the empty darkness of sin, but always in a separation from his loving presence.[34]

Years ago, I was headed into this danger. I'd been walking closely with the Lord when I gradually moved into darkness by listening to others. Before long, my own feelings had entangled me in a controlling, contentious situation. It became harder and harder to hear God's voice and find his peace. Misunderstandings, jealousies, unfairness and lies were heartbreaking. I'd brought turmoil and unrest on myself by seeking what I wanted. The hackneyed phrase, "I wanted, what I wanted,

---

[34] Scripture suggests permanent separation from God is true only for those who've known God intimately. I've observed that God's cords of love and mercy can be long for young believers. That said, continuing in wrong choices hardens hearts and drains life from our souls. Sooner or later our own thinking will take us into darkness and futility. According to Hebrew 6:4-6, *It is impossible for those who have once been enlightened, who have tasted the heavenly gift, who have shared in the Holy Spirit, who have tasted the goodness of the word of God and the powers of the coming age—and then have fallen away—to be restored to repentance, because they themselves are crucifying the Son of God all over again and subjecting him to open shame.*

when I wanted it," fit me well. As I listened to others, my own emotions became louder than reason or the Holy Spirit's quiet guidance. I stopped praising God and became compulsively demanding in my prayers. I never thought of asking God what he wanted. I didn't fully appreciate all he had given me or what I had lost. I hadn't learned that gratitude, forgiveness, contentment and humility (or ingratitude, resentment, dissatisfaction, greed and pride) are moral decisions and attitudes that we can choose, learn and nurture. I thought they were emotions that came and went. Forty years later, I'm still learning to discern which desires are Godly and which are temptations and futile fantasies. Bottom line, God is worthy of praise no matter what I want, think or feel and praising him brings me into line with his light.

Back then, facing into darkness, God didn't turn on any magical lights. But when all my resources were gone, by his grace, he spoke a word to free me. He gave me strength to see my need and turn to him. While still in the dark, I remember singing Micah's words over and over again,

> *Rejoice not against me, O my enemies*
> *When I fall, I shall rise.*
> *Though I sit, in darkness,*
> *The Lord will be a light unto me.*
> *Micah 7:8 adapted*

It took a while. God didn't move quickly. I had stopped praising and glorifying God and was trapped in glorifying a few people and seeking their good opinion. As soon as I changed my direction from trying to gratify myself by pleasing people, God changed my heart and circumstances. He quickly drew me out of an entangled situation. He healed wounds, made sense of confusions and established his order and direction for my life out of a chaotic mess. I began to see the futility of my own thinking, the foolishness of my own idolatrous heart. Although I loved Jesus, I understood St. Paul's words about unbelievers,

> *For since the creation of the world God's invisible qualities, His eternal power and divine nature, have been clearly seen, being understood from His workmanship, so that men are without excuse. For although they knew God, they neither glorified him as God nor gave thanks to him, but they became futile in their thinking and darkened in their foolish hearts. Romans 1: 20-21*

Paul's warning to the Romans almost 2,000 years ago still holds. Cultivating an attitude of praise and thanksgiving toward God is essential for all who would know Jesus Christ as their way, the truth and the light. The Holy Spirit invites us to accept Judah's legacy of praise and join with King David in entering God's gates with thanksgiving and praise.

Since God is relational and his Holy Spirit flows like a river and comes and goes like the wind, there can be no hard and fast rules or formulas about praise. Sometimes we praise in the dryness of sheer will power and keep praising until the winds of his Spirit rise to fill our empty sails. Sometimes, we praise God in sorrow; tears come before joy. Sometimes we praise God in darkness where he alone is our light. We learn to praise by asking God's Spirit to help us, and we seek and find his Spirit as we lift our voices in his praise. In praise, the Holy Spirit helps us to put aside our own feelings, thought and agendas. He teaches us to move with him.

That happened to me this very morning. The alarm rang in the middle of a sleep cycle. I woke up feeling heavier than a soggy dumpling. Still groggy, I fed the dog and made a cup of tea. All I wanted to do was crawl back under the covers and sleep—only ten or twenty minutes more. But I couldn't do it, I'd an appointment to keep! In a dull, rather unenthusiastic voice that came out of the depths, the springs in our souls where his Spirit dwells, I started thanking the Lord for the day, telling him I loved him, telling him I was sleepy and saying, "I do praise you, Lord" in a nevertheless-tone and attitude. What began in a sleepy, routine voice began to quicken with resonant life. Maybe I didn't want to start the day, but the Holy Spirit was ready and willing. Half-asleep, my part was turning to him. Then he woke me up. He helped me pray and begin to order my day to meet the people and responsibilities ahead.

All days aren't like that. When we don't feel like praising God, it isn't always that easy or even possible to turn our wills to praise. Jeremiah had reason to lament. Daniel had weeks of Godly mourning. Perhaps the Holy Spirit will lead you to travail for his breakthrough or to groan and weep your way through a grief or a trial before you can begin to praise him. But then again, he might want you to praise God through your difficulties.

Our willingness to praise God at all times and in all things is a question of heart motivation. Do we want to do all things for the glory of God? Is loving him our prime purpose in life? Do we want to live in his faith, hope, joy, peace and love in the here and now, or do we want to stew in our own soup? A man and woman in love don't stop loving and praising their beloveds just because they're having a bad day. Praising God in the midst of difficulties, confusions and chaos often opens the way for his presence to break through with clarity, solutions and order.

God knows our hearts. Unless our goal is God himself, unless our praise is motivated by our love for him, using praise as a tool or technique to get what we want is fruitless. We don't praise for answers; praise simply expresses outwardly the honor to God which the Holy Spirit is giving Him inwardly. In every circumstance, God is always worthy of praise. In the agony of hanging on the cross, when Jesus cried out from Psalm 22:1, "My God, my God, why have you forsaken me?" he knew that the Psalm ended with praise. In praising God for who he is, we too accept that we might never see the answers to our faith in this life; some of our prayers will be answered later, after our death.

An aside on praise: Lately, I've realized that "Praise God!" is an imperative. When we hear "Praise God!" we are to turn our hearts and minds to praising him, not just repeat the words "Praise God" over again like a mantra. Saying "Praise God" makes no focused sense unless it's flowing from our spirits or we're talking with another person about who God is or what he has done and we want to praise him in that context.

Repeating "I praise you" to God can become meaningless too. It can lead to a Godless emotional religious high. The simple song "Praise him, Praise him, all ye little children, God is Love" tells me to praise God for his love. Singing the Doxology is praising God from whom all blessings flow. These musical praises connect us to God in a relational way.

Praising God for his name is praising him for his nature and character. That's relational too. For example, most of us would never praise our children by saying, "I praise you." That sounds silly. We'd say something like, "Being with you makes me happy." or "That's great! Good work!" or "Hearing your voice is wonderful." or "You solved that really well—it's praiseworthy." It makes sense to simply say to God, "Lord, I'm flabbergasted, awed, humbled by who you are." I don't want to praise God into the empty air with empty words from a religious habit. I want to focus on connecting with him and thanking and praising him for specifics.

As I write about the tabernacle, it's been easy to praise God for what he showed Moses. It boggles my mind to realize how fully that little tent in the wilderness foreshadowed God's love. It amazes me to see how his plan has steadily unfolded through centuries of messy human history. I can honestly say, "Father, thank you! Thank you for the tabernacle. It's a wonder far beyond me." On current earth-bound levels, I can also praise God for my daily bread, for the Skype call I'll make this afternoon and for healing a friend last week. I've hundreds of specific and relational things to praise God for. I can praise him through difficulties, for I can put them in his hands and trust him to solve them or to see me through. That's relational praise. It's directed specifically to him, a precious communication. But I can take this too far. If you're like me, sometimes praise overrules my thoughts; it simply bubbles up until all I can say is "Praise you! Praise you Father. Praise you, Lord!" When that happens to you or me, I'm sure we are praising Jesus and our Father for who they are; we're not numbing ourselves into our own emotional highs of empty ritual.

As we leave the tents of Judah and draw near to the tabernacle courts, we don't leave praise behind us. We take the Lord's praiseworthiness into our very beings until a heart of praise becomes a part of us and our relationship with him.[35]

---

35 Modern classics with encouragements to praise include Judson Cornwall, *Let Us Praise*; Merlin Carothers, *Prison to Praise*; Dick Eastman, *A Celebration of Praise* and Bob Sorge, A *Practical Guide to Praise and Worship*. Sorge's guide is available as a pdf. download.

THE COURT YARD

THE TABERNACLE FENCE AND CURTAINS

Standing with the tents of Judah's praise at our backs, we're looking straight ahead toward the tabernacle fence. Right before our eyes is an area smaller than a residential lot that is clearly separated from the camp by a fence of white linen hangings. These white curtains visually impress the idea of God's separateness upon us. The white linen prophetically represents Jesus's holiness, his spotless purity and separation from the world. It also pictures the righteousness of all who trust in him. We earthlings find his absolute otherness, his separateness from his creation and from all moral evil hard to grasp. Yet, he is calling each one of us into holiness too.

> *For it is written: "Be holy, because I am holy." 1 Peter 1:16*

> *Let us rejoice and be glad and give him the glory. For the marriage of the Lamb has come, and His bride has made herself ready. She was given clothing of fine linen, bright and pure. For the fine linen she wears is the righteous acts of the saints. Revelation 19:7-8*

THE TABERNACLE

The white linen curtains around the tabernacle form a clear boundary between the camp and the courts of the Lord. Since white linen symbolizes Jesus's holiness, purity and separation from the world, the curtains also illustrate that if we want the kind of close and powerful relationship that Jesus had with our heavenly Father, we, too, must be separated unto him.[36]

They were hung from sixty silver curtain rods. All the silver had been brought out of Egypt. Now, in the desert, it was melted, purified and shaped into rods as part of a dwelling place for God himself. How like many of us—pulled by God from servitude in ungodly places, put in a desert place where we need to depend on him, melted by the purifying fires of his love, and reshaped until our appearance and purposes are totally transformed. Then, God puts us in a place of usefulness that's just right for us.

---

[36] Brother Lawrence's account of God's love makes separation from all but God simple, understandable and within reach. *Practice of the Presence of God,* https://www.pathsoflove.com/pdf/Practice-of-the-Presence-of-God.pdf

THE SILVER OF REDEMPTION

The original silver used in the tabernacle construction came from silver coins, tokens used as a medium of secular exchange. The silver became holy when it was offered or dedicated to God for his use. The silver's symbolic prophetic significance as a ransom or atonement money looks forward to Jesus's redemption. Each man paid half a silver shekel as a ransom for his life. On the mount, the Lord directed Moses to take a census to number the army:

> *. . . every male individually, from twenty years old and above— all who are able to go to war in Israel. Numbers 1:2, 3 NKJV*

But before the census was taken

> *The LORD said to Moses, "When you take a census of the Israelites to number them, each man must pay the LORD a ransom for his life when he is counted. Then no plague will come upon them when they are numbered. Everyone who crosses over to those counted must pay a half shekel, according to the sanctuary shekel, which weighs twenty gerahs. This [silver] half shekel is an offering to the LORD.*
>
> *Everyone twenty years of age or older who crosses over must give this offering to the LORD. In making the offering to the LORD to atone for your lives, the rich shall not give more than a half shekel, nor shall the poor give less. Take the atonement money from the Israelites and use it for the service of the Tent of Meeting. It will serve as a memorial for the Israelites before the LORD to make atonement for your lives." Exodus 30:11-16*

God further established silver's symbolic connection with redemption when he told Moses that every firstborn son needed to be redeemed by silver.

> *The firstborn of every womb, whether man or beast, that is offered to the LORD belongs to you. But you must surely redeem every firstborn son and every firstborn male of unclean animals. You are to pay the redemption price for a month-old male according to your valuation: five shekels of silver, according to the sanctuary shekel, which is twenty gerahs. Numbers 18: 15-16*

Filling in the blank spots, it's as if God is saying, "I don't want you to sacrifice your first-born sons to me. I value each one and want them to live, to be part of your family; your sons belong to you. I didn't choose you to mimic the surrounding nations. You are My children, you're not Egyptians. When the Egyptians enslaved you and refused to set you free, I sent the death angel to take their first born. I spoke to them in a language they understood. Now I am teaching you a new way, my way. Remember how I provided a ram for Abraham? I didn't want him to kill Isaac. I am teaching you; I'm calling my people to be different from the Canaanites who hope to worship and appease Molech and Baal by child sacrifice.[37]

God's abhorrence of human sacrifice continues through the Old Testament. The prophet Micah wrote,

> *With what shall I come before the LORD*
> *when I bow before the God on high?*
> *Should I come to him with burnt offerings,*
> *Shall I present my firstborn for my transgression,*
> *the fruit of my body for the sin of my soul?*
> *He has shown you, O man, what is good.*
> *And what does the LORD require of you*
> *but to act justly, to love mercy, and to walk humbly with your God?*
> *Micah 6:6a, 7, 8*

---

[37] 2 Kings 3: 26-27 tells how the Moabite king sacrificed his first-born son.

Every man numbered for war knew that God valued his life. Every family who redeemed a son for five shekels of silver would think twice about sacrificing that child to a god. Each one of those Israelite couples who redeemed their first-born baby boys would have a firsthand experience of the vast difference between the God of Abraham, Isaac, Jacob and Moses and the worship of Canaanite and Mesopotamian gods who asked for appeasement by human sacrifice.

This redemption money was paid to the priests. All families gladly gave, never dreaming that centuries later, in a curious reverse twist, future Israelite priests who had become control-freaks and worshipped the gods of this world and political power more than they respected Abraham's and Moses' living God of love would one day pay Judas thirty pieces of silver to betray Jesus, God's own Son. When Pilate ordered Jesus's crucifixion to appease a demanding crowd, he didn't know that God himself was giving his first-born to redeem all people from sin and the deadly claims of Satan.

Now, Christ makes himself the price of our redemption. In other words, he is our redemption money; he buys us out from under the law. By paying himself as our ransom,

> *Christ redeemed us from the curse of the law by becoming a curse for us. For it is written: "Cursed is everyone who is hung on a tree." He redeemed us in order that the blessing promised to Abraham would come to the Gentiles in Christ Jesus, so that by faith we might receive the promise of the Spirit.*
> *Galatians 3:13-14*

Was God thinking about you and me when he began to set the Israelites free from a culture of death and a mind-set of slavery? Is it possible that the church in our age might grow into the maturity of life and freedom which God asked Israel to model and give to the world? I believe so. When Jesus Christ lived and died to ransom and redeem his followers from the curses of legalistic slavery and death and offered them freedom and eternal life, he became the historical epicenter of God's plan. When God told Moses to collect the silver redemption money, he was prophetically looking ahead to Jesus and our redemption. In his intentional plan for the silver that the ex-slaves brought out of Egypt, God symbolically foreshadowed our freedom in Christ Jesus from the enslaving law of sin and death. Was all of Heaven in a wonder over the hidden prophetic significance of those silver shekels? Did they know God's plan as the workers, under the desert sun, began to heat the pots of silver to the melting point and reshape it to build a strong and beautiful tabernacle in the wilderness?

When God, who knows all, specified silver to typify ransom and redemption, he surely anticipated the clouds of greed and control that have continued to roll over people and nations. Surely, he was watching over you and me, anticipating our redemption from bondage to slavery and the triumph of Jesus's life of love over death in all its forms.

THE TABERNACLE DOORS

Finally, we reach the tabernacle entrance. It is a thirty-foot section curtained off by a veil of white linen worked with blue, purple and scarlet thread. One door alone breaks the continuity of the white-curtained fence. No one can slip under the fence or into the holy court by a back or side door. One single door opened into the outer court, one into the inner court and one into the holy of holies. These single doors symbolically prefigure the truth in Jesus's words when he said,

> *I am the way, the truth and the life. No one comes to the Father except through me. John 14:6*

I am the door. If anyone enters in by Me, he will be saved, and will go in and will go out and will find pasture.
John 10:9 BLB

THE PILLARS

The white curtains hung from sixty brass pillars set in brass sockets, standing straight and upright, like men on guard around the holy place. At the entryway, four pillars upheld the veil. Although not substantiated by Scriptures, Bible teachers suggest these four pillars might represent the books of Matthew, Mark, Luke and John. As the four pillars once stood at the entrance to the place of God's presence in the tabernacle, reading the four gospels has been a doorway to faith for countless believers.

Another sermon illustration that preachers have drawn from the tabernacle compares the ropes securing the pillars with God's love. The love of Christ alone draws us to his courts. His love upholds the fence and secures the boundaries enclosing his holy activities.

I led them with cords of kindness, with ropes of love.
Hosea 11:4

THE BRASS PINS

The pins or pegs of brass securing the fence represent judgment. Buried in the ground, they rise above it, just as Jesus rose up from death and was lifted above the earth in his ascension to heaven.

When I first heard that the brass sockets and pins symbolized Jesus's judgment holding up the fence, I'd simply accepted it as Bible truth. So, when a friend asked me why, I didn't have an answer. After hours of Bible searching, here's what I discovered.

Scripture repeatedly connects brass with both strength and judgment. The metaphorical association between brass and judgment is fascinating. When God judged Samson and King Zedekiah, they were captured by enemies and bound with fetters of brass.[38] When the Israelites disobeyed God's voice and ignored his commandments, the heavens became like brass. God judged them by refusing to listen to their prayers for rain. That led to crop failure and hunger, a consequence of disobedience.

> *Your sky that is over your head shall be brass, and the earth that is under you shall be iron. Deuteronomy 28:23 WEB*

According to the New Testament, our loveless prayers are jarring to his ears. Instead of hearing the voice of his beloved children, he hears an unwelcome, brassy clang. Neglecting his law of love results in a dissonance between us and God. The automatic consequence is form of judgment.

> *Though I speak with the tongues of men and of angels, but have not love, I have become sounding brass or a clanging cymbal. 1 Corinthians 13:1 NKJV*

The biblical trail connecting judgment and brass with Jesus and the brass footings for the tabernacle gets even hotter:

In Numbers 21, a brass serpent prefigures Jesus in an incident of judgment and redemption. During a bout of discouragement in the wilderness, the Israelites bad-mouthed both God and Moses with grumbling complaints. As judgment, the Lord sent fiery serpents. After many people died of snake bites, the people repented and asked Moses to pray for them. The Lord told Moses to make a bronze [brass] serpent and lift it up on a pole. God promised that,

---

38 You can read about Samson's judgment is in Judges 16:22 and Zedikiah's in 2 Kings 25:7.

If anyone who was bitten looked at the bronze[39] [brass] snake, he would live. Numbers 21:9

Two thousand years later, Jesus identified himself with that brass serpent in the wilderness when he told Nicodemus,

"Just as Moses lifted up the snake in the wilderness, so the Son of man must be lifted up, so that everyone who believes in him may have eternal life." John 3:14, 15

When Jesus's talked to Nicodemus about significance of brass as a symbol of judgment, Nicodemus easily understood what the Lord meant. What he caught onto immediately is hard for us to see. Because he was an educated first century Pharisee who knew scripture, Hebrew history and tradition, he got nuances we miss, they go right over our heads.

One expression he understood was *lifted up*. In the first century AD, being *lifted up* was a common term for crucifixion, just as "getting the chair" is a common idiom for the death sentence today. Nicodemus knew that Jesus was predicting his own inevitable death on the cross.

Another bit of common knowledge shared by Nicodemus and Jesus was the significance of the serpent. Satan disguised himself as a serpent in the Garden of Eden. After he deceived the woman[40] and tempted her to disobey God, God cursed him to crawl on his belly. Thus, almost from day

---

39 One Hebrew word, *nehoshet*, has been translated in various Bible versions as copper, brass, brazen and bronze. The original material was either copper or bronze, an alloy of copper and tin. Brass, a mixture of copper and tin, was unknown; it was first used in Germany in the 10th century.

40 Before their disobedience, man and woman were named by the same word, *Adam*, a plural noun. They were one. Their two halves complemented one another. Each represented a distinct type of personhood; together they were a complete whole, one that reflects the complete image of God whose Spirit incorporates the characteristics of both. When disobedience destroyed their unity in a community of love for one another and God, the woman became known as Eve. Dietrich von Hildebrand discusses the wholeness and beauty that God intended for the union between man and woman in *Marriage, the Mystery of Faithful Love*, Sophia Institute Press, 1997.

one, the serpent came to symbolize Satan, both for his sin of deception and rebellion against God and for God's judgment or curse on him. By using this metaphor, Jesus was telling Nicodemus that the bronze serpent Moses lifted up in the wilderness was a prophetic picture of his own death on the cross that would bring life and healing to those who truly saw it. Christ knew that when he was *lifted up* or nailed onto the cross, those who looked upon him in faith would be healed. Christ knew that he would bear the weight of all our human sin as well as the entire weight of God's judgment on it. He would break the curse, the snake bite of sin, that Adam put upon us. On the cross, he would take God's judgment, die for our sin, and redeem us from the curse put on the natural born children of Adam because of disobedience. When Jesus was *lifted up*, spiritual rebirth would become possible for all who looked upon him in faith. Redemption from Satan's curse was implied in Christ's words to Nicodemus, if he had a heart to hear and understand.[41]

> *Christ has redeemed us from the curse of the law by becoming a curse for us. For it is written, "Cursed is everyone who is hung on a tree." Galatians 3:13*

In other words, on the cross, Jesus defeated the power of sin and death. On the cross, Jesus willingly accepted God's judgment on our human sin and released God's forgiveness for sinners. Because of his innocence, he overcame the power of Satan. He extended love and mercy to all. Our death was defeated in his resurrection. (This truth will come up again and again because the tabernacle pictures it in many ways.)

---

41   I've a hunch Jesus and Nicodemus had many more conversations. Nicodemus must have grown to love Jesus greatly because after Jesus's crucifixion, John tells us that *Joseph of Arimathea, who was a disciple of Jesus (but secretly for fear of the Jews), asked Pilate to let him remove the body of Jesus. Pilate gave him permission, so he came and removed His body. Nicodemus, who had previously come to Jesus at night, also brought a mixture of myrrh and aloes, about seventy-five pounds. So they took the body of Jesus and wrapped it in linen cloths with the spices, according to the Jewish burial custom. John 19:38-40*

Jesus's connection with brass and judgment doesn't end there. Scripture clearly describes the glorified Christ as having feet that appeared like brass. Daniel wrote,

> *His body was like beryl, his face as the appearance of lightning, his eyes as torches of fire, and his arms and his feet like polished brass. Daniel 10:6 adapted*

When John, on the Isle of Patmos, saw the revelation of Jesus Christ,

> *His feet were like burnished brass, as if they had been refined in a furnace*[42] *Revelation 1:15 WEB*

Because Jesus's death took our judgment for sin and defeated Satan on the cross, God put all things under Jesus's feet.

> *He [God] raised him [Jesus] from the dead and seated him at His right hand in the heavenly realms, far above all rule and authority, power and dominion, and every name that is named, not only in the present age but also in the one to come. And God put everything under His feet and made him head over everything for the church, which is His body, the fullness of him who fills all in all. Ephesians 1:20-22*

Thus, Jesus's feet like brass harmonize with the truth that God has put all things under his feet, including judgment.

---

42 As said, in the Old Testament, the words *bronze* and *brass* can refer to either copper or bronze, an alloy of copper and tin. Brass, as we know it today, is an alloy of copper and zinc that didn't come to use until the 13th century. The word *brass* suggests a metallic hardness. A metal purified by fire would refer to Christ's footing and position. The refining fire of his incarnate life, suffering and death, strengthened him and qualified him to be our Great High Priest.

And He has given him authority to execute judgment, because He is the Son of Man. John 5:27

You have put all things in subjection under His feet. Hebrews 2:8 quoting Psalm 8:6 NKJV

Then comes the end, when He delivers the kingdom to God the Father, when He puts an end to all rule and all authority and power. For He must reign till He has put all enemies under His feet. The last enemy that will be destroyed is death. For "He has put everything under His feet."[43] 1 Corinthians 15:24-27a NKJV

Putting it all together, about 3500 years ago, God intentionally specified brass sockets and pins as the footing for the curtains enclosing his courts. The brass was a prophetic symbol of future judgment, of a day still ahead of us when Jesus will judge all evil. All things will be under his feet. In that day, Satan will meet his final defeat, death will be no more, and the tabernacle of God, in all its completeness, will be with us.[44] Surely, in every detail the beauty, truth and order of the tabernacle metaphorically foreshadow God's eternal plan. Surely God was thinking of you, me and our descendants when he began to teach his ways to these fearful Egyptianized former slaves.

Enclosed within the white linen hangings of God's outer court, the Israelites were set apart to God and surrounded by a carefully planned sequence of concrete objects that were designed by God to meaningfully symbolize not only Jesus's life, work and righteousness but also his church. Today, as believers choose to live in agreement with his righteousness (imputed to us as a gift), his Holy Spirit separates us from the

---

43 Paul is quoting Psalm 8:6
44 See Revelation 20, 21

tents of the world and draws us to live in the holiness of God. We walk in Jesus's footsteps in fulfilment of the tabernacle's imagery.

> *Such a high priest truly benefits us—One who is holy, innocent, undefiled, set apart from sinners, and exalted above the heavens; Hebrews 7:26*

THE VEILS

The tabernacle veils were valuable hangings, perhaps more like rugs or medieval tapestries than our 21st century curtains or draperies. They were hung to cover the main entrance to the outer court, the doorway to the inner court and the doorway between the inner court and the holy of holies. Veils imply a separateness, a hiddenness that might conceal a mysterious something in reserve. Whether they're over faces, paintings, sculptures, or doorways, veils suggest ownership and protective privacy. The covering of a dusty burlap curtain or a ragged oil-stained tarp suggests that what's underneath is of little value and the covering can be lifted with impunity. But some veils must not be lifted, some veiled thresholds may not be crossed without permission.

A bridal veil of fine lace, a curtain of flowing velvet or a heavy intricately woven tapestry imply that whatever is hidden and protected behind the veil might be of great value. Jesus's birth, hidden away in a stable, hid his infinite value. The tabernacle, from start to finish, from the curtains to the roof coverings and covered doorways is a veiled object lesson about the inestimable worth of God's treasure in Jesus, about God's separateness and the hiddenness of his ways.

> *The glory of God [is] to hide a thing, And the glory of kings [is] to search out a matter. Proverbs 25:2 LSV*

God's ways can be like Jesus's parables, hidden in plain sight, yet needing interpretation.

> *Jesus spoke all these things to the crowds in parables. He did not tell them anything without using a parable. So was fulfilled what was spoken through the prophet: "I will open My mouth in parables; I will utter things hidden since the foundation of the world." Matthew 13:34-35*

Jesus was revealed in the tabernacle, and the tabernacle was revealed in Jesus. Both are a

> *revelation of the mystery concealed for ages past but now revealed and made known through the writings of the prophets [including Moses] by the command of the eternal God, in order to lead all nations to the obedience that comes from faith— Romans 16: 25b-26a NKJV*

Lord! Help us get it. Please.

The beautiful tapestry-like veils that hung over the doors into the outer court, the inner court and holy of holies were different, just as the meaning and function of each place differed. Crossing each threshold into the interior of the tabernacle required a new and different level of consecration and purity. Each passage required a relinquishment, a leaving something behind, and each required a fuller identification with Jesus's death and a greater appropriation of his life.

The first veil or hanging we pass through on leaving the busy activity of camp life and entering the outer court was beautifully woven of blue, purple and scarlet threads. It was "curiously wrought" or as some translations say, "variously mixed" Later on, we'll look at the veil before the holy of holies; it was woven and embroidered with the same yarns, but it was cunningly embroidered with cherubim.[45] This difference is far more than a matter of decorative design. It reflects the distinct differences between the outer court, inner court, and holy of holies.

God's house is a bit like ours. When others come, we meet them at the front entryway or foyer. If they're welcome, we invite them further in—perhaps to an office or living room. For most of us, only our closest friends and family are welcome into our personal space, rooms like our bedrooms and closets. I don't enter my sister's room without her invitation. In visiting Queen Elizabeth, you might go from the waiting area to the reception hall, but only those who qualify are welcome inside her majesty's most personal quarters.

Comparisons between the cherubim embroidered inner court veils with the outer court veil of variously mixed colors illustrate the truth that the closer we approach the Lord the more details we see of his beauty, truth and love. We don't see heavenly things as clearly from a distance as we do when we draw closer to God. Perhaps the most significant prophetic truth about every doorway and veil is its prophetic picture of going through Jesus; he is the only way to draw near to God.

> *I am the way, the truth and the life. No man comes to the Father but by me. John 14:6 NKJV*

> *Therefore, brethren, having boldness to enter the Holiest by the blood of Jesus, by a new and living way which He consecrated for us, through the veil, that is, His flesh,*
> *Hebrews 10:19-20 NKJV*

---

45 Was the veil thick or thin? There is no way of knowing. Scripture doesn't say. The traditional idea that it was four inches thick or the breadth of a man's hand comes from the Mishnah, but the rabbis themselves said that four inches was hyperbole. Thick or thin, it's logical to imagine that the embroidery was heavy enough to act like a room darkening shade so that the light of God's glory would not shine through and harm the priests who ministered in the inner court. (Personally, although most likely wrong, I like to imagine faint rays of God's presence shining through.) https://cbumgardner.wordpress.com/2010/04/06/the-thickness-of-the-temple-veil/

LOOKING AROUND, MORE OUTER COURT THOUGHTS

Can you imagine you've parted the first veil and entered the outer court? Can you look around and picture yourself enclosed in the white linen fabric fence? Let's take a moment to reflect on this fence around us. The white linen represents Christ's righteousness, hanging from the silver clasps and cross bars that symbolize his redemption. The bars that hold up the hangings are secured and held upright in brass sockets and pins symbolizing God's judgment.

Here, within the tabernacle court, we stand at a most significant time and place in human history. Here, in beauty and in carefully structured order, God is beginning to teach the human race lasting truths about his historical plan for all people. He's doing it by walking his people Israel through a concrete, objective pattern of heavenly worship that foreshadows the spiritual realities of worship available to you, me and all peoples everywhere.

It's most unlikely that the Israelites saw much (if anything) of the prophetic meanings built into the linen curtains or bronze footings, the brazen altar or the laver. But the men who led and carried their sacrifices into the outer court didn't need anyone to tell them about the significance of the silver hooks and rings. They knew that the silver had redeemed and ransomed them and their sons. They understood temporary redemption from sin by sacrificing animals. Slavery and redemption had marked their personal natural lives.

Now their father's God was starting to teach them about freedom—not earthly economic, political, or social freedom—but the freedom of his responsible eternal love. God knew that eventually his word of love would spread to all the peoples of the world.

It's worth repeating that because the court was sanctified by the blood of animals, the white linen curtains of righteousness prophetically pictured you, me and every believer who puts on the righteousness of Christ. The white curtains not only illustrate putting on Jesus's righteousness, they also picture how he surrounds and encloses us. Jesus's righteousness, imputed to us as a gift from God, separates us from the outside world. All who freely come to Jesus and choose life in his courts become holy or separated unto God. We begin a journey toward ever increasing holiness.

The white curtain fence shuts us in with God, and it shuts out all that is not God. Enclosed within the linen curtains there is grace and faith to accept God's love and begin to get to know him. He gives us grace to drop off our worries, fears, self-sufficiencies, servitudes and pride. He gives us grace to conform to his moral standards and character, to become merciful and honest, to love goodness and to hate all that he calls evil.

Once inside his courts we begin to leave our small worlds and enter God's glorious one. Our journeys begin with our conscious desire to know God and be separated unto Him. It takes a teachable willingness to follow the Holy Spirit. As we agree with and receive his grace, we begin our journey, our transformation from self-willed independence and slavery to the world's systems into the freedom of God's own beloved children.

The brazen altar that stands before us foreshadows our own redemption at the cross of Jesus. Will we approach it? Will we say yes to God? Looking beyond it, we see the laver, a symbol of our sanctification.

> *How much more shall the blood of Christ, who through the eternal Spirit offered himself without spot to God, cleanse your conscience from dead works to serve the living God?*
> *Hebrews 9:14 NKJV*

The brazen altar and laver illustrate God's pattern for cleansing us from dead works, for setting us free from every attitude and activity that lacks the luster and energy of God-life. They teach us how to receive God's grace, peace, love, joy and strength. Here, standing within the Lord's court, the Holy Spirit can open the eyes of our heart to receive Jesus's love. God himself becomes our security. In the courts of the Lord, we don't need to lean upon our own tents, that is, our own thoughts and feelings, our own positions, families, money, reputations, achievements or stories. We begin to discover our identity in God. We're safe at home—known, accepted and loved by our Father in heaven.

David's Psalm 84 captures the joy living within God's courts.

> *How lovely is Your tabernacle, O Lord of hosts!*
> *My soul longs, yes, even faints*
> *For the courts of the Lord;*
> *My heart and my flesh cry out for the living God.*
> *Even the sparrow has found a home,*
> *And the swallow a nest for herself,*
> *Where she may lay her young—*
> *Even Your altars, O Lord of hosts,*
> *My King and my God.*

> *For a day in Your courts is better than a thousand.*
> *I would rather be a doorkeeper in the house of my God*
> *Than dwell in the tents of wickedness.*
> *For the Lord God is a sun and shield;*
> *The Lord will give grace and glory;*
> *No good thing will He withhold*

From those who walk uprightly.
O Lord of hosts,
Blessed is the man who trusts in You!
Psalm 84:1-3 and 10-12 NKJV

Within the Lord's courts, we discover that our separation from the world, the flesh and the devil doesn't come from our own will power or by rigid adherence to religious rules and regulations but from adhering to God; it is prompted by love. As we learn more about Jesus through the tabernacle symbolism, a strong and vibrant love begins to draw us on and motivate our daily choices. Responding by faith, we can set our eyes upon Jesus, open our hearts to his love, and let the Holy Spirit guide us into a close and trusting relationship with him and our Father in heaven.

THE BRAZEN ALTAR:
THE CROSS

Going back in time and reaching out our hands to part the veil and step into the outer court, the brazen altar stands smack dab front and center before us. The altar is hot and smoky. The air around it is rich with the smells of blood, dripping fats, burnt and roasting meats. The ground around the altar and the once shining brass of the altar are splattered with the blood of sacrifices; so are the priest's white linen tunics. The blood-stained fabric is identified with the life-blood of the animals offered to God.

Bible scholars agree that this ancient altar represents the cross. This place of death, where the blood of animals was poured out on the ground in the Old Covenant and where Christ's blood was poured out for us in the New Covenant, stands at the entrance to our relationship to God. Since God is pure, holy and eternally alive, impurity and death are the first

THE TABERNACLE

things God's people need to take care of when coming to him. Since Jesus overcame all our sin and death on the cross, the brazen altar foreshadows the sacrifice of Jesus. Let's turn our thoughts from Moses and the bright desert sky over the Sinai and look ahead to consider why.

Early in Jesus's ministry, he went to the synagogue in Nazareth and read the first verses of Isaiah 61 to the people.

> *The Spirit of the Lord is on Me,*
> *because He has anointed Me*
> *to preach good news to the poor.*
> *He has sent Me to proclaim liberty to the captives*
> *and recovery of sight to the blind,*
> *to release the oppressed,*
> *to proclaim the year of the Lord's favor. Luke 4: 18-19*

Then Jesus closed the scroll and said,

Today this scripture is fulfilled in your hearing. Luke 4:20

If the Lord had continued reading Isaiah's prophesy about himself, he would have read,

I will rejoice greatly in the LORD,
my soul will exult in my God;
for He has clothed me with garments of salvation
and wrapped me in a robe of righteousness,
as a bridegroom wears a priestly headdress,
as a bride adorns herself with her jewels. Isaiah 61:10

Jesus wore garments of salvation. Because of his sinless purity and unbroken love for his Father, God wrapped him in a robe of righteousness. Jesus was, is, and forever will be the only worthy, perfect, spotless sacrifice for sin. His obedience of faith and love led to a crown of thorns, the spattered blood of flogging and his death on the cross for our sin. As Isaiah prophesied and Paul wrote,

God made him who knew no sin to be sin on our behalf, so that
we might become the righteousness of God in him.
2 Corinthians 5:21

Jesus lived and died in the certainty that his death was necessary for our righteousness. More than any of us, Jesus understood the grim reality of sin and death and the glorious reality of a righteous life in God. He knew that the warm and pulsing life-blood that flowed through his own veins and arteries would atone for our sins. First century Jewish believers accepted the reality of sin and understood atonement by blood sacrifice. Jesus knew his place in history. He knew that the righteousness by faith of all who believed on him and identified with the cleansing power of his blood, was visibly foreshadowed by the animal sacrifices and the blood spatters upon the white linen tunics of the priests who served at the bronze altar in the Sinai Peninsula so long ago.

After Jesus's death, he took John, his beloved disciple, up to heaven in the spirit, where in a vision, John heard a roar, like a rumbling of thunder, crying out,

> *Hallelujah!*
> *For our Lord God, the Almighty, reigns.*
> *Let us rejoice and be glad and give him the glory.*
> *For the marriage of the Lamb has come,*
> *and His bride has made herself ready.*
> *She was given clothing of fine linen, bright and pure.*
> *For the fine linen she wears is the righteous acts of the saints.*
> *Revelation 10:6b-8*

In John's vision, we're the righteous ones. You and me. But our righteousness is not our own. Our clothing of fine linen, enclosing us like the tent, put on and wrapped around us like Jesus's robe, bright like Joseph's coat of many colors and pure and white like the light of God, is given to us because we live by faith in Jesus Christ.

> *The gospel . . . is the power of God for salvation to everyone who believes, first to the Jew, then to the Greek. For the gospel reveals the righteousness of God that comes by faith from start to finish, just as it is written: "The righteous will live by faith."*
> *Romans 1:16-17*

Those faith-filled turbaned priests, putting sacrifices on the grate, feeding the fire and shoveling the ashes out under the open sky, don't look like any priests or pastors we've ever seen. To us, their blood-spattered linen garments and down-to-earth service to God would look messy and menial, more like a slaughterhouse than a place of worship.

Bloody not, we cannot enter further into the place of God's presence without stopping before this brazen altar. Our sacrifice is not an animal, it is Jesus Christ. We bring ourselves to him. When he died on the cross, he identified with human sinfulness and accepted the just consequence of death for sin. But because he had committed no sin, because he was pure and spotless, he did not die for his own sin. He died for the sin of those who crucified him, he died for his friends, and in his identification with the entire human race, he died for the sin of all who will believe in him.

Ever since Calvary, whenever a person humbly comes before the altar of the cross with faith in Jesus's blood sacrifice and identifies with his death, he or she personally receives his full atonement, his expiation, his reparation, his forgiveness for our inborn sinful human nature. In other words, by identifying with Jesus's death, confessing our sin and accepting that Jesus gave his life as a substitute for ours, we are redeemed. We are set free us from the consequences of Adam's rebellion and reunited with God. We become a part of God's family and enter into his historical plan. We also participate with Jesus in fulfilling the truth prefigured by the brazen altar.

When we acknowledge our own unworthiness and need and turn to faith in the reality of the power of shed blood of Jesus's sacrifice on the cross, we are saved. The word *saved*, so often dismissed as a religious cliché, is the English translation of the Greek word *sozo* which means safe. To be *saved* is to be kept safe and sound. It's far more than Jesus's promise of eternal life and an insurance policy against torment in the hellfire and brimstone of God's eternal judgment. To be *saved* in this life on earth includes all the joys of relationship with Jesus. Full salvation, *sozo,* includes healing and deliverance from emotional and psychological injury and imbalances and from physical illness and diseases. *Sozo* includes God's guidance, protection and strength through every threat of danger and destruction.[46]

To sum up, the brazen altar foreshadows the cross of Jesus Christ where God forgives us and takes away the weight of hidden wrong-doing, pours out his love on us and plants the seed of his Spirit within us to give us new life. Stopping at the altar to accept Jesus's blood sacrifice (typified by imperfect animal sacrifice) and to give ourselves to God is imperative. It's absolutely necessary, because God is clean and pure; he is holy, totally loving and just—and we aren't. We are of the flesh and of the world, impure and imperfect in love. God is Spirit and is of heaven, beyond all dimensions. We need the indwelling Holy Spirit to give us God's nature and to teach us to live in relationship with our Creator.

But when we first approach the brazen altar, most Christians don't know any of this history, theology or doctrine of salvation. We don't need to know it either. All we need to know is Jesus and his love.

For some new believers, salvation is joyous decision. For others, particularly small children raised in Christian homes, salvation is a simple quiet almost unrecognized automatic faith-acceptance of Jesus. For still others it's a growth process; we come to believe so gradually that we hardly know the moment we cross faith's threshold and enter God's family. But for some, new birth into God's kingdom is like natural childbirth—transitioning from the old self-life to the new life in Christ takes effort. When the light of God's holy love begins to reveal his truth and beauty and expose our sin and need, we cry out for forgiveness; we're broken and repentant; we long for forgiveness and peace with God. As we cry and pray through to peace, the Holy Spirit never fails to bring

---

[46] *Strongs Exhaustive Concordance* number 4982 and *Theological Dictionary of the New Testament* entry 7:965, 1132 found on https://www.biblestudytools.com/lexicons/greek/nas/sozo.html

us through. God never condemns us, he covers our pain with his love. As we confess and turn from sin and unbelief to faith in God, he forgets our failures to love. All he sees is the blood of Jesus, shed for us. As our heavenly Father welcomes us into his family, he thanks his Son for living and dying to bring another rebellious child back home. There is no formula or "best model" for salvation. Jesus is our way to God.

When I first went to the brazen altar, the place that symbolizes the cross where we give ourselves to God, I'd never heard of it. The cross meant little to me personally (beyond being a horrible thing), and I didn't have any idea what I was doing. Oh, I'd heard about Jesus; I knew the Christmas and Easter events and a few stories about his miracles. I'd even experienced God and sensed traces of Jesus's presence in songs, people and places. Back then, when I was a child, his nearness was always like the sunshine, making the atmosphere bright and peaceful and making me feel happier, safer and more peaceful too. But those glimpses of spiritual reality and truth beyond my normal daily life never lasted. When the song was over, the person gone, the class done or I walked away from the grace-filled place, the light and gladness dimmed. It was years before I could link those childhood memories of brightness and energy surrounding special times and people with the Jesus of our holidays and with our Father God, Creator of all creation.

Testimonies about finding Jesus are fascinating and varied. A relative came to faith while reading a book; a dear friend surrendered to Jesus's love at her first communion; C.S. Lewis came to faith on a motorcycle side car. I was at church, listening to the pastor, when God's love reached out to me in a life-defining moment. That Sunday night, sitting alone on a hard wooden pew in a Swedish Covenant church, I met Jesus at the brazen altar (a type of the cross) and gave him my heart. I cried and cried. My offering or sacrifice was myself. I must have confessed my sins and said the words aloud, because when the service was over, and I walked out of the church, an elderly handshaking man at the door said I was "born again." I didn't understand what that meant, but that night, all that light, gladness, peace and energy of Jesus was no longer outside me; holy love had filled my spirit and Jesus filled me with joy! For five years that brightness and peace stayed with me. I didn't even recognize it as Jesus (or maybe his Holy Spirit), but he went with me—even when I ignored him and didn't live by his ways of love. His light might withdraw now and then when I did wrong, but perhaps because I was young and untaught God didn't seem to hold me guilty, because his light always came back. I soon got so used to him that I never connected his light with that night of tears at the altar and took it for granted as a part of me.

Five years later, that all changed in less than an hour when a college religion teacher convinced my mind (not my heart) against Jesus. I left the classroom in tears and cried deeply once again—this time from grief and loss. I lost the inner light and gladness that I'd thought were my own. Twelve years after that, when the light came back, it was a tiny pinprick. To get closer to Jesus, I had to fight demons, dirt and lies left by wounds, grief, and patterns of doubt. I went to church and prayer meetings. I read my Bible, I made friends with people who knew God, and listened to music alive with his Spirit. I had to seek him.

And seek I did, because it had become a matter of life and death and I knew it. When I'd first met Jesus, as a girl, I was naïve and untaught in the ways of God. I knew Jesus lived in my heart, that's about all. When I came back to him as an adult, I knew I was a sinner who was ignorant of his ways. Starved for his love and eager to learn, I hungrily took a series of inductive, college-level home-study courses in the Bible. Gradually, one thing at a time, God's word began to educate my conscience to his standards and holiness. The Holy Spirit began to reveal my pride and uncover places of resentment and unforgiveness. Life was my larger classroom, the proverbial school of hard knocks. Financial needs and problems, workplace injustice and clashes with friends and family were God's lessons in the futility of my own independent self-sufficiency. Disappointments and closed doors exposed my own control issues, self-pity and an unwillingness to trust outcomes to God.

Some of his lessons were about hidden sins and repentance; other lessons were about hearing his voice, obedience, maturity and growth. All of God's lessons were, and still are, about learning to love him and others. In teaching us to love, so many of God's lessons and tests were (and continue to be) about weaknesses I hadn't seen. Most of my unhealthy responses to challenges were rooted in family patterns and firmly held inner vows that I'd made as a child coping with powerlessness. Under it all were old, hardened scabs covering unhealed (often forgotten) wounds.

As a simple illustration, Jesus repeatedly tells us, *"Fear not."* Peter repeats it,

> *"Do not be afraid of their threats, nor be troubled."*
> *1 Peter 3: 14 NKJV*

As a young child, I'd learned to fear both of my parents and one of my sisters. Fear strangles love. My father did not like scaredy cats, so I became afraid to be afraid. I coped variously, by pretending courage, by avoidance and by silence. I was outwardly confident and inwardly fragile. My habits of denying, squelching and holding emotions inside were so strong that I almost stopped feeling anything except occasional undeniable out bursts of anger. A thinker might have gotten away with it, but according to every psychological test I've ever taken, feeling is my modus operandi. Eventually, all my suppressed and stored-up fears reached the tipping point and began to spill over. After the 1965 Palm Sunday tornado had killed a high school classmate's father, left some of our friends homeless, and leveled the homes and traumatized two sweet pre-teen girls who kept reliving

THE TABERNACLE

the pain in a Daily Vacation Bible School class I taught that summer, I developed an unreasonable fear of tornadoes. Years of fear spilled over and burst into an obsession about tornado safety. I gradually recovered. Five years later, triggered by a combination of losses, violence and trauma, I was blindsided again by unrealistic fears. The psychologists I consulted didn't help.

How did I get over it? By turning to God. Again and again and again. Initially, his encouragement to "Fear not," didn't penetrate my protective armor or change the fearful synapses wired throughout my nervous system. Eventually, God's love and my longing to love Jesus with all my heart and soul and mind and strength got through. One choice at a time, the Holy Spirit led me out into moments of courage. He gave me the strength to do whatever I believed he wanted. If I thought the Holy Spirit wanted me to go somewhere, I'd pray and go. If I thought he wanted me to speak up at a meeting, I'd pray hard to myself, take the risky plunge and speak out. If I heard, "Call that person on the phone" I'd pray again for courage and make the call. One step at a time, by clinging to God's word in the obedience of faith, hope and love, God covered the old fear-circuits in my brain with new faith-pathways and led me out into freedom.

Today, with fresh fearful circumstances in the world, the obedience of faith continues. This process all began at the cross (symbolized by the brazen altar). After my initial confession of sin, the Holy Spirit began to teach me how to wash my mind and attitudes in his word (symbolized by the laver—more about that later). I kept at it, because I'd lived in the death and darkness of self-life outside his courts and I knew the difference now.

It awes me to realize that the simple, untaught steps I took toward God, first as a child and then as a troubled woman in my thirties, were not unique. Over 4,000 years ago in the Sinai wilderness, God had directed, ordered, established, and symbolically illustrated the way to seek him and find him. The design of God's tabernacle foreshadowed my own path, my own need to grow from a baby Christian into a more mature likeness to Jesus. That's why, here and now, in the 21st century, it matters that the brazen altar prophetically points to Jesus's blood sacrifice at the cross.[47]

Since every animal sacrificed on the altar represented some aspect of the death of Christ, our substitute, let's look more closely at how the altar, as an actual object, foreshadowed the place where Jesus secured our atonement, our justification.

The brazen altar was the biggest piece of furniture in the tabernacle. It stood five cubits high by three cubits square (17 ½' x 4 ½') and it represents God's most significant revelation to us. Some Bible students suggest that the dimensions, three cubits square, refer to Jesus as part of the Trinity. The altar was five cubits high. Bible students who associate the number five with God's grace,[48] suggest that the height of five cubits has come to represent God's grace to us through Jesus Christ. The identical four-square sides speak of one cross and Savior; Jesus is the same for all who turn to him, the downs syndrome child or the university professor, the murderer or the priest. Because the altar rested upon the bare earth, the approach from every side is lowly and humble. It was quite unlike pagan altars which were raised up high and elevated the pagan priests. God forbade steps so that no naked flesh would ever be exposed beneath the skirts of those who might climb up any steps to reach the grate.

---

47 The Appendix entry, "Why is the Brazen Altar that Important?" discusses in greater details how the brazen altar prophetically corresponds to Jesus.

48 Kevin J. Conner, *Interpreting the Symbols and Types*, City Bible Publishing, 1980, p. 53

THE TABERNACLE

The brass-covered wood pictures the humanity of Christ taking our judgment. Just as the brass withstood the heat of the fire without weakening, Jesus endured God's wrath toward sin on the cross without faltering or weakening. The fires of judgment could not destroy him.

The four horns, one at each corner of the altar, represent Christ's power and might. They were functional. The priests used them to bind the sacrifices to the altar, to hold them fast. Some commentators suggest they are a type of the restraint that held Jesus to the cross.[49] Pointing in all four compass directions, the four horns metaphorically illustrate Christ's saving-love extending out from the cross unto the four corners of the earth.

Because the altar was holy, whoever touched the horns of the brazen altar was made legally, or positionally, holy. The Lord instructed Moses to

> *Purify the altar by making atonement for it, and anoint it to consecrate it. For seven days make atonement for the altar and consecrate it. Then the altar will be most holy, and whatever touches it will be holy. Exodus 29:36b-37 NIV*

The altar's holiness was not a nice abstract metaphysical idea. It was a lifesaving reality. King David's son Adonijah once saved his life by holding onto its horns. Although David had openly chosen Solomon as his successor, Solomon's brother, Adonijah, was secretly plotting a coup to usurp Solomon and set himself up as king before David's death. King David found out about it. When Adonijah heard that his plot had been uncovered, he feared for his life. He immediately went to the altar for safety—and found it.

---

49 Was Jesus held to the cross by nails or by ropes? The evidence is inconclusive. Bottom line, it doesn't matter. Love held him fast. Some translations of John's description of Jesus's wounded hands support the use of nails. Other Bible scholars say the Gospel texts aren't clear about whether he was nailed or tied to the cross. There is historical evidence that the Romans used both nails and ropes. https://theconversation.com/was-jesus-really-nailed-to-the-cross-56321

> *And Adonijah feared because of Solomon, and arose, and went, and caught hold on the horns of the altar. 1 Kings 1:50 KJV*

In the New Testament, Jesus clearly said that the holiness of the altar, its separation to God, was imputed to all that was offered upon it. In rebuking the Pharisees, he said,

> *And you say, "If anyone swears by the altar, it means nothing; but if anyone swears by the gift on it, he is bound by his oath. You blind men! Which is greater: the gift, or the altar that makes it sacred [holy]?" Matthew 23:18-19*

Our sanctification, or holiness, comes from Jesus, not from any altar. But interestingly important to us today, Paul says that our holiness as Christians is transferable. Not only are spiritual truths often more caught than taught, Paul suggests that a believer's true holiness has power to bring safety and a degree of sanctification to our immediate family.[50] Was Jesus alluding to that when he said that a "light gives light to everyone in the house?"

> *You are the light of the world. A city on a hill cannot be hidden. Neither do people light a lamp and put it under a basket. Instead, they set it on a stand, and it gives light to everyone in the house. In the same way, let your light shine before men, that they may see your good deeds and glorify your Father in heaven. Matthew 5:14-16*

It makes sense. In the natural realm our life choices, conduct and values will usually influence the sphere around us and the people closest to us. In the spiritual realm, the light of Christ's holy life within us

---

50 See: 1 Timothy 3:4-5, 1 Timothy 5:4, 8

influences others too. As we yield to God's love, the Holy Spirit can change the atmosphere around us so that others will glorify our heavenly Father. This partially explains the mystery of holiness, but there's an inexplicable dimension to receive by faith in Paul's words that

> *The unbelieving husband is sanctified through his believing wife, and the unbelieving wife is sanctified through her believing husband. Otherwise your children would be unclean, but now they are holy. 1 Corinthians 7:14*

The power of this realm of solid faith in God (not fantasy or human imagination) is a mystery to all who have not known its reality.

The mercy that Old Testament believers found by grabbing onto the horns of the altar is another illustration of how Jesus fulfills every object lesson in the tabernacle. Everything about the brazen altar speaks of Christ. Everything! Symbolically, Jesus is the altar itself; he also was the sacrificial gift offered upon it. He was also the priest who offered the sacrifice. God grants us a reprieve from death when we hold fast to Jesus's death for us. God accepts his blood as payment for our sins and grants us eternal life.

This prophetic illustration of finding God's mercy by holding onto the horns at the corners of the brazen altar is one more golden thread of truth that runs through four thousand years of Judeo-Christian history—right down from the Sinai wilderness to you, me and our families.

> *Seeing then that we have a great High Priest who has passed through the heavens, Jesus the Son of God, let us hold fast our confession. . . . Let us therefore come boldly to the throne of grace, that we may obtain mercy and find grace to help in time of need. Hebrews 4:14-16 NKJV*

Not only did Jesus foreshadow the altar, the sacrifice and the priest, it was Jesus's fire, God's own holy fire, that consumed the offering. It was the same fire that St. John of the Cross[51] described as

O living flame of love
That tenderly wounds my soul
In its deepest center!

THE FIRE

The fire in the brazen altar was hot and smoky. It burned like any other natural fire, but its origin was supernatural and its flames burned with a life-changing holiness. When the first offering was placed on the altar,

Fire came out from the presence of the LORD and consumed the burnt offering and the fat portions on the altar. Leviticus 9:24

---

51 You can read all of St. John's *O Living Flame of Love* at https://www.jesus-passion.com/LivingFlameLove.htm

The heavenly fire on the brazen altar was carefully tended and not allowed to go out. Every animal offered was consumed by God's ongoing flame.

> *The Lord your God is a consuming fire.*
> Deuteronomy 4:24

> *For our God is a consuming fire.*
> Hebrews 12:29

God's fire is holy. All that comes out from God's presence is holy. His fires purify, refine and test his own people.

> *And I will bring the third part [of my people] through the fire,*
> *Refine them as silver is refined,*
> *And test them as gold is tested.*
> *They will call on My name, And I will answer them;*
> *I will say, 'They are My people,'*
> *And they will say, "The Lord is my God."*
> Zechariah 13:9 NASB

His fires also bring judgment and rebuke to his enemies.

> *For behold, the Lord will come in fire*
> *And His chariots like the whirlwind,*
> *To render His anger with fury,*
> *And His rebuke with flames of fire.*
> Isaiah 66:15 NKJV

Many human fires are not holy or just. Our fires arise from the sparks of natural passion within our very own hearts. They can hurt others and often call attention to us, to our wounds, styles, faults, needs and personal goals. Some are demonically fed. Our fires are defiling, restless, untamable and never satisfied. Jesus said that

> *A man is not defiled by what enters his mouth, but by what comes out of it . . . the things that come out of the mouth come from the heart, and these things defile a man. For out of the heart come evil thoughts, murder, adultery, sexual immorality, theft, false testimony, and slander. These are what defile a man."* Matthew 15:11, 18-20

Jesus's brother James compared the words that come out of our mouths to fire.

> *The tongue is a small part of the body, but it boasts of great things. Consider how small a spark sets a great forest ablaze. The tongue also is a fire, a world of wickedness among the parts of the body. It pollutes the whole person, sets the course of his life on fire, and is itself set on fire by hell. All kinds of animals, birds, reptiles, and creatures of the sea are being tamed and have been tamed by man, but no man can tame the tongue. It is a restless evil, full of deadly poison. James 3: 5-9*

God's fires satisfy; they illuminate, they guide, cleanse and purify; they burn in us with a holy love for God and others.

Because Jesus is God, a holy consuming fire is part of his very nature. Not only did he substitute for the animal on the altar, he is, was, and will always be the divine fire that comes down from heaven to consume the offering. His fire does the work, not the altar itself. For only God's holy fire can consume our sin. Only in Jesus can we be reconciled with a pure and perfectly holy God. He wants us to know his fire. John the Baptist prophesied of Jesus that

He will baptize you with the Holy Spirit and with fire.
Matthew 3:11, Luke 3:16

Jesus's words began to come true when the Holy Spirit came to earth at the first Pentecost and filled believers with God's presence and power.

What seemed to be tongues of fire that separated came to rest on each them. Acts 2:3

The fire on the brazen altar, Jesus's sacrificial death on the cross and the Holy Spirit's fire at Pentecost were onetime events. Although the fire on the historical brazen altar eventually went out, Jesus's fulfillment of the truths it foreshadowed are eternal. His flames of love continue to consume sin. One day, his holy fire will judge all that is from the world, flesh and devil. As we say "Yes, Lord!" to him today, he ignites the fires of his love within our very own hearts and souls. Every one of us must pass through his holy purifying flames before we can come boldly into the presence of our Father in heaven.

Oh, how much we need the cleansing flames of the Holy Spirit to help us die to self and live in union with Jesus. His love is hot enough to burn away sin, to consume our self-centered motivations, to ignite the very light of Jesus within us and to empower us to do his will. As our human natures surrender to his love, his healing warmth moves out through us to touch others; his light illuminates the truth of his word to us, in us and through us.

Every flame that rose up to consume an animal sacrifice on the brazen altar sent forth a prediction of Jesus's body as a burnt sacrifice for us. Every type of sacrifice at the brazen altar prefigured the practical steps that believers walk through in learning God's two greatest commandments.

> "Hear O Israel, the Lord our God, the Lord is One. Love the Lord your God with all your heart and with all your soul and with all your mind and with all your strength. The second is this: Love your neighbor as yourself. No other commandment is greater than these." Mark 12:29-31[52]

Loving God and others isn't always easy. Not only is our own love not enough, God's love is qualitatively different than ours. To love as God loves requires dying to our own ways and choosing to live God's way by the power of his Spirit. The altar, with its undying flames, is a metaphor for both our vicarious identification with Christ's death (dying to our own ways) and our resurrection into new lives of holy love. Long ago, in the 1980's, I wrote a poem to describe my own experience with the fire on God's altar.

Burnt Sacrifice

I climb upon the grate—
or am I placed?
I crawl across the top—
or am I led from edge to edge?

Expecting to be burnt
by the glowing coals below,
waiting for hot flames to flare
and loss consume my soul,
what a surprise to find
God's heat is kind.

---

[52] Matthew 22:37, Luke 10:27, Galatian 5:14b, James 2:8

THE *Tabernacle*

His fires energize
His flames melt down all chains that bind,
His burning coals transform our minds,
with warming love He realigns
each life that yields to his designs.

Climb upon his altars,
Surrender to his fires,
He burns all false device
if we give our all to him
to be burnt sacrifice.[53]

---

53 "Burnt Sacrifice" was first published in *Places*, 2011© Ginny Emery

THE LAVER

What is a laver? The word is out of use today, but familiar words, like Lava soap and lavatory come from its root, *lavatorium,* the Latin word for washing. A laver is a large washbasin, often set on a pedestal. Lavatoriums are designed for communal wash up times. In the middle ages, monks gathered around a communal lavatorium to wash before meals. The tabernacle laver was also a community washbasin. It sat in the outer court, between the brazen altar and the door to the inner court. Scripture doesn't specify the exact position of the laver. Some scholars place the laver to the side of the brazen altar, in a step-saving location so that the priests would not need to walk around it to enter the inner court. Others, who see a cross in the furniture's placement, place the laver directly in line with every tabernacle door.

Both before and after participating in the sacrifices at the brazen altar, the priests would walk straight to the laver and wash themselves. No priest would dare to enter the inner court without washing his hands and feet or inspecting his face in the mirrors to wash off ashes, soot and his bloody spots and stains.[54] Being set aside to serve the Lord did not automatically cleanse them and does not automatically cleanse us from worldliness and the impurities hidden within our own souls

THE WATER

A dry laver is useless for cleansing. Water is essential. In the natural, water sustains life and growth, refreshes, energizes, cleanses, heals, moisturizes, balances, flushes out toxins and both transports and absorbs other elements necessary for well-being. In the spirit, water pictures the same things. Without water, life as we live it on earth would dry up

---

54   Whether or not the priests inspected their faces in the mirrors is conjecture. What matters is the concept of ongoing cleanliness, of washing away all dirty spots and stains.

and die. Without the water of God's life, we dry up and die spiritually. Biblical stories about natural water include God's life-saving provision for the thirsting children of Israel and for Hagar and Ishmael. For Naaman, the leper, dipping into the Jordan's waters brought healing. Jesus used water as a metaphor for both himself and his Holy Spirit when he told the Samaritan woman at the well

> *"Everyone who drinks this water [from Jacob's well] will be thirsty again. But whoever drinks the water I give him will never thirst. Indeed, the water I give him will become in him a fount of water springing up to eternal life." John 4:13-14*

Since Moses gave no dimensions for the laver, we've no idea how much water it held. It's an interesting omission, possibly intentional, since God places no restrictive dimensions or limits on the application of his word for cleansing, for slaking our thirst or for the water of his life-giving Spirit.

> *And let him who thirsts come. Whoever desires, let him take of the water of life freely. Revelation 22:17 NKJV*

Water is a consistent Bible metaphor for spiritual realities. From the words in Genesis 1:1 where the

> *"Spirit of God was hovering over the face of the waters"*

all the way through the Bible to Jesus's baptism in the Jordan (to identify with us) and to the believer's baptismal immersion in water (that testifies to our faith that Jesus's blood has cleansed us from sin and we have died and buried our old life and risen to new life in Jesus)[55] right down to the final chapter where the

---

55 Acts 2:36-38 and Romans 6:1-4

> *"pure river of the water of life, clear as crystal, proceeds from the throne of God and of the Lamb" Revelation 22:1*

Jesus clearly identified water with the cleansing power of his word when he told his disciples,

> *Now you are clean through the word which I have spoken to you. John 15:3 and*

> *Sanctify them by Your truth, Your word is truth. John 17:17 NKJV*

GETTING CLEAN

The laver full of water is a type of the ongoing cleansing work of Jesus Christ as the living word of God. The cleansing power of God's word is not found by memorizing Bible verses and building intellectual understanding. It's in letting the Holy Spirit put God's word into our hearts, where it can correct us, teach us and strengthen and encourage us. We can relate to God and receive the light of his love through his word.

Often one word, phrase or thought takes hold of us. Meditating on a word like l*ove, mercy, Father* and *forgiveness* can fill an hour or more. Recently, on a Zoom prayer meeting, as someone read from the book of Romans, I was gripped by the little word *let*. Phrases like *"let* this mind be in you that was in Christ Jesus" and "don't *let* sin reign in your mortal body" filled my thoughts. I looked *let* up in the dictionary and saw my part in *letting*, that is, in allowing or giving permission to ungodly thoughts. I saw the significance of intentionally turning toward Jesus and allowing, permitting or *letting* the Holy Spirit's light fill my mind. That little word, *let*, stuck with me. It's working in me now as I write. It is helping me be more trustingly open to a moment by moment surrender to Jesus's love and the mind of Christ. As a deposit of the Holy Spirit, when Gods puts his word into us like that, it works in us quietly and effectively, like good leaven. Once received, if we let it, God's word continues to live in us without any conscious effort on our part.

The Holy Spirit cleans us up and keeps us clean by bringing our lives into alignment with God's word. Firmly but lovingly (if we agree) he will wash away every bit of contamination and dirt that gets in the way of our right relationship and union with Jesus and our heavenly Father. The Holy Spirit shows us ourselves as we read God's word.

The base of the laver was constructed of highly polished brass mirrors that belonged to the women who served at the door of the tabernacle. Perhaps they were a sign that these women had turned from looking at themselves to serving God. Perhaps they were mirrors for the priests to see themselves and inspect their faces for dirty spots. If so, those mirrors would reflect how God's word reveals us to ourselves as it teaches, reproves, corrects and convicts. In the word of God, we can see where we need cleansing, discipline or transformation.

All scripture is God-breathed and is useful for instruction, for conviction, for correction, and for training in righteousness.
2 Timothy 3:16

Knowing God's word is vitally important.
How can a young man keep his way pure?
By guarding it according to Your word.
With all my heart I have sought You;
do not let me stray from Your commandments.
I have hidden Your word in my heart
that I might not sin against You. Psalm 119:9-11

Believing lies and acting on them pushes us away from God. Believing truth and acting on it moves us closer to God. When God's word comes alive by the power of the Holy Spirit, we see truth; we also see if we measure up to it or fall short. That reminds me of a story.

A relative of mine, not a Christian until years later, but a fairly honest man at the time, taught his children to be honest. To his family's chagrin, this man always had to be right, and he usually was. Right or wrong, in most conflicts of opinion, he would skillfully debate or dominate until his own view won. One evening his young daughter overheard him on the telephone. She caught enough of the conversation to know that he was clearly agreeing with a friend that it was okay to cheat insurance companies. She confronted him. His first reply was, "Insurance companies are different. It's not the same as lying." She was indignant and reminded him of God's laws, *"Don't steal"* and *"Don't bear false witness . . ."* [56] When she held the word of God up to him, he must have seen his own dirty face in comparison with God's word. The conversation ended. For once he did not attempt to win a debate, justify his opinion or press his point.

God's truth has a mysterious power to free us. Often, at the very moment we see our stains and smudges in the mirror of his word, the very same light that reveals our sin brings conviction, confession, repentance and—Whoosh! Quickly, before condemnation, accusation or shame can begin to shadow our souls, our spots are erased. We're clean. Could that be why the mirrors and water basin of the laver are one piece of furniture? I think so. Jesus's word both reveals the truth to us and cleanses us. He is the living word of God.

> *In the beginning was the Word, and the Word was with God and the word was God. John 1:1NKJV*

---

56 Commandments 8 and 9 are: You shall not steal and you shall not bear false witness. Exodus 20:15,16

And the Word became flesh and dwelt among us, and we beheld His glory, the glory as of the only begotten of the Father, full of grace and truth. John 1:14 NKJV

He told his disciples,

You are already clean because of the word which I have spoken to you. John 15:3

The laver pictures our sanctification. Sanctification is a big word that simply means keeping all that is holy and set apart for God pure and clean—it's the ongoing process of changing our old habits and thought life and getting free from everything that is not Godly. The transformation of believers from sinners to saints is so vital that believers have many words to describe how the Holy Spirt clean ups and changes his children: healing, cleansing, delivering, discipling, transforming, edifying, exhorting, maturing, sanctifying, perfecting, making holy, being made perfect, and being conformed to his image.

Our identification with Jesus's death to self in the fire at the brazen altar anticipates how the cross makes us legally right before God. Our resurrection to new life in the power of the Holy Spirit justifies us before God; our cleansing at the laver sanctifies us.

After giving our lives to God, most cleansing comes through the water of God's word (prefigured by the laver). But if we find a hang-up or habit of self-life that we just can't get rid of, it makes sense to me to go back to the cross, confess it and identify with Jesus's death again. We know that Jesus's

Divine power has given to us all things that pertain life and godliness, through the knowledge of Him who called us by glory and virtue. 2 Peter 1:3 NKJV

In our grateful love for Jesus, by God's grace and power, our part in growing-up into the maturity of Christ's character is to take our failures to the cross. Most of us get annoyed when others sting us with one of our pet peeves. We get grumpy when we're overtired, feel snappy and defensive when hurt, fearful, protective or jumping to the offensive when attacked, impatient when interrupted or delayed and critical of insensitivity and brutishness. We can choose to feed these natural human negatives with contempt and judgment of others (and ourselves) or we can decide to forgive others. In forgiving, we let go of (or die to) our judgments, turn away from our unholy reactions and release offenses by taking them directly to the Lord and confessing them as sins of unlove. Every time we repent, choose love and affirm the death of our sin nature and the reality of our new life in Jesus Christ, we choose the cross. At the cross, we die a little more to our old selves and live more fully in Jesus's resurrection life. It's the same for larger roadblocks to living in God's love. Jesus suffered for every pain of injustice, violence and betrayal. He suffered for all our critical attitudes, jealous comparisons, selfish desires, mean thoughts, resentful feelings and lingering discouragements. As we establish habits of confessing and surrendering our weaknesses and failures to him and continue to identify with his death for us and life in us, he transforms us to agree with the encouragement, generosity, patience, faith, hope and love of the indwelling Holy Spirit.

But some theologians are fussy and insist that the ongoing work of cleansing and deliverance is all pictured the laver. I think God is bigger than our attempts to systematize our confessions or be legalistic about the tabernacle typology. He looks at our hearts.

Not only did Jesus say

If anyone wants to come after Me, he must deny himself and take up his cross daily and follow Me. For whoever wants to save his life will lose it, but whoever loses his life for My sake will save it. Luke 9:23b-24

He also taught that,

If we confess our sins, he is faithful and just to forgive us our sins and to cleanse us from all unrighteousness. 1 John 1:9

After the laver reveals sin and washes it away, it provides water for refreshment. The word of God, alive by the Spirit, is refreshing; it has life-quickening power within us; it renews and restores.

My first recalled successful experience of bending down before God's laver and letting his water wash me clean and restore my health was over cigarettes. I'd backslidden for about ten years and had just come back to God. I didn't know many scriptures, yet one especially began to talk back to me, loudly.

Do you not know that you yourselves are God's temple, and that God's Spirit dwells in you? 1 Corinthians 3:16

The idea that my body was a temple of the Holy Spirit got into me and stuck. Peaceful yet unrelenting thoughts convinced me that stopping smoking wasn't just a-good-idea for my health, it was a God-idea. The Holy Spirit was beginning to show me how he works from the inside out to help us live up to the standard of his word. He was starting to change me.

I needed changing: my addiction was extreme. I'd often have two cigarettes, occasionally more, lit at once. I was coughing up blood, not once in a while, but every morning. Not little flecks, like at first, but more.

I hid it. A campaign against cigarettes at the local grade school turned my children into zealots against tobacco. They begged me to stop. They pleaded. They lectured me with facts. They got angry. My ten-year-old tore up my cigarettes. They'd lost their dad to divorce and they didn't want to lose me.

To make a long story middling short, I set aside the first week in January 1972 to stop smoking. I tried and failed. After every lapse, I'd destroy all cigarettes I found, start again, and fail again. I scotch taped torn cigarettes together, dried wet ones, looked in the bottom of basement trash cans and under the automobile floor mats for stray butts. I spent hours curled up in bed weeping. The only thing I didn't do was buy another pack.

I was about to learn that God HIMSELF will help us do anything that he asks us to do—if it is truly him and if we persist in seeking his help. Often, his help comes when we've reached the end of our own resources and given up. I was in the midst of a huge failure and thought it was all on me. Back then I'd no idea that God would do for me what I couldn't do for myself.

That Friday night I went to a Catholic charismatic prayer meeting. The living room of a small house was crowded with worshippers. Feeling beaten, I sat out of sight in an unlit corner on the front stairs by the entryway. I kept apart from all the teaching, talk, prayer and praise. Toward the end of the meeting, Carole, the leader, asked if anyone needed prayer. Edging into the room, apologizing for my failure, I said something like, "I think God wants me to stop smoking. I've been trying all week and can't do it." Someone placed a folding chair in the middle of the room and said, "Come sit here." I crawled on my hands and knees across Carole's living room floor to the chair. A crowd gathered around me and began to pray. Some read scriptures. Tears flowed. I'd never felt so loved in my life. With my eyes closed, I saw a puff of smoke leave my chest and disappear. I knew I'd never smoke again. That was a miracle.

Then an even bigger miracle began. This was 1972—when people still smoked in restaurants, on the streets, everywhere. Knowing how vulnerable I was, God protected me. For three years, with no effort on my part, I was not once, ever, in a restaurant, store, automobile, or group, with anyone anywhere who lit up a cigarette. The next time I met a cigarette, the first night on a new job, I was sitting next to a woman who pulled out a pack of Winston's (my old favorite). She offered me one and lit up. I said, "No, thank you." The smell was putrid not inviting. I was silent—in awe of God's protection and how I'd changed.

That illustrates the laver. It's where we come into agreement with God's word—where his Holy Spirit puts life into black and white typed letters, words of scripture printed on paper or visible on our computers, iPads and cell phone screens. The Spirit takes them right off the page and applies them to our hearts, our minds and our lives. It's where we splash his words on us, rub them in, soak in them and let them clean us up. It's where our wills move toward doing what he asks and then he does it. God gives his power to his words to make us holy and free us from all the wrong thinking, personal habits, unruly emotions, worldly teachings and demonic resistances—all the stuff-and-stuff—that blocks us from living in him. It's a journey, and I'm still on it.

God wants to fill us with his love—for himself, for ourselves and for others. He wants close communion with us. If we refuse his Holy Spirit's pricks to our conscience and refuse to let him begin to clean up our disorderly messes, he will withdraw until we're ready. If we keep rejecting the truth of his word, his Spirit will eventually leave us.

Seven years after the Lord had set me free from cigarettes, I actually began to fear that he might leave me. That's because he tells us repeatedly to stop judging and to forgive. I absolutely could not forgive a particular person. I tried. I asked for God's help repeatedly. I asked others to pray for me. I was like the woman pestering the unjust judge. Once again, I wanted to keep God's word; I'd tried and failed. The same sense of conviction that led me to stop smoking was pressing me toward a forgiveness that wasn't in me.

Finally, one sunny summer afternoon, as I was hanging wash on the clothesline, I saw Jesus in an open vision with the person who had hurt me. Jesus's love and sorrow were beyond my imagination. The air around him was golden but the colors were clear. I knew it was real. I could not have imagined it. His love for this man, his sorrow for the one who'd hurt me, was profound. In my vision, Jesus said to the man, "I can't do anything. She hasn't forgiven you." I felt the man's pain. In this vision, I knew the man had died and gone to heaven. He'd never fathomed how much he'd hurt me until Jesus showed him. Jesus must have taken over my heart at that moment because I was filled with his compassion. Instantly, without thinking, I knew that I could never intentionally cause anyone the quality or degree of pain I saw and felt before me. My forgiveness for the man was instantaneous. Jesus's word to "Forgive your enemies" came to life in my heart.

God works in many ways. Often, going to the laver and applying God's word is quite easy. We know our sins. We can see our own temptations to lust or greed. We feel our anger at drivers who cut us off on the road and recognize our impatience when slowly-moving lines at the post office rob of us peace. We know fretting gets us nowhere and can sense the hardness in our own hearts when we recall the faults and wrong-doings of others to justify, excuse and defend our opinions about them, to bolster our pride, defensiveness and self-righteous judgments. Warning lights blink in our minds when our outrage at social injustice degenerates to demonizing our opponents with non-productive accusations. We also know that all these thoughts and temptations are either from the world, the devil or our own character. They're not one bit like Jesus.

Because Jesus already made provision for our clean-up at the cross, most often, all we have to do is ask the Holy Spirit for it. We do this by simply turning our thoughts to Jesus and saying, "Lord, forgive me. I put it in your hands. Please give me your response." And, simple as that, God does exactly what we ask. It's naturally as easy for us as it would be for a small child to trustingly reach up and put his or her hand into the great big hand of a consistently wise and loving parent.

Occasionally, though, the dirt is ground-in and scrubbing it off takes effort. We go to the word and prayer again and again, but God doesn't supernaturally intervene to change our unruly hearts. We might need to ask, seek and knock for faith to change. We may need help from friends or counselors to see what triggers our ungodly responses. Often old wounds and traumas need healing. We may need to cooperate with God as he tears down a stronghold[57] in our thinking. We have to work

---

57 Strongholds are safe, fortified places. In the Old Testament, they are literal fortresses; high walled cites built to keep out enemies. In the New Testament, Paul speaks of strongholds in our soul—mindsets or habits that are hard to penetrate and get inside, places in our thinking and feeling that resist change. Most of us have strongholds we're not aware of. I've a delightful friend, I love everything about her except her way of handling criticism. She becomes so defensive that honest dialogue is impossible. She protects herself with impenetrably thick walls of denial. I've a relative who can't stop worrying. It's a stronghold, a habit of thinking that she can't break. Both my friend and my relative are Christians, but both of them have strong walls of denial and many self-protective reasons to justify their habits. They're not able to let God be their safe place these areas. I've been working for years to dismantle the final timbers of a stronghold built of unrealistic fears. I want to let God be my safe place in all things. Many non-believers put up a vast defense system to protect themselves from the truth of Jesus Christ. A former friend of mine, a member of an occult group, refuses to hear anything about Jesus's atonement because her religion says it's negative and negativity is against her religion. They teach a mental-construct of a gnostic christ-spirit; it's a mental stronghold that walls out truth. As Christians, we must agree with God to recognize and tear down strongholds in our own thinking. We need God's weapons of truth in love and power when we encounter strongholds in the minds of others. Our own judgments, standards and negative opinions can imprison others and get in God's way. When we forgive others and withdraw our judgments and opinions, God works in them and in us. In 2 Corinthians 10: 3-5 Paul writes, *For though we walk in the flesh, we are not waging war according to the flesh. For the weapons of our warfare are not of the flesh but have divine power to destroy strongholds. We destroy arguments and every lofty opinion raised against the knowledge of God, and take every thought captive to obey Christ.*

at repentance and fetch the water for ourselves, one splash or bucketful at a time. Because washing at the laver (our sanctification) is absolutely vital to continuing on for more of God's glory, I'll detour to illustrate its importance with one more personal example.

Once, when my daughter and I were driving through an almost white-out blizzardy snowstorm in the Colorado Rockies, God showed me some deeply ground-in grime. We were without snow tires on a narrow, unfamiliar mountain road with hairpin tuns and deep drop-offs. Our lives were in danger; one slip and we'd be goners and I wasn't ready to die. The reason was right in my face—I was angry at a Christian leader who had made unjust and false public accusations against me. I was unable to refute his lies and could not forgive his slander.

I knew that I had to forgive him. Jesus's words "Forgive us our sins as we forgive those who sin against us" hammered away, working to soften my heart. The mirror of God's word was unrelentingly clear and I was not ready to die. I had to get right with God before I could face Jesus in death or return to this man's sphere of influence in my life. After making it safely through the storm, I left my daughter at school in the calm of Eastern Colorado and set out on the fifteen-hour drive from Boulder to northern Illinois. My one-day trip took three days. I drove south, through Kansas and then north through Minnesota and Wisconsin, repeating over and over again, mile after mile, "I forgive him. I forgive." At Lacrosse, I paused, uncertain of my direction. Did I need to keep praying? To head further north, to the Upper Peninsula? With great peace I turned south toward the Wisconsin Dells and home, secure that I'd prayed through to complete forgiveness. Although it seemed wise to cut relationship with the gentleman and leave his church, and although he most likely died believing his untruths, every time I remember that sad time, my heart warms with Jesus's love for the man. I anticipate meeting him in heaven.

Agreeing with God's word will eventually dismantle personal strongholds and bring paradigm shifts. It changes longstanding habits, cultural assumptions and false ideas. Because we're all different, God's transformative work in us is usually delightfully specific and individual. Was it a divine set-up that after meeting a woman whom God healed of a genetic disease by supernaturally changing her DNA, I was able to begin to admit the possibility that maybe—if God could do that—maybe, just maybe Mary, the mother of Jesus might have been a virgin? I'm quite sure my salvation didn't depend on that point—but clearly, at that time, my view of what God could or would do was far too small and needed enlarging. Now, years later, convinced of the truth of God's word, I've seen enough miracles to believe in God's capacity to do whatever he chooses.

Far too many Christians are content to stop at the brazen altar. Getting saved is enough for them. We all need teaching, discipleship and encouragement to wash up and mature. Without it, we remain baby Christians, carnal like the Corinthian church. We don't even see or begin to understand how much we all need to be transformed by the power of God's word. It's sad. Romans 14:3 says that whatever is not from faith is sin. Since God's realm is all faith, doubting his word cripples our capacity to receive his love. Hardened doubt is fatal to our souls. Ignorance of his word and refusal to align our lives with his commands is like staving off spiritual starvation with a crust of bread when a banquet is available in the next room. Oh Lord, may your church grow up, in this day, to the full stature of Jesus. Help us, Father. Send the Holy Spirit to teach us the lessons you prophetically patterned in the laver. Show us our need to live your word, to apply it to our stains.

Only the Holy Spirit sees our sins, blind spots and wrinkles. Only God knows where, when and how to clean us up and teach us his ways. Our outward legalistic attempts to "be good" so often fail. His work is lasting. By the blood of Jesus and the washing of the water of his word, the Holy Spirit takes us into the fullness and the glory of God's presence. And that's where we are headed. But first, we must be washed in his laver and be transformed by his word. As Jesus prayed,

Sanctify them by the truth; your word is truth. John 17:17

Maybe, in fact, I, and perhaps a reader or two, would hear Jesus speaking to us right now if we put down this book of mine and opened our Bibles. Washed in God's word, we might step from the outer court toward the veil over the entrance to the holy place, the room of the tabernacle lit by the light of the Holy Spirit and set apart for the priest's fellowship with God.[58] Unless the Holy Spirit lights the words before us, time with God is far better than time reading or writing books about him.

---

58 Text Note: Recently the Holy Spirit has used a little booklet called *Transformation* written by Peter Payne to reveal my continual need for the cleansing of His Word as represented by the laver. The booklet is available at https://givenwordnow.com/downloads/

THE TWO COURTS:

Thoughts on Inner Court & Outer Court Ministries

Before we leave the outer court and step through the veil into the inner court, it might be wisely helpful to reflect a bit on the distinctions between the two courts. Since both are vital components of every Christian life, we must take care not to get hierarchical about them, not to think one is "better" than the other. Bread needs liquid and flour. One is not more important than the other.

In Moses's tabernacle, only Moses and the priests went into the inner court. Only the high priest went into the holy of holies (and that only once a year on the Day of Atonement.) Those restrictions were not always enforced when the nation fell away from God and the temple needed cleansing and repair. But, followed or not, the official protocol instituted by God remained intact for every Jewish temple built in Jerusalem until the moment of Jesus's death. In that instant, the veil of the Jerusalem temple split in two, the old restrictions were lifted and the way to the inner court and the holy of holies was opened to you and me. Matthew tells us that

THE TABERNACLE

When Jesus had cried out again in a loud voice, He yielded up His spirit. At that moment the veil of the temple was torn in two from top to bottom. Matthew 27:50-51

"At that moment," Jesus opened the way into God's presence for us all. The torn veil vividly pictures God's accessibility.

But, since the kingdom of God, is both now and not yet, both positional and experiential, the veil also illustrates the many differences between what is available to us and what we actually appropriate.

There are differences

- between life in the world and life in the courts of God,
- between living out of relationship with God and Jesus and living in relationship with them,
- between the camp, the outer courts, the holy place and the holy of holies,
- between reading and hearing about God and knowing him and doing his will,
- between living in our own thoughts and feelings and living in God's word,
- between salvation and sanctification,
- between receiving God's gifts and being fully one with Jesus in character,
- between God's omnipresence and God's manifest presence,
- between intellectually believing in God's good works and receiving Jesus's faith and ability to get out of the Holy Spirit's way so that he can do God's good works

- between our limited natural awareness of God in the outer courts and an intense awareness of his resplendent Holy Spirit light in the inner courts.

God is calling his people to stop focusing on outer court activities and move into the holy of holies. There, in his manifest presence, surrendered to his Holy Spirit, we will worship before his power, glory, wisdom and majesty. There, we will keenly and clearly experience the vast difference between him and us. There, he delivers us from our own works and equips us and empowers us for his works.

The tabernacle in the wilderness symbolically embodies this distinction. Veils covered the three doors between the camp, the outer court, the holy place and the holy of holies. The metaphor of passing through the veils illustrates our transformation in Christ from unbelief to mature, fully equipped, in-love-with-Jesus discipleship.

So, are you ready to leave the outer court? To pass through the veil into the inner court? Do you actually want to get closer to Jesus, really close? To share in God's very nature? When he is near, it's easy to voice an enthusiastic, "Yes, Lord, I want more of you." But it's not all up to him. Developing an intimate relationship with Jesus often begins with ardent love, eagerness and desire. But keeping love alive in a stable long-term relationship may require decision and commitment. It takes time and self-denial to learn another person's ways. Some of us, with trust issues, need to build a history with God. Jesus understands. If we keep open and teachable, the Holy Spirit guides us. Step by step, prayer by prayer, outcome by outcome we learn that God is trustworthy. As we trust in Jesus through difficult circumstances, sorrows and temptations we learn humility. Agreeing with God becomes easier as practice strengthens our faith in his all-knowing love.

We may need to forgo perfectly normal activities and interests to give Jesus more time. Our settled routines, our very lifestyles can encourage his presence or pull us away from his love. Distracting thoughts and feelings might rise up to dull our enthusiasm for seeking Jesus. Friends, family, things, money worries, responsibilities, old habits, hobbies, entertainments and addictions, even our own self-images, can divert us from Jesus. When we consecrate ourselves to put God first and love him with all our hearts and souls, the Holy Spirit responds. He invites us, he entreats us, to align our thinking patterns with his own. One thing at a time, he asks us to refuse all that does not lead to God. That's not always easy.

In the months after my husband's death, I turned to God during the days, but in the evenings after supper I ran from the initial pain of loneliness and loss by compulsively turning on the television until I fell asleep. All my friends and family understood and said, "There, there. It's normal." The Holy Spirit disagreed. He didn't like it. As my dependence on the Hallmark channel grew, so did the unrest in my conscience. The Holy Spirit's conviction intensified. I longed to break the compulsion, to turn off the TV and get free from an unwanted time and sleep-robbing habit. I prayed and asked others to pray. The answer came one afternoon in the after-glow of an interlude of profound worship and silence before God. The contrast between the Lord's Spirit and my own mind, so often busy with happily-ever-after romances and repetitive detective stories, was so great that I called up Direct TV and cancelled my subscription.

If we determine to love God and learn to rest in his peace and joy, he may ask us to do far more than turn off the TV. He will lead us to courageously face the pain of recovery from every bit of unlove we've ever known. Some few saints have grace to surrender to God quickly and fully with ease, but for most of us, giving our all to the Lord is a journey. Receiving and responding to divine love may require disciplined growth, healing, and changing our habits. It's a learning curve.[59][60] Building new neural pathways for faith may come suddenly, by divine intervention or may take time, by divine healing, discipline and training. Either way, the result is the same, more of God's loving presence and peace.

> *His divine power has given us everything we need for life and godliness through the knowledge of him who called us by His own glory and excellence. Through these He has given us His precious and magnificent promises, so that through them you may become partakers of the divine nature, now that you have escaped the corruption in the world caused by evil desires.*
>
> *For this very reason, make every effort to add to your faith virtue; and to virtue, knowledge; and to knowledge, self-control; and to self-control, perseverance; and to perseverance, godliness; and to godliness, brotherly kindness; and to brotherly kindness, love. For if you possess these qualities and continue to grow in them, they will keep you from being ineffective and unproductive in your knowledge of our Lord Jesus Christ. But whoever lacks these traits is nearsighted to the point of blindness, having forgotten that he has been cleansed from his past sins. 2 Peter 1:3-9*

---

[59] To nurture the presence of the Lord, a little book from Seed Sowers, *Practicing the Presence of God* by Frank Laubach and Brother Lawrence is a valuable guide. Free download pdfs of Brother Lawrence's book are available on line. Both Laubach and Bro. Lawrence found God's presence by thinking about him and talking with him. Mme. Jean Guyon, in *Experiencing the Depths of Jesus Christ* describes how to find Jesus through silent prayer and devotional reading of scripture. Martha Wing Robinson's biography, *Radiant Glory* by Gordon Gardiner (also available as a free pdf download online), teaches believers to find God's presence in their inward hearts, not their minds, by a turning of will. Each approach appeals to a different personality/learning style. The Holy Spirit wants all of us to know and love God with all of our hearts, souls, and minds.

[60] See Appendix, entry on "Inwardness" for Martha Wing Robinson's brief teaching on inwardness as a way of practicing God's presence.

Fortunately, Jesus knows all about our weaknesses. That's why he died, to give us the Holy Spirit. We've got the very best teacher, guide, helper and coach in heaven or on earth. He goes with us on every step of our journey.

The Holy Spirit does not force us. He always gives us grace to do what Jesus asks for. He knows our hearts. If we truly want God, he will woo us by showing up in unexpected places and giving us vivid experiences of Jesus's love. His great love propels us through the veil. His Spirit often surprises seekers with God's revelations. Then, tasting his goodness, we will pray, "More, Lord. More of you." Since relationship with Jesus works two ways, we don't always have to ask.

For example, once, while reading a most boring list of family genealogy in the book of Numbers, God's light fell on the words and I began to weep. Suddenly, every strange name I read became a husband, a father and the head of a family. I saw that God had entrusted each man with an assignment to provide for, to protect, care for and lead others. I wondered if any of them had living descendants who knew the Lord, so I asked the Holy Spirit. The very moment that I began to pray, the Holy Spirit moved me from the outer court of human thought into the inner court of Spirit-led prayer. The Holy Spirit had illuminated a dull text to reveal layers of hidden meaning and love. He transformed the dead words on paper into living words in my heart. I felt my heart fill with our heavenly Father's love for families.

Has that happened to you? Have you ever been reading God's word when it talked to you? Have you ever been talking with the Lord and suddenly realized that he was listening attentively? Have you ever casually turned up the volume on an MP3 or started to sing a familiar song when the veil unexpectedly parted and you heard God's voice through the music?

The Holy Spirit also moves us through the veil and into closer relationship with God when our conversations begin to honor God and glorify Jesus. For all we know, we may even be living in the day Malachi prophesied, a day when the evil doers prospered and the arrogant were described as blessed. It was a day when many people thought that it was futile to serve the Lord, but

> *At that time those who feared the LORD spoke with one another, and the LORD listened and heard them. So a scroll of remembrance was written before Him regarding those who feared the LORD and honored His name.*
>
> *"They will be Mine," says the LORD of Hosts, "on the day when I prepare My treasured possession. And I will spare them as a man spares his own son who serves him. So you will again distinguish between the righteous and the wicked, between those who serve God and those who do not." Malachi 3: 16-18*

Often, when we talk about God's goodness and lift up Jesus, we can sense that our words, prayers, and creative responses come from the Holy Spirit, not ourselves. When we deny our own thoughts and yield to the Holy Spirit's thoughts, feelings and truth, we are in the inner court. At such times we know what the elders, apostles and church in Jerusalem meant when they said,

> *It seemed good to the Holy Spirit and to us. Acts 15:28*

But, repeating myself again, getting closer to Jesus and hearing from God isn't always automatic. At times, he is silent. At times he disagrees with us. Our heads butt up hard against his. Finding his mind and accepting it might take tedious stretches of waiting on him in prayer. Years ago, while very upset with a friend's decision, I pulled an exercise mat into the middle of my living room floor and said, "Okay, Lord. I'm not going to get off this mat except for necessities until I get an answer." I wanted to change the situation. I prayed. I railed. I begged. I reasoned my head and heart out. I voiced everything I could think of until I could think of nothing more to say; I ran dry and gave up. Fortunately, at that moment, there was grace to put it all in Jesus's hands. Immediately, I moved (or was moved) from my own anxious thinking and efforts into the inner court of God's presence, a place that was ruled by peace of mind. In his light, I saw that my young friend's decision was from God. The Holy Spirit put brief words into my mouth. He changed my distraught thinking to acceptance and blessing. He moved me from my own natural outer court prayer to the Holy Spirit's inner court prayers of agreement with his plan.

It's not always easy to put people and situations in God's hands. I'm still learning how to let go of my own thinking, feelings, wishes and work—my outer court faith and requests. Jesus told us to "count the cost of discipleship." He said,

> *If anyone comes to Me and does not hate his father and mother and wife and children and brothers and sisters—yes, even his own life—he cannot be My disciple. And whoever does not carry his cross and follow Me cannot be My disciple. Which of you, wishing to build a tower, does not first sit down and count the cost to see if he has the resources to complete it? Otherwise, if he lays the foundation and is unable to finish the work, everyone who sees it will ridicule him, . . . In the same way, any one of you who does not give up everything he has cannot be My disciple.*
> Luke 14:26-30; 33

The cost of yielding to God is prophetically illustrated in the tabernacle—and Jesus knew it. He knew that every priest assigned by God to perpetual inner court ministry had to leave lesser alliances behind them. When inner court priests gave up their outer court work and when God told Aaron, the high priest, not to grieve at his son's death, they were foreshadowing Jesus's separation to God. The Bible mentions several occasions when Jesus chose to turn away from his family to follow God.[61]

God's pattern hasn't changed. For decades, a dear friend of mine served the Lord as a missionary in difficult places. Following the Holy Spirit's lead, her ministry encompassed every gift—the whole nine yards—evangelism, healing and deliverance, wise counsel through words of wisdom and knowledge, baptism of the Holy Spirit, Bible instruction and meeting practical needs. Several years ago, the Lord told her, "No more. I want you to give up all that. I'm asking you to create a place for me alone. I want you to spend your minutes, your hours, your days loving me." Many serve Jesus, fewer are called and willing to pay the price to be the lovers he longs for. She retired from the ministry organization that had supported and sponsored her. The invitations to speak slowed down and then stopped. She closeted herself with the Lord in prayer and followed his lead. At one time, in a country under siege and filled with terror and tension, the Holy Spirt told her to stay in her small two room apartment for sixty days to establish his peace and fearless presence within the four walls of that tiny place. Her family did not understand. Following in Jesus's footsteps, she had to let go of her own relatives to follow the Holy Spirit. Miracles, fully known to God alone, and barely hinted at to a trusted few have followed her obedience.

---

61 In Luke 2:41-52, as a twelve-year old boy, Jesus did not return with his parents to Nazareth after Passover. He stayed in the temple. When his distraught parents discovered him, he said, "Why do you seek me. Don't you know that I must be about my Father's business?" Matthew 12:48-50 describes how Jesus's mother and brothers tried to curtail his ministry. Jesus told them that his mother, brothers and sisters were those who do God's will. In John 7:4-28, his brothers seem to be egging him on to go to Jerusalem and show himself off publicly. He listens to God and tells them that it is not his time. Later, he goes secretly.

Whether the Holy Spirit assigns us to outer court or inner court service, he wants to deliver us from seeking recognition for our service and from finding our identity in what we do for him or what he chooses to do through us. Our true identities are discovered in knowing Jesus in a loving unity with the Godhead. At the age of eighty-two, I'm still journeying on for more of who I am in him. His words of encouragement, words like, "I'm with you; don't be afraid; I'll help you; let go and trust me to work it out" are not what I grew up hearing. I grew up hearing words like "Have you done anything to deserve it?" and "What have you done to justify your existence today, young lady?"

Despite years of loving the Lord, the influence of those early words about justifying my existence and needing "to do" something to please my mom lingered on and occasionally came out sideways in my service to God. In one God-given assignment my desire to please others and deserve and win their acceptance rather than please God, coupled with an insecure longing for affirmation and positive recognition, made it almost impossible for me to hold a steady course against criticism, speak out truth in wisdom and follow God's leading. In mercy, the Holy Spirit led me out and taught me a great deal. Maybe, from his point of view, that was what it was all about.

I've often tried to finish a work prompted by God by my own efforts. I have to laugh, because in his love, he quite often intervenes to correct me. This book is a good example. God began it. He will help me finish it. But along the way I've repeatedly forged ahead of God. I've been carried away by my own enthusiasm and relied on unreliable sources and incomplete knowledge. God doesn't like that. He honors his word. As he corrects me, I've thrown many, many pages into the wastebasket. It's easy to stray from depending on the Holy Spirit.

Prayer meetings are another example where my self-effort can get in the way. At times, in praying with others, I've monologued my own thoughts rather than talk with God. At other times, I've spring boarded off the prayers of others in a group conversational prayer style rather than listen to what the Holy Spirit might be saying. At times, in group settings, when I've shared my thoughts aloud with him rather than wait in silence until a warmth in my heart or an inner-knowing releases me to speak. It can sound very nice, even appropriate, but it never brings God's presence. When I do wait, when God does use me, humble gratitude and fulfillment take over. I need no human affirmation or recognition. I'd rather run and hide than take any credit.

I feel like God is smiling at me as I write. He knows that we're all imperfect people in an imperfect world and he loves us and uses us just as we are. He so often turns our weaknesses, including wanting recognition for outward service, toward his purposes. I can chuckle in gratitude for his kindness over so many of my own memories now. When my mother could no longer care for herself, the Holy Spirit led me to become her caretaker. The family applauded in relief and rallied around to help. Although I was obeying God, my follow through was a mixture. Most days and hours were marked by willing acceptance and love, but when she couldn't be left alone for long and I had to cut short a visit with friends or rush through the grocery store when I wanted a leisurely dawdle through the produce and bakery, my attitude at times drained all Godly strength away. I felt enchained by Mom's needs, more like a resentful lackey than a devoted daughter or willing servant of God. The Holy Spirit overlooked my ambivalence. During those difficult years, he brought my Mom to faith in Jesus and healed longstanding tensions between us.

After my Mom's death, the Holy Spirit said, "I want you to go back to school." I went, but my obedience there was mixed too. As a graduate teaching assistant in teaching English to college students who spoke other languages, the Holy Spirit often helped me talk with students from the 1040 window [62] about God's love. More than one lively class discussion was sparked by student questions like "Why is *Jesus* a swear word?" Or "What is *Easter*?" One class wanted to know the salvation plan. In another group, a Japanese PhD candidate thought that we all were gods. I sat back and listened while his classmates, of various faiths, from Japan, Columbia, South Korea and Thailand, successfully stretched their limited English to explain the concept of a creator God who is above all other gods. The face of the *small-g-many-gods* student exploded into smiles of recognition when he finally understood the idea of a *big-G-one-God*, God. The whole class smiled, laughed and sat back in relief. Our classroom discussions about faith were good practice in conversational English. Sharing Jesus like that in a state university was all by God's grace; I couldn't have made it happen. It was humbling and wonderful. But at the same time, my attitude about earning an MFA from an internationally high-ranking department in a Big Ten school was prideful. Ouch!

When that season ended, the Holy Spirit led a few friends and me to start a publishing company. We edited and published several books the Lord wanted, but my personal longings for worldly visible success were totally dashed; the business failed utterly.

I say all this to illustrate that I've honestly tried to serve God. I've followed wherever he's led me and from time to time, not to my credit and despite my mixture of carnality, immaturity and personal flaws, the Holy Spirit has intervened in my life, just as he has most likely intervened in your own life. He lives to help us do his own Kingdom of God wonders for Jesus's glory. Not for our own. Often, to lovingly protect us from

---

[62] "The 10/40 Window is the rectangular area of North Africa, the Middle East and Asia that is approximately between 10 degrees north and 40 degrees north latitude. The 10/40 Window is often called "The Resistant Belt" and includes the majority of the world's Muslims, Hindus, and Buddhists." For more information see: https://joshuaproject.net/resources/articles/10_40_window. More than one semester I was assigned to teach classes in the Language Building Classroom Number 1040. A coincidence? I don't think so.

getting a big head or taking any glory for ourselves, we don't even learn that God has used us until years later.

The Holy Spirit knows us. He knows that our love for Jesus and our obedience of faith are often mixed with frailty and weakness. He also knows that his work in through us will be everlasting. As long as we are willing to follow him, the Holy Spirit will lead us on and draws us closer and closer to the holy of holies.

In one way or another, physical death or death to self by identifying with Jesus's death, all of our journeys are preparing us to die. Just the other day I was thinking of songs I'd like my children to sing at my funeral. Perhaps I'll not walk in Jesus's full manifest presence until I get to heaven. Through all these years, despite all the books I've read about practicing God's presence, despite my inner yearnings and repeated attempts to focus on Jesus and live more fully in his love, despite many visits to his inner courts, I've not consistently drawn close to the measures of his presence that I've read about in others. Believers like Bro. Lawrence, Jeanne Guyonn, Fenelon, Martha Wing Robinson, Frank Laubauch, A.W. Tozer and an almost ninety-year-old neighbor who consistently does and speaks good have set the human standard for following Jesus high. Have I given up? No way! In the last month or so (it's now January 2022, in the umpteenth revision of this book) I've wondered if God has assigned angels to give a spiritual jumpstart to energize Bible truth for readers of a recently published book, *Wrecked for God* by Dianne Leman.[63] I hope so. Dianne's 21st century account of her journey to find loving union with Jesus is not written for super-saints. It makes a life of loving communion with Jesus accessible for folks like you and me.

For years, Jesus had continued to invite me to still my busy mind, to lay down my ego-driven motives for outer activities and surrender more fully to his love. His invitation to spend more time in his inner courts

---

63 Dianne Leman, *Wrecked for God*, Chosen Books, © Dianne Leman, 2021

stayed open. One particular afternoon, while seeking the Lord, he drew near. I wept as song after song rose in my heart, not songs of "I will love him" but songs of "I will serve him." I was still stuck on serving.

Serving is a good place to be—when it's an overflow of love; when God's Holy Spirit flows through us in his obedience of faith. Who were God's servants? His list is long: Abraham, Moses, Joshua, Samuel, Job, David, all the prophets, Nebuchadnezzar, Ezra, Nehemiah, the apostles, Paul and, of course, Jesus himself, are all described as God's servants. But that particular afternoon Jesus wasn't asking me to serve him, he was asking me to love him. Much as I wanted to sing "I will love you," Jesus was so near that any superficial "right" answer, any hypocritical pretense was impossible. The only words I could honestly utter were "I will serve you." I was like Peter, who answered Jesus's question, "Do you love me—with the love of God do you love me?" by replying, "Yes Lord, I love you—with all my human love." I felt miserable and conflicted and asked the Lord to help me get over my works mentality. [64] Help came, fairly soon, too.

One Monday morning, on a Zoom prayer group call, as a gentle man taught on sanctification,[65] he said, "God deals with us one thing at a time. We take out one bag of trash at a time." With my computer on mute, I asked, "What is it, Lord? What trash do I need to get rid of now?" I wasn't thinking of my Martha vs. Mary mentality, [66] but Jesus was.

---

64 My misery was clearly prideful; I was stuck on myself and my own spirituality. I clearly hadn't learned the lesson Brother Lawrence illustrates when he wrote, "... I simply admit my thoughts, saying to God, 'I shall never do otherwise if you leave me to myself. It is you who must stop my falling and it is you who must amend that which is amiss.' After such praying, I allow myself no further uneasiness about my faults." *Practicing His Presence*, Bro. Lawrence and Frank Laubach, The Seed Sowers, 1973, p. 46

65 See the *Transformation* booklet by Peter Payne recommended on page 109 footnote number 59

66 Mary, Martha and their brother Lazarus were close friends of Jesus. In Luke 10:38-42 Martha's love for Jesus expresses itself in service; Mary's love puts relationship first. Both are vital, but service should flow from relationship.

His response was life-changing. Tears began to flow. Instantly, I knew that I was still listening to my mother's lies. I was still hearing that I needed to achieve, deserve and justify my existence by obedient service.

As my mother aged, I had washed her clothes and her body, cooked her meals and cared for her home. We read the Bible daily. One day, I gave her a copy of Walter Martin's *Kingdom of the Cults* [67] and asked her to read it. While she read, God changed her ideas about justification and acceptance by works and replaced her occult faith in reincarnation into a solid faith that Jesus died for her sins. Then, he began to slowly transform her from a critical mother into a grateful sister in Christ. But the chains of childhood training and expectations can be strong, I still idolized her and served her.

I was raised to believe that being a good daughter meant serving obediently. In a Godly way, that's good. Adam got us all into trouble by disobedience and scripture says,

> *Blessed rather are those who hear the word of God and obey it. Luke 11:28*

and

> *Children, obey your parents in the Lord, for this is right. Ephesians 6:1*

But my thinking got distorted. I'd reduced love to obligatory obedient service.

If my arms were loaded with clean laundry to put it away when someone asked for a glass of water, I'd put down the laundry to fetch their water. It felt unloving to say, "Sure, but can you wait a sec?"

---

67   Walter R. Martin, *Kingdom of the Cults*, revised edition, Bethany Fellowship, 1977

I'd mixed up loving God with my ideas about serving until that day on Zoom when the Holy Spirit opened my eyes to truth. I saw that my thinking was incomplete. I was still hearing my parents' voices and seeing through distorted childhood lenses; my thoughts were off balance.

Accepting reality was painful, but it wrought a heart-change. Today, it's easy to spontaneously sing "I love you Lord." In God's kingdom our service is not to earn points or deserve love, it overflows, freely and gladly, from hearts engaged with God's own in trusting affection. All the Lord wanted from me that afternoon was loving worship.

The truth sets free. God wants us to learn that we don't need, at any level, to try to deserve acceptance and approval, anyone's or God's. We don't need to justify our existence. God made each and every one of us. He loves us with a love too great for any of us to deserve. He wants our love in return. He created us for his pleasure and the blood of Jesus is our justification.

> *"You are worthy, our Lord and God, to receive glory and honor and power, for You created all things; by Your will they exist and came to be." Revelation 4:11*

Taking care of my mom was outer court service. I didn't know it then, but the moment I said yes to the Holy Spirit's promptings to move back home and care for her, he enrolled me in an intense training program. Although human pressures often motivated me—my own, my mother's, our family system and a legalistic drive to do the right thing—God was always in charge. He often uses circumstances and other people (who are far more difficult than my well-meaning mom) to try our human love and drain our strength so that he can teach us to turn to him and depend upon his supply. He wants to teach us the contentment, peace and joy of leaning on him in all circumstances. He wants to draw us closer to his manifest presence in the holy of holies.

Many good works, many churches and ministries are birthed by God's direction but are continued by more reliance on human vision, direction and ability than on trust in God and continued prayerful seeking for his vision, guidance and power. They are outer court works. And if there's a good, a better, and a best, many of these outer court works are laced with good. But since God alone is truly good, only what is totally of him, from him, by him and for his glory is best.

The outer court illustrates our first steps in beginning to get to know God. Under the open skies in the natural light of sunrise and sunset, God's grace begins to act upon our wills. Looking on the animal sacrifices offered to God and laid on the brazen altar, we see a prophetic picture of God's grace in sending Jesus to offer himself to God for our sins. These animal sacrifices also prefigure us as we offer ourselves and our inherited sin nature to God in exchange for his Holy Spirit. Once we have given ourselves to God, we can move toward the laver where we will find sanctification in the washing of the water of his word.

The inner court, with the lampstand, table of showbread and altar of incense, is a prophetic picture of our continuing on with God under the light of his Holy Spirit. In the golden glow from the lampstand, we see walls and furniture of gold. We discover and enjoy Jesus's companionship; we eat his bread; we draw closer to him; intimacy increases. He begins to work in us and through us. We begin to leave our own works for him and seek his works alone.

In our daily lives, the tabernacle-metaphors describing our journeys with the Lord will often overlap and merge together. Generally though, because our Father in heaven is a good teacher, who knows that most of his children learn and grow sequentially, we thrive on object lessons that teach us step by step.

Not all believers want to leave the outer courts and move closer to God. Because of childhood wounds, a friend of mine is scared to. Others rightly rejoice in the outer court's white linen, the forgiveness of sins, the cleansing of God's word and fulfilling service. But many believers are like Apollos; he eloquently taught others all he knew about the Lord, but until Priscilla and Aquila explained God's ways to him more fully, he didn't know that more was available.[68]

> *There are different gifts, but the same Spirit,... different ministries, but the same Lord.... different ways of working, but the same God works all things in all people. 1 Corinthians 12:4-6*

All members of Christ's body are essential parts of one body. There can be no inner court ministry without outer court ministry first. It's important to remember that no one, not even Moses or Aaron, lived inside of the tabernacle. We all enter through the outer court.

God alone knows where he wants us to serve. Jesus loved Mary, Martha and Lazarus, but they stayed in Bethany. He didn't call them to journey with him. In drawing close to Jesus, every one of us will begin in the outer court. Essential, God-birthed, kingdom work is accomplished there. One of the Sons of Korah wrote

> *For better is one day in Your courts than a thousand elsewhere. I would rather be a doorkeeper in the house of my God than dwell in the tents of the wicked. Psalm 84:10*

In the outer court, the natural man or woman can study and receive the facts of Jesus's life and ministry. We can think and build clear and

---

68   See Acts 18: 24 ff.

sound doctrines about God. Much of my writing on the tabernacle is outer court work, putting commonly known facts on paper. Occasionally the Holy Spirit gives me specific words, but more often he brings thoughts to mind that I must wrestle to express. Often, in inadequacy, I pray, "Lord, I can't do this. If you want this book, if this sentence matters to you or a reader, you've got to help." Clarity usually comes—that's a gift. But when the Holy Spirit reminds me of Scriptures, he doesn't drop them into my mind, I must open the concordance or do a web search to look them up. Typing the first drafts, revising for clarity and proofreading are all done in the natural light of computer skills and human learning. Sitting here at the computer this afternoon, I'm thinking of Jesus with part of my mind, but I'm certainly not in the holy of holies worshipping my Lord or seeking the Holy Spirit's heart to pray before the altar of incense. Although I am listening for the Holy Spirit's thoughts, I feel no anointing, nothing other than a peaceful trust. Whenever the peace gets cloudy, I stop, reread what I've written and revise a bit. Many valuable concordances, Bible dictionaries and encyclopedias, books of Bible history, geography and archeology have been written by outer court believers. The musicians whose worship can turn our hearts to God and bring God closer to us practice scales and hone their skills in the outer court—and so on.

Solid evangelism and teaching can be outer court work. Many supernatural gifts of the Holy Spirit, such as wisdom, strength, guidance and healing are also available in the outer court. Jesus's gifts and anointing are not his manifest presence. Many believers don't know the difference between an anointing and God's presence. Our language doesn't help because the word *anointing* means to be smeared with his ointment, his Holy Spirit.

Let me give an example. Have you ever visited a church where there is a special grace, a presence or deposit from the Lord? It's truly anointed.

You know there's something of Jesus in the air. Good ministry goes on. Prayers are answered. Jesus touches people; they get healed, delivered, and taught, and you might think, "Thank you, Father! I've found a place where I can find you. A place where I can serve and worship." So, you go back and get connected, sometimes so connected that you begin to think of the church as your own, not God's. And week after week, month after month the meetings are the same. You get hungry. You want more than the anointing that is resident in that place. Your hunger, restlessness and frustration are usually never a sign indicating that it's time for you to pick up and move on to another church or complain against the leadership. Most often, it's God's invitation to begin to pray for a closer relationship with him. You don't want a resident anointing or a deposit of God. You want GOD! You don't want the same food week after week. You want Jesus, more of his love, his truth, more of himself—in all his freshness. He's healed and delivered and taught you up to the limit of the grace upon that particular place, but you know there's more. And you want it. You want to be a part of a fully mature body of believers who all live and move in Jesus.

If you start criticizing the pastor, you're pushing Jesus away and adding to the problem. As soon as we try to perfect others, we stir our own imperfections into the mix. Don't do it—that church belongs to God. It is Jesus's body. His anointing is there. Get on your knees, humble yourself, love your brothers and sisters in Christ and seek the Lord. Ask for his presence to take you to the holy place. Keep after him until you can love his church as he loves it and he can use you to bring fresh encouragement in the Lord to everyone you touch.

Does that help clarify the difference between his anointing and his presence? Jesus didn't invite all of his followers to be apostles. God alone knows our best fit into his Kingdom plans. Only Peter, James and John saw his transfiguration and heard God's voice.

He was transfigured before them. His face shone like the sun, and His clothes became as white as the light. . . .a bright cloud enveloped them, and a voice from the cloud said, "This is My beloved Son, in whom I am well pleased. Listen to Him!" When the disciples heard this, they fell facedown in terror. Matthew 17:2, 5-6

I have been unusually fortunate to meet a few sane, stable, credible men and women who have actually seen Jesus and talked with him today. He changed their lives. I've also known those whom he took to his throne room. Although God is calling us to the Holy of Holies, not all of us are ready or willing to go there.

If we're impure, God will mercifully back off and protect us from the premature judgment of his holy presence. In his manifest presence, we must, and I emphasize *must*, either repent of all sin and agree with God or God's very presence will judge us. In the 1980's I attended meetings led by a man of God who carried an unusually strong anointing to release God's presence in worship. The meetings he led were life-changing. When the Holy Spirit came, God's power was present to save, deliver, heal and give life-direction to many. I once heard this missionary-pastor say that he followed the Holy Spirit's directions exactly to avoid bringing judgment on anyone. If the Holy Spirit wasn't moving, he did nothing to invite God or release the anointing he carried. He feared what might happen if God drew near. If, in God's manifest presence, anyone insincerely sang words they didn't believe in their hearts, they would be mouthing lies. Lies, mockery, deception, hypocrisy and unbelief do not survive in God's manifest presence. God's innate and total purity will always expose and judge falsehood. Do you recall what happened to Ananias and Sapphira? In the early church, when God's Spirit rested in power on the apostles, Ananias and Sapphira dropped dead after lying to the apostles?⁶⁹ We don't get it that God is HOLY. No one can sin in his presence.

Living and serving God on the outer court outskirts of God's purity and power may be God's assignment for us. It never indicates that Jesus might love us less. He knows us better than we know ourselves and wherever he puts us is best for us. Although Jesus singled out Peter, James and John to be with him on the Mount of Transfiguration and see his resplendent, earth-dazzling, heavenly glory, he also said to Thomas, who hadn't seen his transfiguration and wasn't with the other apostles when they first saw Jesus's resurrection body,

> *Because you have seen Me, you have believed; blessed are those who have not seen and yet have believed. John 20:29*

I'm glad that Thomas wasn't there the first time the risen Jesus appeared to some of his disciples. I'm glad Thomas needed more concrete proof than the testimony of others. He needed to see Jesus and touch his wounds. He needed to know for himself. I think Thomas yearned to believe, longed to believe. I think his heart cry was "Lord, let it be true.

---

69 Most of us have lied—and we've gotten away with it because it was not deliberate, or we did not lie in the fullness of God's manifest presence. We are so unfamiliar with the holiness of his manifest presence that we read the words about it without understanding their serious truth. This incident illustrates the reality of judgment before God. Because I believe that God wants to visit some who will read this book with the immediate reality of who he is, I quote the story below. Ananias and Sapphira could have kept the money and lived, if only they had told the truth.
   Now a man named Ananias, together with his wife Sapphira, also sold a piece of property. With his wife's full knowledge, he kept back some of the proceeds for himself, but brought a portion and laid it at the apostles' feet.
   Then Peter said, "Ananias, how is it that Satan has filled your heart to lie to the Holy Spirit and withhold some of the proceeds from the land? Did it not belong to you before it was sold? And after it was sold, was it not at your disposal? How could you conceive such a deed in your heart? You have not lied to men, but to God!"
   On hearing these words, Ananias fell down and died. And great fear came over all who heard what had happened. Then the young men stepped forward, wrapped up his body, and carried him out and buried him.

Show me." If that's your heart-cry, give voice to it. Tell Jesus. At one time in our journey, all of us need to reach out and touch Jesus ourselves. We need to ask for God's gift of faith, the kind of faith that brings forth what it purposes.[70] Without true faith, any acceptance, belief, conviction or credence, by whatever name you call it, becomes a powerless, intellectual acknowledgment. As Jesus's brother, James, said, it's dead.

> *So too, faith by itself, if it does not result in action, is dead. But someone will say, "You have faith and I have deeds." Show me your faith without deeds, and I will show you my faith by my deeds. You believe that God is one. Good for you! Even the demons believe that—and shudder.*
> *James 2: 17-19*

Whether we stand beside Jesus, as Thomas once did, or further out on our journey toward knowing him in the Holy of Holies, we always need faith. While God rejoices in faith that believes without seeing, he repeatedly encourages us to seek him, to get closer, to want more.

> *Draw near to God, and He will draw near to you.*
> *James 4:8*

> *I count all things as loss compared to the surpassing excellence of knowing Christ Jesus my Lord, for whom I have lost all things. I consider them rubbish, that I may gain Christ and be found in him, not having my own righteousness from the law,*

---

[70] Charles S. Price clarifies the distinction between real faith and intellectual assent in *The Real Faith for Healing*, Bridge-Logos, 1997.

> *but that which is through faith in Christ, the righteousness from God on the basis of faith. I want to know Christ and the power of His resurrection and the fellowship of His sufferings, being conformed to him in His death, and so, somehow, to attain to the resurrection from the dead.*
>
> *Not that I have already obtained all this, or have already been made perfect, but I press on to take hold of that for which Christ Jesus took hold of me. Brothers, I do not consider myself yet to have taken hold of it. But one thing I do: Forgetting what is behind and straining toward what is ahead, I press on toward the goal to win the prize of God's heavenly calling in Christ Jesus. All of us who are mature should embrace this point of view. Philippians 3: 8-15*

Although God's relationship with each of us is uniquely personal, our approach to him must be in his way, through Jesus's holy sacrifice, through his holy fire on his altar, not through our own efforts. Two of Aaron's sons died for putting God's fire, taken from his altar, in their own censers and burning incense to glorify themselves, not the Lord.

> *Now Aaron's sons Nadab and Abihu took their censers, put fire in them and added incense, and offered unauthorized fire before the LORD, contrary to His command. So fire came out from the presence of the LORD and consumed them, and they died in the presence of the LORD. Leviticus 10: 1-2*

Before Aaron, the high priest, was permitted into the holy place of God's presence, God gave Moses very specific directions on how to prepare Aaron. Moses called the whole congregation to assemble at the doorway of the Tent of Meeting. There, before the eyes of all the people, Moses washed Aaron and his sons with water.⁷¹ After washing them, Moses clothed Aaron in his high priestly garments.

> *He put the tunic on Aaron, tied the sash around him, clothed him with the robe, and put the ephod on him. He tied the woven band of the ephod around him and fastened it to him. Then he put the breastpiece on him and placed the Urim and Thummim in the breastpiece. Moses also put the turban on Aaron's head and set the gold plate, the holy diadem, on the front of the turban, as the LORD had commanded him. Leviticus 8: 7-9*

Finally, Moses anointed the tabernacle and all its contents and poured oil on Aaron's head to consecrate him. After that, Moses offered the sin offering, the burnt offering, and the ram of ordination. He anointed Aaron and his sons as God had commanded him to do. Then Moses told the priests,

> *You must not go outside the entrance to the Tent of Meeting for seven days, until the days of your ordination are complete; for it will take seven days to ordain you. What has been done today has been commanded by the LORD in order to make atonement on your behalf. You must remain at the entrance to*

---

71   Cleanliness matters to God and he wanted his people to know it. In chapters 11 to 15 of Leviticus God gives the people specific instructions about what's clean and unclean. He tells them what they can touch and what to avoid, what can be cleansed from contamiation and what must be destroyed. His standards for human hygiene are high and, in the light of modern knowledge, sensible. His concerns include clean and unclean animals, dead people and creatures, contaminated water, protective guidelines for women after childbirth, human infection, wastes, discharges of many kinds and mold in leather, cloth and buildings. Making natural distinctions (drawing lines) between clean and the unclean were foundational for a people separated unto God, a people unlike the surrounding nations. Domestic and personal cleanliness was a daily, tangible, practical reminder that their God was clean and pure. In time, personal cleanliness came to picture holiness. And while cleanliness is not next to godliness, a friend who often saw angels and demons and discerned the differences between light and darkness, once commented that she often saw more demons in filthy, messy homes than in clean and orderly ones.

the Tent of Meeting day and night for seven days and keep the LORD's charge so that you will not die, for this is what I have been commanded." Leviticus 8: 33-35

After all that, Aaron and his sons were prepared for their priestly duties. Surely, they knew that they were set apart to God. We've got to remember their example, that ordination into the priesthood did not give them liberty to approach God willy-nilly. Once a year, on the Day of Atonement, Aaron, the high priest carefully followed God's directions and prepared himself once again before he dared to approach the manifest presence of God. He was specifically warned against presumption.

The LORD said to Moses: "Tell your brother Aaron not to enter freely into the Most Holy Place behind the veil in front of the mercy seat on the ark, or else he will die, because I appear in the cloud above the mercy seat. Leviticus 16:2

Today, because of Jesus, we can draw near to God at any time by faith.[72] Every yearning in our heart to know him more is his invitation to us.

I love those who love me, and those who seek me early shall find me. Proverbs 8:17

You will seek Me and find Me when you search for Me with all your heart. Jeremiah 29:13

Ask, and it will be given to you; seek, and you will find; knock, and the door will be opened to you. Matthew 7:7

---

72 Hebrews 9 describes how Jesus's blood is a better sacrifice than the blood of animals. He died that we might all draw closer to him and know God as our Father in heaven.

What is our response? If you're like me, you might waffle at times, wondering if you really do want a fuller revelation of God's glory. Despite longing for more of God, I've been scared about what a fuller revelation of his glory might mean. I've gone through successive stages of determination and failure. You might relate to some of my hurdles.

I've feared losing control. I've been self-centered rather than God-centered. I've known uncertainty and misunderstanding about complete union with Jesus. In wanting to achieve, I've and drawn back in concern that "I" might fail if Jesus asked for more than I could give. Some fears were dramatically grandiose. I don't have St. Francis's zeal for poverty. I don't want to beg for food or go barefoot in wintery snow. I don't know if I could sell all I have and give it to the poor. Other fears were based in reality. My practice of the spiritual disciplines of prayer and Bible reading has been sporadic.

Bottom line, all of my hurdles centered on myself and my own self-efforts and poor-me unworthiness, not on God's loving grace, ability and provision in Jesus. While I longed to live fully in Christ and be filled to overflowing with God's love, I was double-minded in looking at myself, not at Jesus. Looking to him inspires confidence and resolves all hesitation. He is altogether lovely. One sight of his tender-hearted mercy and loving kindness is enough to dissolve our fears and fill us with longing to know him.

Knowing God is all about relationship. And it is all so simple. All it takes is accepting the truth that he loves us and wants a relationship with us. We act on the truth by accepting his love and intentionally turning our thoughts toward him. Again and again and again. On that foundation, we ask for what we want and begin to learn to listen to him for what he wants. Are we asking, seeking, knocking and trusting Jesus for more? He invites, but we must respond.

Calvinists say that drawing near to God is all by his grace; Arminians say we have a choice in the matter.[73] I don't think the prodigal son[74] thought much about grace or choice. He simply he humbled himself, admitted his mistake, rejected the pig slop, turned his back on the distant country and set his face toward home. He traveled on until he finally saw his father—waiting with open arms. Only then did he feel the warm embrace of steadfast love and feast on the fatted calf. [75]

Many journeys toward God parallel the prodigal son's. God's holiness requires humbly turning away from our own mistaken choices and thinking. The journey into our Father's loving arms may take a while, but the reward will be glorious—Jesus himself! In more love, life, joy and light than human minds can fathom. He said,

> *I am the light of the world. Whoever follows Me will never walk in the darkness, but will have the light of life. John 8:12*

And as his disciple John witnessed of Jesus,

---

73 Calvinists believe that God is supremely sovereign; mankind is totally depraved; God has predetermined who will choose to believe in Jesus and be saved; it's impossible for them to resist His saving grace, and once a person is saved, they'll always be saved. Arminians believe that in God's foreknowledge and sovereignty, he gives mankind free will; salvation is not predetermined; it is his will for all people to choose to believe; God's grace enables us and helps us believe, but it is resistible and salvation can be lost.

74 See Luke 15:11-35

75 *There was a man who had two sons. The younger son said, "Father, give me my share of the estate." So he divided his property between them. . . .The younger son journeyed to a distant country, where he squandered his wealth in wild living. . . . A severe famine swept through that country, and he began to be in need. So he went and hired himself out . . . to feed the pigs. He longed to fill his belly with the pods the pigs were eating, but no one would give him a thing. Finally he came to his senses and said, . . ."Here I am, starving to death! I will get up and go back to my father and say, . . .'Father, I have sinned against heaven and against you. am no longer worthy to be called your son. Make me like one of your hired servants." So he . . . went to his father. But while he was still in the distance, his father saw him and was filled with compassion. He ran to his son, embraced him, and kissed him. The son declared, "Father, I have sinned against heaven and against you. I am no longer worthy to be called your son." But the father said to his servants, "Quick! Bring the best robe and put it on him. Put a ring on his finger and sandals on his feet. . . . Let us feast and celebrate. For this son of mine was dead and is alive again! He was lost and is found!" So they began to celebrate. Luke 15:11-22*

In him was life, and that life was the light of men. The Light shines in the darkness, and the darkness has not overcome it.
John 1:4-5

THE INNER COURT:
ITS STRUCTURE

In the outer court, under the open sky, God reveals himself through natural light. Passing through the scarlet, blue and purple veil, we move out of the natural light of the sun, moon and stars and enter the holy place, under the tabernacle roof.

Within the holy place, all light comes from the lampstand. The pure burning oil represents the light of God's Holy Spirit. He is the Spirit of Truth. He alone can reveal Jesus to our natural minds. We already discussed the tabernacle's division into the outer and inner courts as a picture of our own bodies and souls. This division between outer court and inner court also pictures Jesus's body and soul as the temple of God. Jesus's final self-denial of the outer court of his physical body was his sacrifice on the altar of the cross, out in the open, on a busy road outside of Jerusalem, for every passerby to see.

[Jesus] himself bore our sins in His own body on the tree, that we, having died to sins, might live for righteousness.
1 Peter 2:24 NKJV

By comparison with the wooden cross, the inner court of Jesus's inner person, the holy place of his soul, is pure gold. Can you imagine stepping into the holy place with me for a quick first look? All the walls and furniture are pure gold. Looking around in wonder at the beauty we will notice another veil separating the holy place from the holy of holies. The inner court is divided into two rooms, the holy place and the holy of holies—the place of God's manifest presence at the mercy seat, above the ark between the wings of cherubim.

THE FOUNDATION

Foundations are crucially significant. The tabernacle foundation had to be strong, enduring and unshakable. A shaky, weak, uneven, cracked foundation results in a shaky, uneven building. A strong, even, firm foundation stabilizes and supports what is built upon it. I learned about foundations the hard way. Years ago, when starting publishing company, I asked a trustworthy business counselor for advice. He prophetically said, "Look to the foundation. Check it for cracks." I didn't understand the wisdom of his words until the business began to fall apart. Too late, I realized that our foundation was full of cracks. Relationships between the founding partners, all Christians who initially cared deeply for each other, split apart as tiny cracks from control issues, poor communication, stonewalling, criticism, back-biting and incompatible visions surfaced. As CEO, much of the responsibility on a business level was mine. Our marketing expectations were unrealistic and I had no clue. Because of rapid, recent changes in the publishing world, our team was totally out of synch with the times. On a relational level, I didn't speak out and ask questions soon enough. Too late, psychological testing revealed I was an artist-intellectual and business was toxic for me. One professional counselor said, "Get out. Fast. You're dead in water." God must have agreed. He orchestrated the company's closure and made publishing provisions for the author's we'd worked with. We'd built on a cracked foundation and despite encouraging several authors and publishing a few good books for the Lord, our company and many friendships fell apart. Fortunately, God's foundations are not cracked, they are sure. Consider his creation.

In the beginning God laid the foundations of the earth, and the heavens are the work of His hands. Psalm 102:25 adapted

Eternally enduring values are the foundation of God's throne.

*Righteousness and justice are the foundation of God's throne; loving devotion and faithfulness go before him.
Psalm 89:14 adapted*

Faith in God's son, Jesus is a sure, unshakable foundation. Isaiah prophesied of him,

*"See, I lay a stone in Zion, a tested stone, a precious cornerstone, a sure foundation; the one who believes will never be shaken
Isaiah 28:16*

Jesus said that everyone who acts on his words builds on a strong sure foundation,

Therefore everyone who hears these words of Mine and acts on them is like a wise man who built his house on the rock. The rain fell, the torrents raged, and the winds blew and beat against that house; yet it did not fall, because its foundation was on the rock. Matthew 7:24-25

Jesus Christ is the only sure foundation of God's kingdom that cannot and will not ever be shaken.

He [God] has promised, "Once more I will shake not only the earth, but heaven as well." The words "Once more" signify the removal of what can be shaken—that is, created things—so that the unshakable may remain.

Therefore, since we are receiving an unshakable kingdom, let us be filled with gratitude, and so worship God acceptably with reverence and awe. Hebrews 12: 26b-28

Jesus Christ is the only foundation on which the Holy Spirit will build us, God's people, into a holy temple. The Holy Spirit will build Jesus's church, his holy temple, on our current individual faith in God's word and our relationship with Jesus, our Father and himself. If we try to build on our baptism, our doctrines, our gifts, anointings or experiences, we'll make cracks in the foundation. Years ago, I temporarily based my contribution to the body of Christ on an experience. It didn't work. I don't know if I became a bump, a hole or a crack, but I sure was a hindrance to unity.

It began after attending a conference with extended times of worship. While there, the Holy Spirit plugged me into a power outlet and charged me up, again and again. At the time, it was very humbling and turned me toward Jesus. But after returning to the pressures and imbalances of the young church I attended, I thought my experience of God's power gave me authority to challenge my pastor and another church leader. I presumed that my experience and Bible College background had made me more anointed or special than I was. No one else thought that. In basing my presumption on my experience rather than God's word and Jesus, my foundation was faulty. (Oh, I do hope my experience will help some young reader avoid a few of the growing pains and pitfalls I've stumbled into on my journey toward God's peace and joy.)

That experience reminds me of my critical attitude toward a highly anointed Bible teacher I knew in the 1980's. Both stories illustrate the as-you-judge-you-will-be-judged principle.

Do not judge, and you will not be judged. Do not condemn, and you will not be condemned. Forgive, and you will be forgiven. . . .For with the measure you use, it will be measured back to you." Matthew 5: 37-38b

I loved to listen to this pastor's preaching. Sadly, he came to think that the anointing the Lord had given him to teach carried over to other areas of his life and that his opinions outside of his keen exegesis of God's word were as true and solid as his Biblical studies. His foundation was faulty. He became critical of other pastors, then his congregation and board became critical of him. Sadly, this brilliant teacher was asked to retire early.He trusted that his anointing gave Godly authority to his own thoughts. Remember Jesus's warning to his disciples after he had sent them out to heal the sick and say that the Kingdom of God was near them?

The seventy-two returned with joy and said, "Lord, even the demons submit to us in Your name."
So He told them, "I saw Satan fall like lightning from heaven. Behold, I have given you authority to tread on snakes and scorpions, and over all the power of the enemy. Nothing will harm you. Nevertheless, do not rejoice that the spirits submit to you, but rejoice that your names are written in heaven." Luke 10:17-20

Our names are written in heaven by virtue of Jesus's redemptive blood, not our own. Another question to ask ourselves is, are we building on our denominations? Saying, "I'm a Baptist or a Lutheran or a Catholic." Or might a person be at the core of our faith? That happened to the Corinthian believers. Paul wasn't happy about it when he wrote

> *Individuals among you are saying, "I follow Paul," "I follow Apollos," "I follow Cephas," or "I follow Christ." Is Christ divided? Was Paul crucified for you? Were you baptized into the name of Paul? ... For when one of you says, "I follow Paul," and another, "I follow Apollos," are you not mere men? What then is Apollos? And what is Paul? They are servants through whom you believed, as the Lord has assigned to each his role. I planted the seed and Apollos watered it, but God made it grow. So neither he who plants nor he who waters is anything, but only God, who makes things grow. He who plants and he who waters are one in purpose, and each will be rewarded according to his own labor. For we are God's fellow workers; you are God's field, God's building.*
>
> *By the grace God has given me, I laid a foundation as an expert builder, and someone else is building on it. But each one must be careful how he builds. For no one can lay a foundation other than the one already laid, which is Jesus Christ. 1 Corinthians 1:12-13 and 3:4-11*

Yes, our only sure foundation is Jesus Christ, alive in us and alive in his written word by the power of the Holy Spirit. So, since everything in the tabernacle points to Jesus, what did the first tabernacle's foundation look like?

The boards for the tabernacle walls were set into a foundation of heavy solid silver sockets. There were ninety-two sockets for the wall-boards, four for the corners, and four for the pillars upholding the veils.

> *And of the hundred talents of silver were cast the sockets of the sanctuary, and the sockets of the vail; an hundred sockets of the hundred talents, a talent for a socket. Exodus 38:27*

God himself had directed Moses to set the inner court on a solid silver foundation. Silver! Heavy blocks of silver, the Bible's metaphor for redemption we looked at earlier in the section about the silver of redemption. The silver foundation is a type of the strength, solidity, weight and great value of a structure built upon the precious metal God chose to represent Jesus's redemptive life and death. It was so heavy that scholars who don't accept God word at face value reasonably doubt the weight. Since a talent weighs about 75 pounds, the foundation would weigh about 7,500 pounds or close to 3 ¾ tons of silver! [76] When the tabernacle moved, it would have taken 100 men carrying 75 pounds each to move the sockets from one place to another. That may sound daunting to us, but the Levites had carts and oxen [77] and many of these former slaves were strong wiry men who had made, lifted and carried heavy loads of bricks and mortar for years. During my son's youth, when he worked as an apprentice bricklayer, he lifted 75 pounds easily. The weight is important. The sockets supporting the tabernacle walls represent our unshakable foundation in Christ Jesus. They would not easily be shaken.

This wasn't any old silver. God called the silver of redemption *ransom*[78] money. I'm repeating the discussion and scriptures on silver earlier in the book, to highlight that this silver ransom money was especially collected and designated for the foundation. It came from the offering mentioned earlier, the one required from each man over twenty years old who was numbered for service in Israel's army.

---

[76] 100 talents is approximately 3.77 tons or 3.42 metric tons of silver according to the footnote on on Exodus 38:27 in the Berean Study Bible

[77] Numbers 7:2

[78] According to Merriam-Webster's dictionary a ransom is a consideration paid or demanded for the release of someone or something from captivity. https://www.merriamwebster.com/dictionary/ransom.

The LORD spoke to Moses... He said: "Take a census of the whole congregation of Israel by their clans and families, listing every man by name, one by one. You and Aaron are to number those who are twenty years of age or older by their divisions—everyone who can serve in Israel's army." Numbers 1:1-3

"When you take a census of the Israelites to number them, each man must pay the LORD a ransom for his life when he is counted. Then no plague will come upon them when they are numbered. Everyone who crosses over to those counted must pay a half shekel. . . . This half shekel is an offering to the LORD." Exodus 30: 11-12

The silver from those numbered among the congregation totaled 100 talents and 1,775 shekels, according to the sanctuary shekel. . . from everyone twenty years of age or older who had crossed over to be numbered, a total of 603,550 men. The hundred talents of silver were used to cast the bases of the sanctuary and the bases of the veil—100 bases from the 100 talents, one talent per base. Exodus 38:25-27

The silver ransom money, melted down and recast for the foundation, is symbolic of Jesus Christ. He not only redeems us, he also gave his life as a ransom for us. The noun *ransom* refers to money paid to free a hostage and *redemption* is the act of redeeming or buying something or someone back. The verb *to ransom* means to set free, to deliver from sin, consequences and penalties. [79]

---

79   https://wikidiff.com/ransom/redemption

The Son of Man did not come to be served, but to serve, and to give His life as a ransom for many." Matthew 20:27

For there is one God, and there is one mediator between God and men, the man Christ Jesus, who gave Himself as a ransom for all. . . 1 Timothy 2:5

The goodness of God in Jesus Christ as our redeemer and ransom price is the foundation our salvation and life and Christ.

In Him we have redemption through His blood, the forgiveness of our trespasses, according to the riches of His grace Ephesians 1:7

Jesus Christ is the foundation of our cleansing and sanctification and our fellowship.

If we walk in the light as He is in the light, we have fellowship with one another, and the blood of Jesus His Son cleanses us from all sin. 1 John 1:7

He is the foundation of our service.

How much more will the blood of Christ, who through the eternal Spirit offered Himself unblemished to God, purify our consciences from works of death, so that we may serve the living God! Hebrews 9:14

And Jesus is the foundation of our prayer and worship.

We have confidence to enter the Most Holy Place by the blood of Jesus, Hebrews 10:19

Surely the foundational silver sockets of the inner court pointed ahead to Jesus.

Lord, in these troubled days, help us to build our lives upon you.

For no one can lay a foundation other than the one already laid, which is Jesus Christ. 1 Corinthians 3:11

The LORD is exalted, for He dwells on high;
He has filled Zion with justice and righteousness.

He will be the sure foundation for your times,
a storehouse of salvation, wisdom, and knowledge.
Isaiah 33:5-6

THE WALLS

The tabernacle's inner court walls were awesomely beautiful. The acacia hardwood boards, signifying Jesus's humanity, were completely covered with purest gold to illustrate Jesus's divine nature. The gold overlay pictures heavenly, not earthly revelation. At times, when feeling vulnerable in uncertain relationships and situations, I've asked the Lord to be a boundary around me. Picturing myself surrounded by the golden walls of his love is a comforting steadying reminder of the often invisible and unperceived beauty of his protection.

The boards were not laid horizontally as in the slat homes we are familiar with today. They stood upright in silver sockets. Their stability was reinforced with gold covered acacia wood crossbars. I once heard a preacher speculate that God directed the boards to be placed upright because Jesus is upright in all his ways. I chuckle and shake my head as I write because it's impossible to know all God's reasons. Upright boards make practical sense from a construction viewpoint. But if the pastor was right, it gives us one more tiny glimpse into the seamless, inter-connected, purposeful, meaningful harmony that's intrinsic to all God's works.

THE TABERNACLE COVERINGS OR ROOF

No one but the priests ever saw these beautiful golden walls because an almost impenetrable, protective roof covered the inner court. In writing about the tabernacle roof, I'm keenly aware of our need for protection—from plagues and viruses, from violence and destruction, from toxic people and ideas and even from the negative or ungodly impulses hitting us in the head or hiding inside our own hearts. We need protection. Our relationship with God needs guarding. God recognized and illustrated our need in the pains he took to shield the inner court from the desert sun and storms, from birds, bats and every unwanted intruder. He hid his glory from prying eyes as well. The four different layers of materials covering the roof illustrate God's desire to protect us and cover our close relationship with him. To paraphrase the first two verses of Psalm 91, when we live within the shelter of the Most High God and abide under the shadow of the Almighty, we are under the most powerful protection that exists anywhere. Trusting in God, we can honestly say that he is our refuge and fortress. He will keep us safe.

The outmost visible covering was a sturdy a rain-repellent material that fully covered over the top and hung down to protect all sides. Under that came an insulating protective layer of ram skins dyed red. The third layer was of woven goat's hair. The fourth inner layer was of fine linen. The tabernacle's protection illustrates how we are completely protected and safe in Christ—in life and through death.

From Genesis through Revelation, the tent of God's habitation offers protection to his people. In Greek, the word *tent* is *skene*. [80] In John 1:14 the form *skenoo* describes Jesus. The literal meaning of *"The Word became flesh, and dwelt among us* is "the word pitched a tent among us." One literal Bible translation is *the word became flesh and did tabernacle among us,* [81] that is to say, *the word pitched his tent among us.*

When Jesus said,

> *If you abide in Me and My words abide in you, you will ask what you desire, and it shall be done for you.*
> *John 15:7 NKJV*

It's as if he is saying, "Come into my tent. Live in me and in my life-giving word. I'll be with you and cover you with my love."

When a tornado, blizzard or heavy thunderstorm rolls through our Midwest, the safest place is inside a building. For the children of Israel in the desert, the safest place to find shade from the blazing sun or protection during a storm was in their *skene*, their tent. The safest place for us, spiritually, in any situation, is inside God's tent, abiding in union with his Son.[82] When Jesus Christ, the living word became flesh and pitched his tent among us, he himself was the place of God's glory.

When we abide in Jesus, that is, live inside of Jesus's tent, his desires and concerns become our own. In agreement with him, our Father in heaven answers our prayers. Dwelling in Jesus all we ask moves into harmony with God's will. The tabernacle metaphor points to Jesus's teaching on abiding when he said,

---

80 See Acts 7:44; Hebrews 8:2, 5, and chapter 9
81 *Youngs' Literal Translation*
82 See Appendix entry on Abiding

Remain in Me, [dwell in Me] and I will remain in you. Just as no branch can bear fruit by itself unless it remains in the vine, neither can you bear fruit unless you remain in Me. I am the vine and you are the branches. John 15:4-5

It also points to Paul's truth in Galatians 2:20

I have been crucified with Christ, and I no longer live, but Christ lives in me. The life I live in the body, I live by faith in the Son of God, who loved me and gave Himself up for me. Galatians 2:20

Everything about the heavily covered inner court prefigures Christ's life in us and our abiding communion with God in Christ Jesus. The holy place glowed under the light from the lampstand that prefigured the Holy Spirit. Each piece of furniture pictured different aspects of Jesus and our relationship to him. Beyond the second veil, hidden from our eyes, the holy of holies shone with the supernatural light of God's manifest presence.

When Moses went inside the tent to speak with God between the cherubim, God told Moses exactly what to do. When Moses left the tent, he followed God's direction. With one difference, Moses's coversation with God foreshadows the ongoing communion with Jesus available to all who abide in him. The difference between Moses and us? You're most likely ahead of me. We don't have to leave the tent. Without contradicting the differences between inner court and outer court ministry that we've dissected for understanding, the reality is that if we abide in Jesus, if he lives in us and we live in him, we need never leave the tent.

Just as God's protective presence in the cloud and fire hovered over the tent in the wilderness, God's protective presence and the fire of his jealous love for his Son hover over us as we abide in Jesus.

THE TACHASHIM SKINS:
THE OUTER PROTECTIVE HUMBLE COVERING

The tabernacle's outer layer, the tachashim skin, was most likely a fine weatherproof leather, possibly from a sea creature like the porpoise. It may have been lovely, soft and supple like an eel skin with radiating shades of violets and blues. It may have been ugly; drab, and coarse like tanned hide. No one today knows. We do know it was protective. There is always a protective covering over the place of God's presence. The Psalmist wrote,

> *He who dwells in the secret place of the Most High*
> *Shall abide under the shadow of the Almighty.*
> *I will say of the Lord, "He is my refuge and my fortress;*
> *My God, in him I will trust."*
> *Surely He shall deliver you from the snare of the fowler*
> *And from the perilous pestilence.*
> *He shall cover you with His feathers,*
> *And under His wings you shall take refuge;*
> *His truth shall be your shield and buckler.*
> *Psalm 91:1-4 NKJV* [83]

That is the quality of protection that's available to you and me today. More than once my family and I have called on God to remind him of Psalm 91's promise of deliverance and refuge. After my mother came to faith in Jesus, whenever she feared for her adult children or questioned the safety and wisdom of her teenage grandchildren, she'd

---

[83] For an inspiring account of God's faithfulness to those who claimed his covenant of protection by praying Psalm 91, check out Peggy Joyce Ruth's book, *Psalm 91: God's Shield of Protection*, © Peggy Joyce Ruth, Creation House, 2007. Ruth explicates God's covenant of protection and illustrates it with over two dozen testimonies of his faithfulness to fulfill it. An inspiring story from her book about soldiers who prayed Psalm 91 during the Battle of Dunkirk is available online at https://kinshipradio.org/home/2020/03/25/psalm-91-and-the-miracle-of-dunkirk/

pick up her Bible, prop up her knees to hold it and read Psalm 91 aloud. By faith, she'd substitute our names for the personal pronouns in the Psalm and picture each child of her concern dwelling in the secret place of the Most High, abiding under the protective shadow of our Almighty God.

For years, I've kept a single sheet of paper with a paragraph about soldiers who prayed Psalm 91 during WW I. I don't recall who gave it to me; I don't know who wrote it, but the first paragraph is worth passing on. It reads:

> *Psalm 91 is called the Soldier's Psalm. We are told that in World War I, the soldiers of the 91st Brigade recited the 91st Psalm daily. This brigade engaged in three of the war's bloodiest battles. Other units suffered up to 90% casualties, but the 91st Brigade did not suffer a single combat-related death. God is willing and able to keep his words of covenant promise. Plead God's shield daily in these evil times. We confidently claim his angelic watchers, deliverance and protection. Memorize it, meditate on it, and pray it out loud for your family. It could mean the difference between life and death.*
>
> (Thank you, whoever wrote this!)

We don't know all that God protects us from. Occasionally, we're blessed with such obvious supernatural intervention that it can only be called a miracle.[84] That happened to me once in the 1980s. Early on a brightly cold Sunday morning when the world was sparkling with ice and fresh snow, I was driving along Barrington Road toward Route 72

---

84 A faith-building read for those who doubt the plausibility of miracles and for those enjoy reading about them is Eric Metaxas's book, *Miracles, What They Are, Why They Happen and How They Can Change Your Life,* Penguin Books, 2015

to pick up a friend for church. Suddenly, my wheels hit a slick spot on the freshly plowed road. The car spun out of control and angled off the highway. Looking through the windshield, I clearly saw the car (with me in it) was sailing through the air, up, up and away across the deep ditch running parallel to the roadside shoulder. I was heading straight into the barbed wire fence enclosing the higher ground of a snow-covered farm field. I cried out, "Father!" Next thing I knew, so fast I couldn't see it happen, the car must have turned in midair because I was back on Barrington Road driving toward Route 72 without slowing down or feeling the slightest bump when the tires hit the road. Oh—did I feel God's protective hand that day!

Dwelling in the secret place of the Most High, giving ourselves to abide in Jesus, illustrates entering into a covenant relationship with God. In a covenant relationship with God, he guarantees to care for us. Under the Old Covenant, he guaranteed to care for Israel. And he did, until they broke covenant with him. It's kind of like a marriage vow. We join ourselves to God and then, for better or worse, for richer or poorer, in sickness and in health, since we are his, God is covenant bound to care for us.

We may suffer losses and endure attacks and difficulties, but his protective hand will see us through. I watched my husband live this out. He was a chronically ill man who trusted on the Holy Spirit's power to keep him. With a steady joy and inner light, he lived through and rose above many opportunities and temptations to doubt God. Looking back, I believe that the Holy Spirit gave him the very same faith that held Jesus steady on the cross. He knew that whatever happened to his body, God would protect his essential life. As my husband was dying, we prayed the Lord's Prayer and the 23rd Psalm, knowing that Jesus said,

I give them eternal life, and they will never perish. No one can snatch them out of My hand. My Father who has given them to me, is greater than all; no one can snatch them out of my Father's hand. John 10:28-29

And Paul repeated,

But the Lord is faithful and He will strengthen you and guard you from the evil one. 2 Thessalonians 3:3

Intellectual agreement with the "nice idea" that Christ protects us isn't faith in his protection. We need to reflect upon his word until it gets into us and (whether we feel it or not) we learn to trust the safety of his living, loving presence around us. Taking time to imagine what Jesus's choice of tent imagery meant to his disciples when he urged them to abide in him strengthens my faith.

As descendants of desert dwellers, a sheltering tent signified protection from animals, insects, wind and rain, sun and desert sand. Tents suggest seclusion and privacy as well. They picture the emotional safety we experience whenever we meet with Jesus inside the guarded sanctuaries of our own hearts. Jesus not only lived in union with God, he also saw himself as a tent or dwelling place for his Father God and the Holy Spirit. He allowed no one to intrude upon or disrupt their relationship of mutual love. He wants us to know that holy and loving safety too. Abiding in Jesus shelters us under God's protection.

You are my hiding place;
You shall preserve me from trouble;
You shall surround me with songs of deliverance.
Psalm 32:7 NKJV

Although the outermost covering of the tabernacle was the most sturdily protective, no one today is quite sure what it was. A literal translation of the Hebrew word for the material is *the skin of the tachash*. Christian Bible scholars debate about it and Rabbinical opinions in the Talmud include weasel skin, giraffe hide, or a blue or violet-hued goatskin (sic).[85]

Bible translators' suppositions about *tachashim* range widely. A survey of current on-line translations came up with seven translations of fine leather, one of durable leather, three of badger skin, two of goat skins and ten for some kind of sea creature—three porpoise, three seal skins, two sea cow hide[86], one dolphin skin and one manatee skin. Three other translations referred to color: one was rams' skins of sky blue, one was simply blue skin and another was violet. Finally, my favorite translation simply acknowledged uncertainty by calling the outer covering by its Hebrew word, *tachashim* skins.

Earlier commentators who relied on the King James translation of tachashim as *badger skins* concluded that the outer covering was a complete layer of drab, sturdy unbecoming skins and compared it to Jesus, of whom Isaiah said

> *For He grew up before him like a tender shoot, and like a root out of a dry ground. He had no stately form or majesty to attract us, no beauty that we should desire him. He was despised and rejected of men. Isaiah 53:2-3a*

The image is richly meaningful. Following Jesus is not as glamorous as seeking the wealth, power, success, fame and beauty of this world. He calls his followers to self-denial. They are often misunderstood, maligned and rejected.

---

85 http://www.jewishanswers.org/ask-the-rabbi-category/the-land-of-israel/the-temple/?p=2400)

86 Bedouin Arabs have continued to make sandals out of sea cow (manatee) hides from the Persian Gulf until recent times. (Keil and Delitzsch, *Commentary on the Old Testament*, vol. 1 book 2 Grand Rapids, MI Eerdmans1981 p. 163 translated from German by M.G. Easton

The Tachashim Skins: The Outer Protective Humble Covering

Accurate or not, I like the idea that a plain simple leather covering would speak of Christ sharing our ordinary humanity. An unpretentious practical outer covering is consistent with Jesus's birth in a stable, his life of poverty, his humility in identifying with us and his humble obedience to his Father.

Most likely, Isaiah's description of Jesus was literal. He was probably rather ordinary to look at, not particularly handsome. The crowds who followed him were drawn by the energy of his presence and his messages of hope and love, not by his outward appearance. Those with eyes to see gravitated to him because of the purity of his character, the light of his countenance and the compelling truth of his teachings. They felt and saw the consistency of his loving compassion, recognized his wisdom and were amazed by the convincing power of his many deeds of merciful loving-kindness.

Those who looked on Jesus outwardly, without love or insight into his identity, saw no beauty in him. Even those who loved him weren't seeing beauty when he was betrayed, abandoned by his friends and followers and victimized by false accusations. There is no beauty in the intense degradation or the shame and physical suffering of flogging and death on the cross.

A simple, humble outer covering is also consistent with how foolish and unglamorous [87] the ways of God look to the natural man. The glory of God's revelation is hidden to unbelievers.

> *The god of this age has blinded the minds of unbelievers so they cannot see the light of the gospel of the glory of Christ, who is the image of God. 2 Corinthians 4:4*

---

[87] Self-sacrifice, meekness and refusal to retaliate looks like foolish weakness to "worldly winners" who look down on Christians. Might this be why Jesus said that the meek shall inherit the earth and the last shall be first in His Father's kingdom?

From the outside, Calvary is grotesque and unsightly. Its riches are hidden.

> *For the message of the cross is foolishness to those who are perishing, but to us who are being saved it is the power of God. For it is written: "I will destroy the wisdom of the wise; the intelligence of the intelligent I will frustrate." 1 Corinthians 1:18-19*

Yet every believer who finds mercy at the foot of the cross knows that the place of Jesus's humble obedience unto death is the source of inexhaustible love, hope and joy. So, whatever the outer covering looked liked, one thing is sure; every type of skin has metaphorical possibilities that liken it to Jesus. Beautiful or drab, all we can reasonably know is that the outer covering was durable, waterproof and protective. Whatever it was, the tachashim protected the holy places from the hot sun, from insects and birds, and from desert storms. No moisture, grit or sand could penetrate God's covering over the inner court. It symbolically signified Jesus Christ as our protection from every evil and storm and from all the pollution of the world—and he wants it that way. Hallelujah!

THE RAMS' SKINS DYED RED:
OUR SHEPHERD AND BLOOD SACRIFICE

Directly under the outer layer was a layer of rams' skins dyed red. The red rams' skins speak of Jesus's obedience to death on the cross. The red dye came from a worm and reminds us that while his blood-marked body hung on the cross, Jesus cried out the first line of Psalm 22, *"My God, My God, why have You forsaken me?"* Verse 6 of the same Psalm prophetically describes another aspect of his death in the words,

> *But I am a worm, and no man; A reproach of men, and despised by the people. Psalm 22:6 NKJV*

While the worm is an apt metaphor for aspects of our Lord's willing humility and submission to the humiliation of the cross, Jesus never embraced what we call the worm-mentality. The rams' skins represents male productivity, leadership and headship over the flock. As the head of the flock, Jesus willingly and strongly chose to embrace substitutionary atonement to protect his sheep,

> *He is the head of the body, the church, who is the beginning, the firstborn from the dead; that in all things he might have the preeminence. Colossians 1:18 NHEB*

Finally, and dear to so many hearts in including mine, the rams' skins point to Jesus as our shepherd. Rams' skins are the traditional garb of shepherds. Psalm 23 begins with the words,

> *The Lord is my Shepherd. Psalm 23:1*

Jesus, our Lord, described himself as a shepherd. He anticipated His death by telling His disciples,

> *I am the good shepherd. The good shepherd lays down his own life for the sheep. John 10:11*

The rams' skins' blood-red also symbolized the reality and prophetic meaning of blood sacrifice at Israel's major historical God-encounters. God himself instituted animal sacrifice when he killed animals for skins to cover the nakedness of Adam and Eve. Thus, Adam's sons, Cain and Able, must have grown up knowing animal sacrifice was God's pattern for worship. Able's humble acceptable sacrifice to God was a lamb. Cain's proud inacceptable offering to God was from the fruit of his own labor on the cursed ground. After the flood, Noah sacrificed [88] one of every kind of clean animal when he worshipped God. On the night the Israelite slaves fled from Egypt, they put lamb's blood on the lintels of their doorposts to protect themselves and their children from death.

The red of blood sacrifice would also remind the Israelites of Abraham's covenant with God in Genesis 15 and of the history-changing moment when God tested Abraham's faith by asking him to sacrifice his son, Isaac. Isaac was already bound upon the altar, the knife was in Abraham's hand, when God intervened and provided a ram to stop Abraham from sacrificing his son.[89] That ram and every one of those red rams' skins protecting the tabernacle look forward to the final sacrifice, the death of Jesus, God's only begotten Son, for you and for me. They picture the blood of Jesus protecting us from death and covering our sins as we draw near to God.

> "Come now, let us reason together," says the LORD.
> "Though your sins are like scarlet, they will be as white as snow; though they are as red as crimson, they will become like wool."
> Isaiah 1:18

THE GOAT HAIR: OUR SCAPEGOAT SUBSTITUTE

The next protective covering over the tabernacle was of goat hair. Goats were a significant part of Israel's subsistence. They provided meat, milk, cheese and butter as well as leather for bottles, saddlebags and slings. Fine goat hair was spun and woven into curtains and clothing. Coarser goat's hair was plied into rope and spun and woven into fabric for tents.

---

[88] Judson Cornwall, *Forbidden Glory: Portraits of Pride*, MacDougal Publishing, © 2001 by Judson Cornwall, p. 48-49

[89] Genesis 22

Israel's camp, of thousands of dark goat's hair tents, surrounded the tabernacle.

For the Hebrew children, weaving goat hair for their own tents and for the tabernacle curtains was natural, practical, commonplace and utilitarian. Spun goat hair was familiar and available. It's unlikely they realized all the prophetic and spiritual meaning that's now associated with God's protective covering over them and their families. We'll never know.

It's not surprising that after centuries of scholarly and devotional digging for buried spiritual treasure and hidden lessons in the tabernacle that a few treasure hunters have picked up gravel with the gold and polluted the vast collection of thinking about the tabernacle with horrible and hurtful misconceptions. A couple inaccuracies are related to goat's hair. One is the conjectured interpretation that Jesus is the true Israel, that all those goat's hair tents foreshadowed him and his followers.

That's just not true. The sons of Jacob are still alive. They're still singing, dancing, and bringing up children who will fulfill scripture as part of God's end-time plan. Another extra-Biblical misconception is the tragic antisemitic association between goat's hair and Israel as an international scapegoat. Millions of innocent Jews have been wrongly blamed for situations as different as Jesus's death, the bubonic plague, Germany's economic depression after WW I and the twin-tower bombing. When I did an internet search of "Israel as scapegoat" I was stunned to read that a few misinformed anti-Semites are now blaming Israel for covid-19. But Jesus's identification with us as the scapegoat-substitute for our sins is not extra-Biblical nor is it conjecture; it's a clear foreshadowing of his love.

Eleven goat's hair curtains were under the rams' skins dyed red. The goat's hair was spun into yarn and woven into cloth. We don't know if this particular hair was the coarse variety, used for sturdy ropes and sacks, or a longer, silkier staple, like angora. I'd guess, the finer stuff, tightly woven. *Sair*, the word used for the sacrificial goats chosen for the Day of Atonement, means the hairy one.

Goats were offered for every single one of the eleven prescribed Old Testament sacrifices for sin. Each goat was a type of Jesus's sacrifice for you and me. Every year, on the Day of Atonement, two goats were chosen. The priest sacrificed one goat as a sin offering. Its blood was sprinkled and smeared on the priests and the tabernacle to symbolically cleanse them from sin. The other goat, the scapegoat, was set free to carry away their sin and iniquities.

> *Aaron shall bring forward the living goat; laying both hands upon its head, he shall confess over it all the iniquities of the Israelites and all their sinful transgressions, laying them on the head of the goat and sending it away to the desert. . . . The goat shall bear away their iniquities. Leviticus 16:21-22 Mof*

Just as Aaron once put his hands upon the goat's head and confessed Israel's sins and iniquities, we, as sinners, must reach out our hands to Jesus, our high priest. His death has made atonement for us. When we touch Jesus in faith and confess and repent of our sins, he forgives our sins and takes them away.

How many of us can personally identify with the scapegoat? I can. Years ago, God sent me to Al-anon and ACOA [90] meetings to discover much-needed truth and find support. For a time, I went to twelve-step meetings seven days a week to survive the pain of facing and breaking the denials and dysfunctions of generational alcoholism in my nuclear family. There, I learned about family scapegoats. Most dysfunctional families have them—a person to blame. Was it a blessing or a shame that I so often appeared blameworthy? Today I can laugh about all the opportunities I was given to identify with Jesus as the scapegoat. Half a century ago, it hurt. I gathered guilt. Since I couldn't literally take other people's opinions and coping mechanisms to the cross, I took myself there. The Holy Spirit gave me many opportunities to forgive and let go. Again and again, Jesus healed the pain of misunderstandings and accusations (both valid and ridiculous); he helped me build new thinking patterns and behavior. Then, most lovingly, he began to dissolve almost all the censure against me.

Anyone who has ever felt the sting and shame of blame, justly or not, can be grateful for the scapegoat. We can repent of our guilt (for all have sinned), forgive our accusers, and praise and thank Jesus for taking away every last bit of accusation and condemnation. Why then, do so many of us, continue to nurture guilt and self-condemnation. Are we pridefully disagreeing with God and his word?

---

90 ACOA stands for Adult Children of Alcoholics.

> *Therefore, there is now no condemnation for those who are in Christ Jesus. Romans 8:1*

If, after true repentance, the accusations and condemnations stick or return, we can, by faith, actually ask the Holy Spirit to take us to the courts of heaven. We can ask the Lord to open the books containing every accusation against us. We can acknowledge our guilt (for all have sinned), forgive our accusers (including our own self-accusations) and ask Jesus to advocate for us. He will plead our case.[91] His victory was won at Calvary. Our faith in his blood, that so long ago was symbolized by the red-dyed rams' skins covering the goat's hair, is our strong sole plea and release from every blaming, scapegoating accusation our accusers might throw our way.[92]

Most translations describe the goat's hair as black; a very few say it was white. Either way is metaphorically meaningful. When Jesus's blood (symbolized by the red lambskins) covers our blackest sins, they are washed away and we become white as snow.

> *But if we walk in the light as He is in the light, we have fellowship with one another, and the blood of Jesus Christ His Son cleanses us from all sin. 1 John 1:7 NKJV*

---

[91] *If anyone does sin, we have an advocate before the Father—Jesus Christ, the Righteous One. He himself is the atoning sacrifice for our sins, and not only for ours but also for the sins of the whole world. 1 John 2: 1-2*
For more about Jesus's advocacy for us, check out Robert Henderson, *Operating in the Courts of Heaven,* © 2014 Robert Henderson Ministries.

[92] One helpful healing resource for Christians who want to recognize and reject the principality of blame that has settled over our nation is Emotionally Focused, an online seminar offered by the Mile High Vineyard of Denver, Colorado. This seminar has helped hundreds of believers to become aware of blaming and shaming patterns and reject the defensive, limiting coping mechanisms of a growing shame-based cancel culture. Their program builds healthy Biblical thinking patterns. They can be reached at www.emotionallyfocused.org

FINE-TWINED LINEN OF LOVE: PURITY AND RIGHTEOUSNESS

The tabernacle ceiling is no exception to the astoundingly breathtaking beauty of the inner court. The skillful handwork of the richly embroidered curtains under the golden lamplight reflects the beauty of God's protective covering. This innermost visible layer covering the inner court ceiling was of fine twined linen that had been thickly embroidered with cherubim in blue, purple and scarlet threads. This ceiling was formed by ten curtains: two sets of five each. Bible searches for the significance of ten curtains hung in two sets of five is inconclusive. Some say the curtains symbolize double grace, others say they represent truth, still others suggest they point to the human mind, and one writer asserts that the curtains symbolize the new creation in Christ. We don't know what they stood for, but the idea that I like best (even though it's as unsupported as the others) is that the curtains symbolize the two sets of commandments God gave to Moses. Five commands were about acknowledging and honoring God (and our parents as his representative authority) and five about our responsibilities to others. If so, it's a short logical step from seeing ourselves standing under the law to seeing ourselves standing under Jesus Christ who fulfilled the law. As we abide in and under him, he fully meets all of the law's obligations to fully love both God and others.

Since Jesus said that he fulfills the entire word of God, everything about the tabernacle can help us understand more about our Lord. He said,

> *Do not think that I have come to abolish the Law or the Prophets. I have not come to abolish them, but to fulfill them. For I tell you truly, until heaven and earth pass away, not a single jot, not a stroke of a pen, will disappear from the Law until everything is accomplished. Matthew 5:17-18*

THE INNER-COURT FURNITURE:
THE LAMPSTAND

For with You is the fountain of life; in Your light we see light.
Psalm 36:9

Standing under the heavily covered roof and beautifully embroidered ceiling, we've clearly left the outer court's natural light. We've stepped through the veil into a small room that looks and feels like another world. A soft "Wow!" might whisper from our lips. The room is completely paneled in gold. Looking around, we might blink our eyes as they adjust to the golden glow that's reflected off the walls. The only light comes from seven steadily burning oil lamps on one large golden lampstand. God told Moses,

> *Then the LORD said to Moses, "Command the Israelites to bring you pure oil of pressed olives for the light, to keep the lamps burning continually. Outside the veil of the Testimony in the Tent of Meeting, Aaron is to tend the lamps continually before the LORD from evening until morning. This is to be a permanent statute for the generations to come. He shall tend the lamps on the pure gold lampstand before the LORD continually.*
> *Leviticus 24:1-4*

The word *continually* jumps off the page and into my heart as a reminder that the light of the Holy Spirit is always available; we're to tend our relationship with him continually.

The *pure* olive oil in the lamps reminds us that the Holy Spirit's light burns in us without soot or smoke. (Smudge is from our rubbish, not his flame.) Everything in this inner court is illuminated by clean, pure flames.

The pure gold of the lampstand reminds us of Jesus's purity and divinity. No other piece of furniture in the entire tabernacle was formed from one piece. Repeated blows, both hard hits and gentle taps, were needed to shape the gold into its final form. Each blow added meaning to the lampstand as a type of both Jesus Christ and his church.[93]

---

93 It is so easy for many of us, including me, to stray from scripture and rewrite God's word according to our own imaginations and understanding. Writing this short paragraph on the lampstand taught me a lesson that might be worth sharing. According to scripture, Moses was directed by God to *make a lampstand of pure, hammered gold. It shall be made of one piece, including its base and shaft, its cups, and its buds and petals* and *Make seven lamps and set them up on the lamp- stand so that they illuminate the area in front of it. The wick trimmers and their trays must be of pure gold. The lampstand and all these utensils shall be made from a talent of pure gold. Exodus 25:31, 37-39*

I read that, and supported by trusted resources, I wrote: "If solid, the lampstand would equal the weight of a small man; one hundred and twenty-five pounds of purest gold. The purity reminds us of Jesus's purity and divinity. No other piece of furniture in the entire tabernacle was formed from one piece. Repeated blows, both hard hits and gentle taps, were needed to shaped the large, heavy chunk of gold into its final form. Each blow added meaning to the lamp stand as a type of both Jesus Christ and his church."

Did you catch the mistake? I didn't. Not neither did my trusted resource. Fortunately, a friend who read a draft of the manuscript prompted me to look at the paragraph and the Bible texts more closely. First off, I realized that we've no idea how much gold was used for wick trimmers and trays and we don't know the size or the weight of the lamps that were set upon the stand, so figuring out the amount of gold in the lampstand is impossible. To complicate any suppositions, in the ancient Middle East the weight of a talent varied. One Bible scholar says it's the weight a man can carry. (2 Kings 5:23). A strong man or a weak one? According to *The Illustrated Dictionary of the Bible*, (Herbert Lockyer, Sr., Ed., © 1986, Thomas Nelson, p.1096-97) a talent weighed 3,000 shekels and a shekel weighed in at 11.4 grams. My current kitchen reference for weights and measures puts a pound at 454 grams. The arithmetic on that (never my strong point) turns out to be 75 ⅓ pounds of gold in total for the lamps, lampstand, wick trimmers and trays. Does it matter? Yes. The friend who prompted me to look it more closely commented,

"I think it more likely that the lampstand was beaten work made from sheets of gold, not only due to the enormous amount and great weight that would otherwise be required, but because gold melted down to form a solid piece would have been melted into a mold that was the desired shape, not a shapeless chunk that would then have required beating to form a lampstand. Besides, how could oil flow through the lampstand's pipes if it were solid? . . . No one knows exactly how it was made."

My friend's suppositions led to mistakes too. The Bible says the lampstand was to be made of one piece, not gold sheets. According to the Bible,

Then you are to make a lampstand of pure, hammered gold. It shall be made of one piece, Exodus 25:31

God's word also indicates that the lamps sat on top of the lampstand and could be positioned to face any direction. The oil was in the lamps. It did not flow through the stand.

Then the LORD said to Moses, "Speak to Aaron and tell him: 'When you set up the seven lamps, they are to light the area in front of the lampstand.'" And Aaron did so; he set up the lamps facing toward the front of the lampstand, just as the LORD had commanded Moses. Numbers 8: 1-3

Since everything in the tabernacle points to Jesus, details matter. If you find more mistakes, please let me know.

The next time we wince under the blows of difficult circumstances or bend beneath the challenges of obedience or smart when other people hammer on our souls, we might find strength, endurance and understanding by identifying with Jesus and the repeated blows he suffered at the hands of men. Scripture says, that

> *Although He was a Son, He learned obedience from what He suffered. Hebrews 5:8*

God uses difficulties and blows to shape our characters into agreement with his own and form us according to his will. The Psalmist wrote,

> *Before I was afflicted, I went astray; but now I keep Your word. Psalm 119:67*

We are also shaped by our response to God's word.

"Is not My word like fire," declares the LORD, "and like a hammer that smashes a rock?" Jeremiah 23:29

Every challenge of conforming to God's word in daily life and in difficulty, affliction and enticement presents us with a temptation and a choice. How will we react? I can picture God's watchful eye looking on like a wise and loving father. He gives us freedom of choice, to find our way, and then steps aside to root us on, hoping we'll remember or seek out his instruction, trust his wisdom and call for his help. If we insist on going our own way, our enemies will be many. They include (short list) all the rebellions of self, self-satisfaction, self-will, self-determination, self-pity, self-indulgence, self-entitlement, self-justification and on and on as well as compromise, sloth, denial, blame, contempt, criticism, pride, fear, anger, bitterness, envy, vengeance and doubt.

In my eighty plus years, I've stumbled and fallen into the enemy's hands often. I could bore you with a personal example of every ugly rat listed above. Just recently I blamed someone (in a kind and laughing way) for breaking a glass pitcher that I broke myself. When corrected, I asked forgiveness immediately. I should have left it there, but instead I excused my choice of blame on poor memory because of external pressures. Did you notice the words *excused my choice* and that parentheses (*"in a kind and laughing way"*)? Those stinkers snuck in as a way to pretty up my self-image. Yuck! The first excuse was accurate reporting, but I could have rejected the parentheses. I left it in to illustrate the point. Over the years I've excused my agreements with God's enemies as my "human nature." I've justified negative choices by blaming others, and I've unknowingly accepted many disagreements with God as culturally acceptable, convenient and common.

Our heavenly father is on our side. He sent Jesus to die for us and give us the Holy Spirit's help. When we accept his help, his word increases our awareness of the contrasts between God's holy goodness and his enemies' subtle evil. When we rely on his word and let his character shape us, our responses will thwart and defeat our enemies. They will be humble, honest, authentic, self-controlled, upright, righteous, confident, merciful, just, courageous, peaceful, patient, kind, generous, wise, helpful, healing, forgiving and faith-filled. God's word carries his authority. By agreeing with it, we will separate ourselves from evil and embrace good.

Lord, help us take the life-filled route of conforming to God's word, of dying to self and accepting that Jesus lives in us and we in him. We can praise and thank God that the Holy Spirit is with us to help us agree with God. Lord, help us remember Galatians 2:20 and find our responses in you!

> *I have been crucified with Christ, and I no longer live, but Christ lives in me. The life I live in the body, I live by faith in the Son of God, who loved me and gave Himself up for me. Galatians 2:20*

The first time I recall intentionally and completely dying to self, or "taking the cross" as old-timers say, followed a shaking blow to my self-image. God was hammering me into conformity with his word. At that time, I thought I was financially trustworthy. Although my income was well below the poverty level, I'd lived frugally, was debt-free and had a small bit of savings in the bank. My mother questioned my ability to provide for myself and use money wisely. Financial security was her bottom line; following Jesus was mine. When Mom died, her will specified that my small inheritance go into a trust. Her motives were well-meaning. She didn't approve of my generosity or desire to wait on God for his directions. She didn't trust God to meet my needs; she wanted to take care of me. I understood her thinking, but when my sisters got their inheritance outright, it hurt. At the time, I was living with Mom in her own home, a house my dad had built for her. Three years earlier, when she became unable to care for herself, the Holy Spirit led me to leave my apartment and move in with Mom to take care of her. She'd prayed to die in her own bed, not in a nursing home, and God honored her prayer.

After Mom's death, her house had to be sold to settle her estate. I was given a deadline to move. It all happened too fast. I was weary and depressed from grief; Mom's last year had been hard. Meeting her needs had become all consuming. In the last weeks of life she suffered through a short but wicked bout with dementia and couldn't be left alone. Given the ultimatum to move, I asked for ninety days to recover and plan. My need was ignored, denied. Under great pressure, I couldn't move past my hurt feelings to think clearly or plan. I didn't know what to do. That's when I took the cross.

I'll never forget the moment. It was a cold, gray early evening in mid-January. A damp chill stung my face. The streets were empty and the streetlights went on as I walked Larry Elizabeth, my sons's black and white husky. She'd been pulling on the leash. We were on the east side of Nash Road near South School when grace came. I took myself to the cross and identified with Jesus. I forgave all and put the house and everyone involved into Jesus's hands. Grace not only took me to the cross, it enabled me to die to all the pain of Mom's decision and all my own fear, insecurity, consternation and uncertainty about the next step. I only recall one phrase of my conversation with Jesus. It was, "They can do whatever they want to." The feelings in my heart were new. First, intense pain. Then, piercing bittersweetness. And, at last, sweetness and calm. I'd let go. Peace immediately replaced hurt and blame. Resolve to move ahead replaced uncertainty and fear; sustaining energy replaced fatigue. As I geared up to move out, my "Let go and let God—dying to self—taking the cross" response brought a transformation I can take no credit for. It was all God's grace. By total grace, I was able to live in Mom's house for as long as the Lord wanted. It turned out to be years before I finally moved out. I knew Jesus was with me and, briefly, I'd been on the cross with him. He was using hard blows to shape me—and my future.

> *We do not have a high priest who is unable to sympathize with our weaknesses, but we have one who was tempted in every way that we are, yet was without sin—in all instances He was tempted as we are. Hebrews 4:15*

Jesus knows our frailties, our emotions, our temptations to take things into our own hands. He alone can give us the humility and wisdom needed to bring God's plans to earth. His Holy Spirit alone can strengthen us to oppose and defeat the pharaoh's enslaving forces in our lives. He alone gives us his weapons of warfare.

> *For though we live in the flesh, we do not wage war according to the flesh. The weapons of our warfare are not the weapons of the world. Instead, they have divine power to demolish strongholds. We tear down arguments and every presumption set up against the knowledge of God; and we take captive every thought to make it obedient to Christ. 2 Corinthians 10: 3-5*

The cross is our greatest weapon. When we die to self and live to Jesus, we get out of God's way so that he can move on his own behalf in our circumstances. He wants the best for us, and only he knows what that is. Our battles are won by his Spirit.

> *Not by might nor by power, but by My Spirit, says the LORD of Hosts. Zechariah 4:6*

God alone knows exactly what blows and difficulties will break us and which ones will shape us into vessels he can use. Jesus, the very Son of God, the light of the world, was willingly beaten and bruised by the Roman soldiers. He yielded his body to the Holy Spirit in life and through death, just as the gold of the lampstand yielded to the hammer. And all so that we might live by faith in his love, receive the oil of his Holy Spirit and carry his light today.

THE OIL

Oil is a Bible symbol for the Holy Spirit. When the text reads *anoint*, *anointed* or *anointing*, it refers to the oil of the Holy Spirit that is rubbed on or into a person's physical body. The actual or literal oil is always olive oil.

In the natural, olive oil is valuable for food, for fuel, for illumination, for softening and protecting our skin and for healing. Oil penetrates. It sinks in. A Middle-Eastern gentleman once told me that he was born prematurely, thought dead, and set aside on a pile of rags and laundry while the midwife tended to his mother's needs. His grandmother saw him move and picked him up. For a length of time, he was too weak to nurse from a bottle and his mother was too ill to feed him. His grandmother fed him by rubbing copious amounts of pure olive oil into his skin several times a day. Nourished by the oil on his skin, he began to gain weight and grow until he was strong enough to nurse.

As a type of the Holy Spirit, this nurturing oil was used to anoint prophets, priests and kings. Anointing oil was applied as a sign of God's call upon their lives. It was an indication that God had set them aside for himself. After being anointed, they were (at least symbolically) consecrated and empowered for God's purposes. Moses anointed the priests:

Moses took some of the anointing oil and some of the blood that was on the altar and sprinkled them on Aaron and his garments, and on his sons and their garments. So he consecrated Aaron and his garments, as well as Aaron's sons and their garments. Leviticus 8:30

When Samuel anointed David with oil,

The Spirit of the LORD came upon David from that day forward. 1 Samuel 16:13b.

When Jesus walked into the waters of the Jordan River to humbly identify with us in baptism for repentance of sins, the Holy Spirit came upon him and anointed him as prophet, priest and king. Next, the Holy Spirit led him into the wilderness. There, the devil came to Jesus with three temptations. Each began with the words, *"If you are the Son of God..."* [94] Jesus's anointing from the Holy Spirit, his relationship to his Father and his authority as prophet, priest and king were on the line. If he had fallen into the devil's trap and replied in his divinity, his ministry would have been all over. His opportunity to show the world God's love, complete his mission to reconcile us with our heavenly Father and give us the Holy Spirit would have failed.

With each temptation, Jesus chose to rely on the Holy Spirit and refused to defend or prove himself by supernatural powers. All three times Jesus rebuked the tempter by quoting the word of God, the same Old Testament scriptures that are available to us today. He knew that God's kingdom can come and God's will be done through us on earth only by the power of the Holy Spirit. After overcoming every temptation, he was released to quote from Isaiah 61:1,

---

94 Matthew 4:1-11

The Spirit of the Lord is on Me, because He has anointed Me to preach good news to the poor. He has sent Me to proclaim liberty to the captives and recovery of sight to the blind, to release the oppressed. Luke 4:18

The word *Christ* means the anointed one. Anointed as God's prophet, Jesus edifies, encourages, comforts and teaches us. He is God's greatest prophet, the one the Lord was speaking of when he told Moses,

I will raise up for them a prophet like you from among their brothers. I will put My words in his mouth, and he will tell them everything I command him. And I will hold accountable anyone who does not listen to My words that the prophet speaks in My name. Deuteronomy 18:15-19

Anointed as priest, Jesus advocates and intercedes with God on our behalf. He is the greatest and final High Priest.

Therefore, since we have a great High Priest who has passed through the heavens, Jesus the Son of God, let us hold firmly to what we profess. Hebrews 4:14

Anointed as king, Jesus rules with total governmental authority. He is the only ruler with absolute authority over heaven and earth. He is the only king who rules an everlasting kingdom. He told Pilate,

"My kingdom is not of this world; if it were, My servants would fight to prevent My arrest by the Jews. But now My kingdom is not of this realm."
    "Then You are a king!" Pilate said.
    "You say that I am a king,"

> *Jesus answered, "For this reason. I was born and have come into the world, to testify to the truth. Everyone who belongs to the truth listens to My voice." John 18:36-:37*

Jesus, our anointed prophet, priest and king lived and died to give us the oil of the Holy Spirit that burned within him. Shortly before he was crucified, he told his disciples,

> *But I tell you that I am going to do what is best for you. This is why I am going away. The Holy Spirit cannot come to help you until I leave. But after I am gone, I will send the Spirit to you. John 16:7 CEV*

Jesus wants to fill us to overflowing with the oil of the Holy Spirit. He wants to empower us to silence the devil with God's living word just as he did. He wants God's Holy Spirit to come alongside of us, just as the Holy Spirit remained with him. He rejoices when God's mercy and compassion flow through us to others and he cheers us on when we ask for God's holy love to sustain us through trials. He yearns for us to be one with him and our heavenly Father. He knows how much we need their wisdom and their love. Not a namby-pamby affection or feeling but the strong, unquenchable kind of love that he had for his Father, his friends and for you and me. He knows we need the quality of divine love that held him steady against opposition and through death. He knows all about human weakness and how fully and completely we need the Holy Spirit's oil. How eagerly he must have watched from heaven when the Holy Spirit descended upon his followers in the upper room.[95] With a mighty rushing wind and tongues that looked like flame, the Holy Spirit settled upon the heads of his followers to empower them. How seriously satisfied he must have felt to watch earth history unfold. The burning

---

95 See the Appendix entry on Holy Spirit Baptism

The Oil

oil that been prophetically symbolized by a golden lampstand hidden in a small tent in the Sinai wilderness now rested upon the human flesh of Jesus's friends and followers. [96]

> *When the day of Pentecost came, they were all together in one place. Suddenly a sound like a mighty rushing wind came from heaven and filled the whole house where they were sitting. They saw tongues like flames of fire that separated and came to rest on each of them. And they were all filled with the Holy Spirit and began to speak in other tongues as the Spirit enabled them. Acts 2: 1-4*

God's tongues of fire continue to light his church today. Because the Holy Spirit won't pour more oil into a dirty vessel, some of us will have more or less oil than others. Then too, we may have oil, but if our wicks need trimming our flames will flicker and smoke from self-life and sin. As we yield to God's Spirit and surrender to the transformative, cleansing power of God's word, the Holy Spirit trims our wicks and fills us with more of his oil. He wants us to have more! Just the other night, while reading the parable about the ten virgins who took their lamps out into the night to meet the bridegroom, I was struck by the words *extra oil*.

> *Five of them were foolish, and five were wise. The foolish ones took their lamps but did not take along any EXTRA OIL. But the wise ones took oil in flasks along with their lamps. Matthew 25: 2-3 [emphasis mine]*

I'm not sure how to get extra oil, but I want it, so I've begun praying for it, trusting that if I'm to spend more time resting in the Lord or in

---

[96] Jesus clearly viewed his churches as lampstands. In the book of Revelation, John said, "*I saw seven golden lampstands.*" and he heard Jesus say, "*The seven lampstands are the seven churches.*" *Revelation 1: 12, 20*

prayer, worship or God's word, the Holy Spirit will help me. In the final years of my life, in the tribulations, the pressures of this decade in God's story with man, I don't want to fall into doubt or fear. I don't want to run out of oil or let my light go out and end my life reflecting on a darkening world or the light of past experiences. I want my eyes fixed on the light of Jesus's love and God's redemptive plan for the human race.

Moses said of Jesus, "You must listen to him."

John the Baptist said, "Look on him. Behold him. The Lamb of God who takes away the sins of the world."

Jesus said, "Follow me!"

> *"I am the light of the world. Whoever follows Me will never walk in the darkness, but will have the light of life." John 8:12 BSB*

Jesus received the full measure of the Holy Spirit's anointing.[97] His lamp was full to overflowing with oil. His light was bright enough, hot enough, to accurately and continually reveal our Father in heaven. Think about it: full measure—extra oil. Jesus's love for his Father-God was a constant flame. That's what he wants for us.

Just who is this Holy Spirit who so filled Jesus? One way of getting to know the Holy Spirit is to listen carefully to all the Bible tells us about the anointing on Jesus. It's amazing. He taught God's freeing truth to those who had been bound and misused by the lies of religious legalism. He offered hope to the poor and needy, healed the sick and opened blind eyes to see and deaf ears to hear. He repeatedly delivered the demonized and mentally ill from torment. He comforted the grief-stricken and brokenhearted and he lifted up those in depression and despair by giving them hope and the Holy Spirit's joy. He proclaimed God's Kingdom and

---

[97] See John 3:34 *For the One whom God has sent speaks the words of God, for God gives the Spirit without limit.*

prophesied God's ultimate justice and judgment against injustice and evil. Through all that Jesus said and did, he revealed God's merciful loving kindness. He came to earth to show us what God is truly like and reconcile us to our Creator. And he did it all by the power of the Holy Spirit. Knowingly. After being filled with the Holy Spirit, Jesus himself declared his life's work by standing up in his hometown synagogue at Nazareth and reading the following verses from Isaiah.

> *The Spirit of the Lord GOD is on Me, because the LORD has anointed Me to preach good news to the poor. He has sent Me to bind up the brokenhearted, to proclaim liberty to the captives and freedom to the prisoners, to proclaim the year of the LORD's favor. Isaiah 61:1-2* [98]

When finished reading, he said,

> *"Today this Scripture is fulfilled in your hearing." Luke 4:21*

The very same Holy Spirit who lived in Jesus lives in his church today. As he cleanses us of self, sin and all that impedes his activity, he fills us with himself. He teaches us God's ways and connects us with Jesus. He wants to give us wisdom, power and compassion from God. The Holy Spirt, our Father in heaven and the Lord are working together to give you and me the very same power, love and steadying strength that moved through Jesus. As we accept their influence and direction, they bring the living truth of God's plan, foreshadowed by Moses so long ago in the tabernacle, to this troubled world. The Holy Spirit wants to use you and me to reveal the merciful loving kindness

---

[98] Isaiah's scripture continues, . . . *and the day of our God's vengeance, to comfort all who mourn, to console the mourners in Zion—to give them a crown of beauty for ashes, the oil of joy for mourning, and a garment of praise for a spirit of despair. So they will be called oaks of righteousness, the planting of the LORD, that He may be glorified. Isaiah 61:1-3*

of our heavenly father and to bring Jesus's healing, strengthening love to others.

Father, give us Jesus's humility. We're not worthy, but Jesus is! You are. Give us more of your Holy Spirit. Anoint us with your oil. Help us follow Jesus.

As we step out in faith, the Holy Spirit will open our eyes to see Jesus, the Lamb of God foreshadowed by the tabernacle sacrifices. He will tune our ears to hear Jesus's voice and give us all the grace we need to follow in the courage of Jesus's pure and holy love. God needs all of us to give his hope of ever-lasting life, speak his encouraging words and release his acts of mercy to a broken, sick and troubled world.

We ask again, Father, please give us Jesus's humility. Please, Holy Spirit, anoint us with your oil. We would follow Jesus.

> *As for you, the anointing you received from him remains in you, and you do not need anyone to teach you. But just as His true and genuine anointing teaches you about all things, so remain in him as you have been taught. 1 John 2:27*

Often, when I consider God's oil, I recall a Sunday morning in the spring of 1951 at a Swedish Covenant Church on Foster Avenue in Chicago. A young, slender dark-haired student from North Park College visited that day and taught the congregation to sing a short chorus that he and a friend had just written.[99] I'm still singing it; it has become my prayer.

---

99 *Faber and Faber Piano Adventures* attributes the text of "Give Me Oil in My Lamp" to A. Sevison. I don't know if I learned the song from Sevison or from the friend who wrote the music. In the last seventy years, musicians have added verses and changed words. The records of attribution seem to be lost and the song is considered traditional. I've no reason to doubt my memory or the young man's story. The author's original second verse as he taught the congregation that Sunday was: "Make me a fisher of men, keep me fishing; Make me a fisher of men, I pray; Make me a fisher of men, keep me fishing; Keep me fishing till the judgment day."
Lord, make us fishers of men.

Give me oil in my lamp, keep it burning,
Give me oil in my lamp, I pray,
Give me oil in my lamp, keep it burning,
Keep it burning till the judgment day.
Sing Hosana, Sing Hosana, Sing Hosana to the King of Kings
Sing Hosana, Sing Hosana, Sing Hosana to the King.

Give us oil in our lamps! May our spirits and the lampstands of our churches be aglow like the gold of heaven's lampstands. May your pure oil burn steady, bright and clear in us. Please remember and fulfill Jesus's words to his followers when he said,

You are the light of the world. Matthew 5:14

Help us now, in this day and age, to be the light of the world.

THE GOLD

Consider the properties of gold. It is valuable and beautiful. According to the World Gold Council,[100] it is reliable and versatile. *The Encyclopedia Britannica*[101] says it's "durable to the point of virtual indestructibility." Comparing a common knowledge list of gold's properties with Jesus, we find that:

- Gold conducts electricity. So does Jesus. Believers who have been touched by his energy power compare it to being hit by lightning.

- Gold resists corrosion. It won't weather away or dissolve—that means it's stable, like God's love, character and purpose, like God's very being, who does not change, and like God's word which endures forever.

---

100 https://www.gold.org
101 https://www.britannica.com/science/gold-chemical-element

- Gold is a catalytic substance. That means it speeds up chemical reactions. When God comes on the scene, things change fast—people repent, get delivered, healed and empowered.

- Gold is biocompatible. It gets along with living organisms of all kinds—for that reason, gold fillings can be used in teeth and gold can be used in other implants without causing inflammation or other negative reactions. Gold gets along with us.

- Gold is extremely malleable and ductile. Skilled artisans can pull it into threads so thin that a single ounce can be stretched out for fifty miles. What an image for Jesus's malleability and strength. When I picture him as gold, hammered and stretched out, I think of human balkiness and inflexibility. Why, Lord? Why? What would you have us do? Where do we resist you?

- In its purest state, gold is transparent, like glass and the floor before the throne of God.

- Finally, gold is beautiful. More beautiful than any other metal. Those who have glimpsed Jesus' perfection and felt his love know that he is more desirable, more lovely, than any other affection or longing. As the bride describes the bridegroom in the Song of Songs,

> *This is my beloved, and this is my friend,*
> *he is altogether lovely. Song of Solomon 5:16*

The Lord invites us to surrender to his shaping and to follow his golden threads wherever he leads us. At sixteen ounces to a pound, the twenty-five pounds of gold in the lampstand would stretch 1,000 miles. For me, gold is a stirring visual of missionaries like Hudson Taylor, Johnathon Goforth, Adoniram Judson, Amy Carmichael, Eric Liddell, Nate Saint and Jim Elliott who left their home lands to carry God's love into China,

Korea, Thailand, India and the South American jungles. The oil of the Holy Spirit burned in their souls as they travelled thousands of miles, stretching out the golden threads of God's light around our globe. Ah, how far even one small spark of his golden light can travel.

THE LAMPSTAND ITSELF

The seven branches on the lampstand represent Christ's perfection. For readers interested in the spiritual meaning of Bible numbers, the six lower branches would depict mankind, the central branch, which was higher than the others, depicts Jesus. Six, the number of mankind, added into Christ, equals seven, which is the number of perfection.[102]

The branches also illustrate Jesus's church. According to Wikipedia,[103] Jesus has about 2.5 billion followers on earth today. His church is made up of many members, speaking many languages and living in many different cultures and countries. Every single person and group has a unique combination of God-given callings, ministries and gifts, yet all are one in Jesus. The light of the Holy Spirit burns in us all to empower us to good works and reveal God's words of life to a fearful loved starved world.

> *The body is a unit, though it is composed of many parts. And although its parts are many, they all form one body. So it is with Christ. For in one Spirit we were all baptized into one body, whether Jews or Greeks, slave or free, and we were all given one Spirit to drink. 1 Corinthians 12: 12-13*

Each branch on the lampstand held the bud, blossom and fruit of the almond tree. The almond is known as the "awakening tree" and symbolizes the resurrection of Jesus. The branches, symbolizing the

---

102 Conner, p.54

103 https://en.wikipedia.org/wiki/Christianity

church, correspond to life's seasons. The knops or buds at the bottom are furthest from the oil, suggesting youth and beginnings. The blossoms opening up to him in summer's growth are in the center. And the bowl of fruit, suggesting maturity in Christ, is at the top, closest to the flame where the light is brightest and the flames burn hotly. Those who live closest to God's flame of love willingly burn for him. They know that

Our God is a consuming fire. Hebrews 12:29

THE LIGHT AND THE WICKS

The flames of love in Christ Jesus are God's light to the world. Jesus is God's living word. As he lives in us by the power of the Holy Spirit, we spread his light and life. Whenever God's words ring with loving truth in our ears or rise up off the pages of the Bible to settle into our hearts and minds, God's word comes alive in us. As God talks with us through his word, the Holy Spirit shines his light upon us and lights our way.

Your word is a lamp to my feet and a light to my path.
Psalm 119:105

As we receive God's word and begin to live it out, the Holy Spirit burns within in us. We begin to see people and circumstances under his light. He replaces our opinions with his discernment and compassion. When his flames of love burn brightly in us, he can send light to others through us. Alive *in us*, he can honestly, accurately and effectively speak his truth to others *through us*.

For with You is the fountain of life; in Your light we see light.
Psalm 36:9

I'm seeking more of that light right now. I'm in a situation where several people have varied viewpoints about how to resolve a complicated question. Thinking on it, I pray, "Oh Lord! Give me your light. Give us all your light. And truth. We need your light to guide our lives, to understand our personal situations. We need your light to discern all the conflicting and contradictory reports in our daily news. Help us live in your word."

We can never see ourselves, others, or God accurately in natural light. And vastly more important, only in his own light can we see his glory and Jesus's beauty and worth.

> *But the natural man does not receive the things of the Spirit of God, for they are foolishness to him; nor can he know them, because they are spiritually discerned. 1 Corinthians 2:14 NKJV*

Do you ever slip back and forth between your own natural thinking and spiritual discernment? I do. While copyediting one manuscript revision I became hyper-analytical and critical about the next paragraph. I disconnected and drew a blank at the sentence, "The seven branches also suggest the seven blazing lamps of the seven spirits of God in the throne room of heaven." I'd written it, but "duh?" I didn't get it. It felt out of place. I wanted to cross it off. Then I slowed down and said, "Holy Spirit, I need your help. Should I delete it?" Next, in a small measure of faith, I read the scripture it was based on over again, several times.

> *From the throne came flashes of lightning and [rumbling] sound and peals of thunder. Seven lamps of fire were burning in front of the throne, which are the seven Spirits of God.*
> *Revelation 4:5 AMP.*

An indescribable, undefinable sense of God's presence, began to surround me. I wondered if the Lord was giving me a foretaste of the atmosphere that fills God's throne room in Heaven. My spirit trembled in awe at the seven blazing lamps of the seven spirits of God in his throne room.

I saw another glimpse of Heaven in the prophetic meaning and significance of the tabernacle's lamps.

The steady flames of light from the lampstand reveal layers upon layers of harmonious interconnected spiritual truth about God, the Holy Spirit, Jesus, his church and heaven. I touched on it in writing about oil and the Holy Spirit. The lampstand lights the entire inner court. We couldn't see the table of showbread to eat the bread of God's word without the Holy Spirit's illuminating flame. We can't fellowship with others around God's table without the Holy Spirit's light to unite us in Christ. We don't know how to light the incense of Holy Spirit prayer before the golden altar without his fire.

Each day, as the priests dressed the lamps, they brought new illumination to worship. Each day, we are to seek fresh oil and ask for the light of God's Holy Spirit before eating the bread of his word, joining with others in his fellowship and praying as he would teach us to pray.

> *The Spirit helps us in our weakness. For we do not know how we ought to pray, but the Spirit himself intercedes for us with groans too deep for words. And He who searches our hearts knows the mind of the Spirit, because the Spirit intercedes for the saints according to the will of God. Romans 8:26-27*

As the clean-burning oil of the lampstand illuminates the holy place, it sheds light on the veil to the holy of holies, the place of God's manifest presence. God's light is like a magnet. It draws those who are open to his love into a closer connection with him. It repels all who are not humbly willing to embrace sanctification and holiness.

Everyone who does evil hates the Light, and does not come into the Light for fear that his deeds will be exposed.
John 3:20

God veils the fullness of his glory to protect both believers and unbelievers from judgment.

If we want more of the light of God's presence, it's up to us to keep up our end of our relationship with him and feed the flames of his love. That's one point of Jesus's parable of the virgins who ran out of oil while waiting for the bridegroom.

At that time the kingdom of heaven will be like ten virgins who took their lamps and went out to meet the bridegroom. Five of them were foolish, and five were wise. The foolish ones took their lamps but did not take along any extra oil. But the wise ones took oil in flasks along with their lamps. When the bridegroom was delayed, they all became drowsy and fell asleep.

At midnight the cry rang out: 'Here is the bridegroom! Come out to meet him!' Then all the virgins woke up and trimmed their lamps. The foolish ones said to the wise, 'Give us some of your oil; our lamps are going out.'

'No,' said the wise ones, or there may not be enough for both us and you. Instead, go to those who sell oil and buy some for yourselves.' But while they were on their way to buy it, the bridegroom arrived. Those who were ready went in with him to the wedding banquet, and the door was shut. Later, the other virgins arrived and said, 'Lord, lord, open the door for us!' But he replied, 'Truly I tell you, I do not know you.' Therefore keep watch, because you do not know the day or the hour.
Matthew 25:1-13

Not only do we need extra oil, we also need to tend our wicks. We are God's wicks. A friend who kindly reviewed an early draft of this book summed up the wick's importance for me. He wrote,

> *I really like the imagery of us as the wick in the oil lamps. That makes us the conduit of his life and energy, bringing light to whatever dark place we inhabit. Not only are we fully dependent on the oil of the Spirit, but we are also dependent on the flame of the Spirit. Only the Spirit can light our wick into flame. And if it were to go out, we are once again dependent on the Spirit to relight our flame. Why he insists on using wicks (and not just lighting his own oil) is a testimony to his love for us. He wants so much to include us in lighting his world that he reserved a critical role for us to play—that of the wick. A lot could be said about wicks. Not all wicks are "created equal." Some wicks are better at drawing up the oil. Impurities in the fabric or the wrong kind of material will hinder the flow of oil. Too thin a wick won't hold the flame. If a wick is too long, it has to burn down to the right level above the oil to stop burning wick material and start burning oil (from Holy Spirit).*[104]

May the Lord help us all to keep short accounts and take care of our wicks. Many of us have repeatedly promised to do just that when we've sung,

> *This little light of mine, I'm going to let it shine*
> *This little light of mine, I'm going to let it shine.*
> *Let it shine, let it shine, let it shine.*

---

[104] From an email from Peter Payne, September 8, 2021. Thank you, Peter.

God wants the oil of his Holy Spirit to flow through us. Like the many choruses of the song, Jesus wants our little lights to

> *Shine all over the neighborhood and*
> *Shine all over the whole wide world*

He wants our lights to "shine till Jesus comes." One of the verses promises,

> *We won't let Satan blow them out,*
> *We're going to let them shine.*
> *Let them shine. Let them shine. Let them shine.*

That's a corporate promise. The only way we can shine as God's lights in the world and radiate the light of Jesus Christ is by the power of the Holy Spirit. If our wicks won't draw or we run out of oil, our lights will go out. We won't be welcomed into the feast with Jesus around his banqueting table. Without bonding to Jesus's life in us by the [oil of] the power of the Holy Spirit, we have nothing to offer God but wood, hay and stubble. We may know about Jesus, but

> *No one can lay a foundation other than the one already laid, which is Jesus Christ. If anyone builds on this foundation using gold, silver, precious stones, wood, hay, or straw, his workmanship will be evident. . . . It will be revealed with fire, and the fire will prove the quality of each man's work.*
> 1 Corinthians 3:11-13

If the Holy Spirit isn't illuminating something, if we don't have peace about his direction in our efforts to follow him, then we might as well back off. Without his oil, even if our contributions may look and smell okay to us, they're like smoking rubbish to God.

THE TABERNACLE

When our own concerns overwhelm us, when God seems far away, the heavens feel closed, and scriptures become dry and dead, it may be time to seek the Holy Spirit and ask him to revive our relationship with the living God.[105] Only he knows how to pour out his oil and stir up the fires within us. In our dry times, Paul's advice to Timothy might help,

I remind you to fan into flame the gift of God, which is in you through the laying on of my hands. 2 Timothy 1:6

Oil needs replenishing. As our wicks burn down, oil is burned too. One filling isn't enough. We need the Holy Spirit moment by moment. Keeping filled is as simple as turning our hearts and minds to Jesus and resting in him. Following the Holy Spirit, he will trim our wicks and turn up our lights.[106] He will often refill our lamps by praise and worship, by meditations on God's word and by simple acts of obedience. Sometimes, obedience is as simple as getting a good night's rest. Sometimes it's surprising—and not at all like our "religious" expectations. Not long ago, I wanted to watch a movie. Questioning myself, I said, "Lord? Is this you?" Clear as could be, I knew the Holy Spirit wanted me to watch a particular film. I enjoyed almost two hours of drama. When done, I asked, "Lord, what did you want me to see?" Immediately one small scene of a father and son came to mind. The father couldn't accept his son as he was. He took responsibility for circumstances beyond his control and blamed himself as a failure because God had a different life-plan for his son than the life that father had envisioned and thought best for his boy.

---

[105] Be watchful in this. Seek balance; don't fall into guilt, anxiety or self-absorption with your spiritual state. Unless the Holy Spirit brings conviction or direction, we can trust God and keep on keeping on. At times God seems to withdraw because he wants us to seek him; at times he may be teaching us to live by faith.

[106] Trimming our wicks is a metaphor somewhat like pruning. Jesus said of His Father that, *"He cuts off every branch in Me that bears no fruit, and every branch that does bear fruit, He prunes to make it even more fruitful."* John 15:12

I thought I'd learned that lesson of letting go with my own children. I'd long ago repented of trying to pray my plans and expectations for them into being, but my wick needed a trim again. It was smoking again about others. I'd let discernment turn into judgments. The Holy Spirit couldn't use me to love and pray cleanly for some other dear ones in difficulty. I had to repent and pray, "Father, forgive me for thinking I know what is best for others. Forgive my opinions and judgments. Without your revelation, I'm blind."

Oh, how I laughed to realize that our Father God's desires for them are higher than mine. Once free of self's smoke, the Holy Spirit's oil began to flow and I could pray for his freedom and plans for them with real conviction and sureness."

Above all, the Holy Spirit teaches us to welcome and rest in the presence of God as we do his will. Our job is to seek God's will and follow the Holy Spirit as obediently as the Israelites followed the cloud in the wilderness, trusting always that when we are in his will, he will go before us and make a way.

> *And the LORD went before them in a pillar of cloud to guide their way by day, and in a pillar of fire to give them light by night, so that they could travel by day or night. Exodus 13:21*

This means far more than just knowing God's word; it means living it; it means following Jesus and doing his will. If I keep beating the similar rhythms on the same drum, it's because I'm preaching to myself as well as to any readers. Following Jesus, keeping in tune with the Holy Spirit, means dancing together, each one of us lightly and easily moving to the rhythm and music of "What now Lord? What now?" He doesn't want one or two super saints to do his work. He calls all of us to keep our lamps lit with the Holy Spirit's oil and burn for him. There are seven lamps, burning all at once, not one great big flame. One big flame could be dangerous. Think of the electric lights in your house; the electricity, power, and energy flow best through lots of little wires bound together. That's a great illustration for why the writer of the book of Hebrews said,

> *Let us not neglect meeting together, as some have made a habit, but let us encourage one another, and all the more as you see the Day approaching. Hebrews 10:25*

INNER-COURT MEMORIES

At salvation (foreshadowed by the brazen altar) God's love came to me. Years later, when I first entered his inner courts, God stirred and awakened his love in my heart with a driving desire to get closer to him, to know him. I made many small conscious decisions to seek more of his presence. I wanted more of the Holy Spirit's light (the lampstand) in my life. I wanted fellowship with other believers and more Bible-time and prayer. I don't remember when I first stepped through the veil into to enter God's inner court, but I vividly recall an inner-court season of seeking God intensely. In response, he drew near. Briefly, all of life was illuminated by his light.

To the outer man, it might have looked like I paid a heavy price. I didn't. Jesus had already paid the price and choices that might have looked like sacrifices to others filled my life with joy and meaning. A lifestyle my family considered fanatically imbalanced was actually easy. I read no newspapers, watched no television, and most days prayed an hour in the morning, an hour at noon and another hour in the evening. I read nothing but the Bible during a forty-minute train ride to and from work and read the Bible and prayed again before bed each night. During part of that season, I took Bible correspondence courses. For a time, I worked, taught and studied at a Bible college. I also worked for the local Department of Special Education. God was always near; almost all I did was motivated by love for Jesus. A majority of the poems in *Giving* [107] were written during those foundational years of seeking God.

I clearly remember leaving this season. I mentioned it earlier. Encouraged by others, I left a healthy church, joined an unhealthy one, and walked away from Jesus to follow a deceptive dream. Before long I was trapped in an unhealthy, spiritually abusive, controlling, contentious situation. Jesus didn't leave me, but my disciplines of prayer and Bible reading faltered and fell away. I began to center more and more of my thinking and decisions around people, not around God. Outside of the protection and illumination of the tabernacle's pattern of worship,[108] my mind strayed. Old wounds and weaknesses surfaced. I willfully nursed my own feelings and sought the unattainable—approval from people who could not give it to me. Double minded, I wanted both God *and* what I wanted. I couldn't have both. I flopped like a fish out of water. Brothers and sisters in Christ misunderstood my inconsistency. God was silent and let me flounder for several years. Despite continued prayer, I felt ensnared. One night, in great mercy, it was almost as if God switched on a light and turned off the program I'd been listening to. He changed the channel and tuned me into his station. Maybe he said, "That's enough!" The moment I agreed that, "That's enough!" I changed directions; then circumstances began to change too. My deception became evident. God began to search my heart and Romans 8 became real and true.

---

107 *Giving* by Ginny Emery, ©2018. These poems, mostly written forty years ago, won the 2019 Illumination Award for the best book of Christian poetry published in 2018. Many are as alive as when written. A few continue to minister to my heart and voice my longings almost as if someone else wrote them. They're not widely distributed, but copies are available at amazon.com and on my website, givenwordnow.com.

108 That includes a willingness to repent at the laver, regular feeding on the bread of God's word, worship and fellowship in Holy Spirit's light.

> *The Spirit helps us in our weakness. For we do not know how we ought to pray, but the Spirit himself intercedes for us with groans too deep for words. And He who searches our hearts knows the mind of the Spirit, because the Spirit intercedes for the saints according to the will of God. And we know that God works all things together for the good of those who love him, who are called according to His purpose.*
> Romans 8: 26-28

As soon as God opened my eyes and put his light on reality, I received his grace and direction. Once again, I began to want God's will before my own. God quickly led me out of the darkness of an unhealthy social situation. But he expelled the darkness of my own soul and family generational patterns by increasing his light slowly, like turning a dimmer switch from low to bright. As the light increased, he also lifted the veil from my eyes to see how fully this dark world is also shot through with his glory—the light of his kingdom is near us always, his songs surround us, if we have eyes to see and ears to hear.

Looking back, I can see that God had been in control all the time. My lapse was rooted in buried and unacknowledged childhood wounds. The Holy Spirit did not lead me back to the inner courts of God's light right away. Instead, he sent me to professional counselors and support groups. The Holy Spirit led me through a time of inner healing and deliverance. On occasion, it actually seemed to get darker. I began to learn about trusting God in the dark.

God's plan for me was uniquely individual and personal, just like his plan for you. But our journeys toward Jesus will most often follow the route foreshadowed by the tabernacle. Everything about it was designed to point toward him. The Holy Spirit loves to make him known.

THE INNER COURT:
THE TABLE OF SHEWBREAD

As we pass through the veil into the inner court, all is quiet, clean, peaceful, beautiful and designed to represent the visible glory of God. The activities around the brazen altar's messy, smoking blood sacrifice and the laver's cleansing water are behind us in the outer court. Standing inside the veil, looking around the small closed room, close to the door on our right, to the north, is a small table. Although it was initially cut, carved and sanded from acacia wood, God did not instruct the workmen to wax or polish the wood to bring out the natural grain. Instead, he directed Moses to completely cover it with gold. Similarly, the glory of God, like gold, shone over Jesus's humanity. Before he died Jesus said,

> *I have given them [my disciples] the glory You gave Me, so that they may be one as We are one. John 17:22*

That same glory continues to rest on the followers of Jesus today.

The table's only purpose was to hold the bread of God's presence. The bread is what's important. The table was simply called *the table*. Today, we call it the *table of showbread* because of Tyndale's 16th century translation of Exodus 25:30.[109] He translated the Hebrew phrase *lechem haPanim*,[110] literally *bread of the faces*, as *shewbread*. Most current translations call the bread the *Bread of the Presence* because it rested before the presence of God.

> *And place the Bread of the Presence on the table before Me at all times. Exodus 25:30* [111]

Once each week, on Shabbat, the priests reverently set out twelve freshly baked cakes of unleavened bread made of fine flour as an offering to God. This offering of bread was carefully placed in two rows of six each to represent the twelve tribes of Israel. It rested on the table for a full week until it was replaced with fresh bread.

> *Take fine flour and bake twelve loaves, using two-tenths of an ephah for each loaf, and set them in two rows—six per row—on the table of pure gold before the LORD. And you are to place pure frankincense near each row, so that it may serve as a memorial portion for the bread, an offering made by fire to the LORD.*
>
> *Every Sabbath day the bread is to be set out before the LORD on behalf of the Israelites as a permanent covenant. It belongs to Aaron and his sons, who are to eat it in a holy place; for it is to him a most holy part of the offerings made by fire to the LORD—his portion forever." Leviticus 24: 5-9*

---

109 I don't recall where I read that and haven't been able to find the source again.

110 https://en.wikipedia.org/wiki/showbread

111 God's manifest presence literally dwelt between the cherubim in the Holy of Holies and the bread rested under the light of the lampstand signifying the Holy Spirit in the Holy Place. God blesses us with varying intensities of his presence.

God chose bread to symbolically represent his permanent covenant with Israel. That may look like an insignificant detail to 21st century Christians, but it's not. It's vital. God has never forgotten his covenant with Abraham or the twelve tribes of Israel. God might not fully reveal the covenant's importance until the end of this age, but a quick detour through scriptures and history confirms the ongoing place of all twelve tribes in God's historical plan.

After Moses had finished writing down all the rules and ordinances from God that established God's covenant with Israel, Moses made sure that every one of the twelve tribes understood the significance of entering into a covenant with God. This covenant was not between Moses and God or between one or two tribes and God, but between God and all the children of Israel. Moses

> *. . . built an altar at the base of the mountain, along with twelve pillars for the twelve tribes of Israel. Then he sent out some young men of Israel, and they offered burnt offerings and sacrificed young bulls as peace offerings to the LORD. Exodus 24:4 -5*

God further emphasized the significance of all twelve tribes by directing that

> *. . . twelve stones [that] are to correspond to the names of the sons of Israel, each engraved like a seal with the name of one of the twelve tribes. Exodus 28:21*

These stones were worked into the front of the high priest's ephod. Aaron, the high priest carried the names of the each tribe above his heart and lungs, perhaps as a sign of continual intercession. Following God's directions, Aaron also carried the names of the twelve tribes upon his shoulders. God told Moses to

> *Take two onyx stones and engrave on them the names of the sons of Israel: six of their names on one stone and the remaining six on the other, in the order of their birth. Engrave the names of the sons of Israel on the two stones the way a gem cutter engraves a seal. Then mount the stones in gold filigree settings. Fasten both stones on the shoulder pieces of the ephod as memorial stones for the sons of Israel. Aaron is to bear their names on his two shoulders as a memorial before the LORD. Exodus 28: 9-12.*

Family bloodlines and kinship ties mattered to the Lord. After entering Canaan the land was divided by lots among the twelve tribes. Their family identities and geographic boundaries remained somewhat stable until about 900 BC. After King Solomon's death, they began to erode. When the northern tribes rebelled against the harsh rulership of Solomon's sons, the nation split into the Northern and Southern Kingdoms. In about 700 BC, as judgment for continuous idolatry, the ten northern tribes, known collectively as Ephraim, and now often romantically referred to as "The Lost Tribes of Israel", were captured by the Assyrians. These ten tribes were exiled and dispersed throughout Assyria. Also, about the same time, around 700 BC, Isaiah was warning Judah and Benjamin that God was going to judge their sins too. He prophesied Jerusalem's capture, the fall of the Judah, the nation's seventy-year exile to Babylon, and their eventual restoration to Jerusalem. Not only did Isaiah predict Israel's return from Babylon after seventy years, he also described the return of Jewish people to Israel that began after World War 2.

> *Do not be afraid, for I am with you;*
> *I will bring your offspring from the east and gather you*
>   *from the west.*

> *I will say to the north, 'Give them up!' and to the south,*
> * 'Do not hold them back!'*
> *Bring My sons from afar, and My daughters from*
> * the ends of the earth—*
> *everyone called by My name and created for My glory,*
> * whom I have indeed formed and made."*
>
> ———
>
> *"You are My witnesses," declares the LORD,*
> * "and My servant whom I have chosen, so that you may*
> * consider and believe Me and understand that I am He.*
> *Before Me no god was formed, and after Me none will come.*
> *I, yes I, am the LORD, and there is no Savior but Me.*
> *I alone decreed and saved and proclaimed—I,*
> * and not some foreign god among you.*
> *So you are My witnesses," declares the LORD, "that I*
> * am God.*
> *Isaiah 43:5-7, 10-12*

Israel was God's witness. That has not changed. The existence of Israel continues to witness to the Lord.

About two centuries after Isaiah, around 586 BC, at the very time that Isaiah's prophecies about Judah's exile were being fulfilled and the Southern Kingdom of Judah was living in Babylon, the exiled prophet Ezekiel saw a promising prophetic vision from God. In his vision, all twelve tribes were reunited and God, who keeps covenant with Israel, was once again dividing the land among them.

> *This is what the Lord GOD says, ". . . you are to divide the land as an inheritance among the twelve tribes of Israel. . . . You*

are to divide it equally among them. Because I swore with an uplifted hand to give it to your forefathers, this land will fall to you as an inheritance." Ezekiel 47: 13-14

Fast forward about another 500 hundred years, Jesus's words and the New Testament scriptures about the twelve tribes once confirm their continued existence in history and a coming fulfillment for all of Israel. Note the word *renewal* [112] in this conversation between Peter and Jesus. Peter says,

> *"We have left everything to follow You. What then will there be for us?" Matthew 19: 27-28*

Jesus answers Peter,

> *"Truly I tell you, in the renewal of all things, when the Son of Man sits on His glorious throne, you who have followed Me will also sit on twelve thrones, judging the twelve tribes of Israel." Matthew 19: 27-28*

Paul also confirmed the vision of all twelve tribes alive and restored when he told King Agrippa,

> *I stand on trial because of my hope in the promise that God made to our fathers, the promise our twelve tribes are hoping to realize as they earnestly serve God day and night. It is because of this hope, O king, that I am accused by the Jews. Why would any of you consider it incredible that God raises the dead? Acts 26:6-8*

Finally, God confirms the significance of Jacob's sons in the Book of Revelation when an angel lets John preview the holy city of Jerusalem. The twelve tribes of Israel, that once symbolically rested before God's

---

[112] If the twelve tribes will be judged, their continued existence is sure. Whether it will be in the natural (as we know it) or in a changed renewed existence, I don't know.

presence in the twelve cakes of unleavened bread on a little golden table in a tent in the Sinai, are now joined with Jesus's apostles as an essential and integral part of the city of God.

> *And he carried me away in the Spirit to a mountain great and high, and showed me the holy city of Jerusalem coming down out of heaven from God, shining with the glory of God. Its radiance was like a most precious jewel, like a jasper, as clear as crystal. The city had a great and high wall with twelve gates inscribed with the names of the twelve tribes of Israel, and twelve angels at the gates. There were three gates on the east, three on the north, three on the south, and three on the west. The wall of the city had twelve foundations bearing the names of the twelve apostles of the Lamb. Revelation 21:10-14*

God is purposeful. Despite his mystery and hiddenness, he doesn't make mistakes or confuse us with meaningless random trivia. Since the table's original purpose was to hold twelve cakes of bread representing the twelve tribes of Israel, Israel's sons surely continue to rest before God in a mysterious, yet-to-be-fulfilled way today. Although I can't unwrap all the symbolism, I can't dismiss God's promises to Abraham. His grandson Jacob's sons, the twelve tribes of Israel, are foundational to the city of God and foundational to our Christian faith.

Scriptures also establish that the table and the bread of God's presence illustrate and prefigure Jesus and his church. Jesus lived his life before God's presence and referred to himself as the bread of life. His word becomes the bread of life for all who believe in him. As Jesus lives in us, and we lay down our lives in his service for others, we metaphorically become bread for them.

Once a week, after the holy bread was removed from the table and fresh cakes placed before God's presence, God allowed his priests to eat these aged cakes of fine flour, provided they ate them in a holy place, within the courts of the Lord. Can you picture them? I don't imagine them snacking a quick bite on the run. After a busy week in the outer court caring for the fire on the altar, sacrificing animals and meeting people's needs, I like to imagine the priests slowing down for a Sabbath rest and enjoying fellowship, nourishment and refreshing while eating holy food together around the table in the inner court. It's just as likely that the bread was hard and they carried it to the outer court. If it was cracker-like and crunchy, they'd be careful not to drop crumbs on the inner court floor. They might have dipped it in broth or softened it with wine. God's only stipulation was to eat it in a holy place. They could not put a crumb or two up their sleeves to take home to their own tents.

Whether hard or soft, tasty or bland, every bite the priests ate together foreshadowed our gathering together in fellowship around Jesus, to partake of him, to eat of his body and receive his life. If we could time-travel backwards and join Aaron's sons in lifting a morsel of holy bread to our own mouths, we might recall familiar words of scripture.

> *The Lord Jesus, [who] on the night He was betrayed, took bread, and when He had given thanks, He broke it and said, "This is My body, which is for you; do this in remembrance of Me."*
> *1 Corinthians 11: 23*

When we eat our communion bread in remembrance of Jesus, we can rest in him and the finished work of the cross. With each morsel, the Holy Spirit quickens his life in us. By comparison, every time the tabernacle priests ate the bread of God's presence, their less complete experience pointed toward our fulfillment.

In contrasting the shadow of the Old Testament types with the reality of their New Testament fulfillment, it struck me that the priests who gathered around the table were sons of Levi, a natural, biologically interrelated family. As they served together under the light of the Holy Spirit, they were joined together by kinship ties, by the neighborly community-life of traveling together as a group and by pitching their tents together. They also knew the practical camaraderie, understanding and co-operation that grows between co-laborers in God's service. Eating the holy bread together, they foreshadowed Jesus's family, the priesthood of all believers. Like them, we fellowship with other believers and serve our Lord under the Holy Spirit's light. Like lasting blood kinship, our lasting Christian family ties are not always based on personal preferences. The Holy Spirit unites us under Father God by our union with Jesus Christ. As the body of Christ, we will join one another in worship, in work and in the breaking of bread.

> *And is not the bread that we break a participation in the body of Christ? Because there is one loaf, we who are many are one body; for we all partake of the one loaf. 1 Corinthians 10:16-17*

The offering of cakes made of grain,[113] ground up, mixed with oil, and baked into bread is another rich symbol of Jesus. The night before he died, the Lord used the image of a kernel of wheat to refer to himself,

> *Truly, truly, I tell you, unless a kernel of wheat falls to the ground and dies, it remains only a seed; but if it dies, it bears much fruit. John 12:24*

---

113 Though not biblically supported and not as obvious as the connection between the showbread and Jesus as the bread of life, the grain, a fruit of the ground cursed for human sin, may allude to Christ's human birth. The metaphor of sowing in 1 Corinthians 15 surely alludes to Jesus' death and resurrection and our life after death.
 So will it be with the resurrection of the dead: What is sown is perishable; it is raised imperishable. It is sown in dishonor; it is raised in glory. It is sown in weakness; it is raised in power. It is sown a natural body; it is raised a spiritual body. If there is a natural body, there is also a spiritual body. So it is written: "The first man Adam became a living being;" the last Adam a life-giving spirit. 1 Corinthians 15:42-44

THE TABERNACLE

In a painfully heart moving metaphorical likeness between the nation of Israel, Jesus, and his persecuted followers, the cakes were pierced and baked, an illustration of being in the furnace of affliction.

These pierced cakes not only represented the twelve tribes of Israel waiting before God, they also point ahead to Jesus's twelve disciples and all who have suffered for their faith. According to tradition, every disciple (except John, who was exiled to the Isle of Patmos for his faith) was like a grain of wheat who died for his faith in Jesus.

> *Most assuredly, I say to you, unless a grain of wheat falls into the ground and dies, it remains alone; but if it dies, it produces much grain. John 12:24 NKJV*

Finally, the equal rows of equal sized pierced cakes remind us that Jesus represents all equally before the Father. And, without intending to suggest replacement[114] theology, the unleavened cakes picture Jesus's church, a grafted-in branch of the spiritual Israel of God.

---

114 Replacement theologians assert that the church will replace Israel. They interpret God's word symbolically or allegorically to support their claim that all of God's unfulfilled blessings and curses, plans and promises to Israel will now exclusively apply to and be fulfilled by the church. Although the church has been blessed to receive many of God's Old Testament promises, we cannot replace Israel. Certainly Israel's rebirth as a nation, as prophesied, should surely alert us to the predictive accuracy of God's word. His promises to Israel hold true. A remnant will be saved by faith in Christ. In the following scripture, Paul warns the Gentile church about any prideful assumption that they might replace Israel in God's plans.

Now if some branches [Israel] have been broken off, and you, a wild olive shoot, have been grafted in among the others to share in the nourishment of the olive root, do not boast over those branches. If you do, remember this: You [the church] do not support the root, [Israel] but the root supports you. You will say then, "Branches were broken off so that I could be grafted in." That is correct: They were broken off because of unbelief, but you stand by faith. . . . For if you were cut from a wild olive tree, and contrary to nature were grafted into one that is cultivated, how much more readily will these, the natural branches, be grafted into their own olive tree! I do not want you to be ignorant of this mystery, brothers, so that you will not be conceited: A hardening in part has come to Israel, until the full number of the Gentiles has come in. And so all Israel will be saved, as it is written: "The Deliverer will come from Zion; He will remove godlessness from Jacob. And this is My covenant with them when I take away their sins." Romans 11:17-26

Jesus continues to represents us before the Father as an unleavened cake of living bread. He is also the grain of wheat that fell into the ground to die and rise again to reproduce his life in others. And, extending the metaphor, he invites his followers to be grain, ground up into fine flour under the circumstances appointed by our heavenly Father. Then, in fires of affliction and love, he bakes us into bread for others. That is us, the church.

The praying church is foreshadowed by the memorial portion of frankincense which God told Moses to set on the table beside the bread.

> *You are also to take fine flour and bake twelve loaves, using two-tenths of an ephah for each loaf, and set them in two rows—six per row—on the table of pure gold before the LORD. And you are to place pure frankincense near each row, so that it may serve as a memorial portion for the bread, an offering made by fire to the LORD. Leviticus 24:5-7*

Frankincense's inclusion in the offering is fascinating. Its fragrant aroma arose from grains or nuggets of pure frankincense placed near each row of cakes. Frankincense is a white gum-sap or resin from the Boswellia tree, a gnarly knotted evergreen that grows in Arabia, North Africa and India. This resin can be distilled as oil or dried and hardened to burn as incense. It was more valuable than gold in the ancient world. Its healing benefits were known and highly appreciated over 4,000 years ago and used in ancient Middle Eastern and Chinese and Ayurvedic medicine. Today, researchers continue to recognize frankincense's anti-inflammatory properties. Studies and clinical evidence suggest that it can stimulate the immune system, balance hormones, help digestion, slow aging, fight tumors, relieve stress, aid sleep, and encourage spiritual sensitivity. Its smoke drives away insects and its aroma is a natural fumigant.[115]

Because of its pleasant perfume and health-supportive physical properties, it makes natural sense for the Lord to tell Moses to place a piece of frankincense on the table next to the bread. Even in the natural, an offering of frankincense could symbolize Jesus. It is extremely valuable, pure and good, healthy, healing and free of evil.

But God's reason for directing an offering of frankincense was not all natural. God chose

> . . . to place pure frankincense near each row, so that it may serve as a memorial portion for the bread, an offering made by fire to the LORD." Leviticus 24:7

The word for *memorial* is *azkarah,* a form of the Hebrew word *zakar.* It means to remember or a reminder, a remembrance. [116] God wants to be remembered. Frankincense would stir up pleasant memories. Recent studies have discovered strong neural pathways between odors, emotions and memory.[117] God wanted his reality and works to remain fresh in Israel's hearts and minds. He wants us to remember Jesus, who directed we break bread and drink the wine of communion in remembrance of him. He wants us to remember all he has done for us individually. In their historical context, the frankincense beside the bread would remind the priests of God's hand in their deliverance from death on the Passover

---

115 https://ijirt.org/master/publishedpaper/IJIRT147179_PAPER.pdf
https://www.goodnewsforcatholics.com/bible/what-is-the-meaning-of-frankincense-in-the-bible.html
https://www.healthline.com/nutrition/frankincense
https://draxe.com/essential-oils/what-is-frankincense

116 Strongs, Number 234

117 https://news.harvard.edu/gazette/story/2020/02/how-scent-emotion-and-memory-are-intertwined-and-exploited/
and https://www.sciencedaily.com/releases/2018/07/180723155726.htm

night when their families baked unleavened cakes before their flight from Egypt.

God remembers too. From his place outside of time, God would see wise men bringing frankincense to his infant son.

> *When they [the wise men from the East] saw the star, they rejoiced with great delight. On coming to the house, they saw the Child with His mother Mary, and they fell down and worshiped Him. Then they opened their treasures and presented Him with gifts of gold and frankincense and myrrh. Luke 1:10-11*

What did those three gifts mean? Answers vary, but it's generally agreed that the gold represents Jesus's royalty, his kingship. Significantly, Gentiles were among the first and last to recognize Jesus's kingship during his earthly life. At our Lord's birth the wise men who came from the East came to worship a king. And at his death, Pilate, a representative of the western Roman world, recognized Jesus's kingship.

> *Pilate . . . summoned Jesus, and asked Him, "Are You the King of the Jews?"*
> *Jesus answered, "My kingdom is not of this world. . . . My kingdom is not of this realm."*
> *"Then You are a king!" Pilate said.*
> *"You say that I am a king," Jesus answered. "For this reason I was born and have come into the world, to testify to the truth. Everyone who belongs to the truth listens to My voice." John 18 33, 36, 37*

Also, significant, the wise men's gift of myrrh, an anointing oil commonly used in embalming, points to Jesus's death.

Nicodemus, who had previously come to Jesus at night, also brought a mixture of myrrh and aloes, about seventy-five pounds. John 19:39

The frankincense, an incense (also used in embalming), points to prayer and to a pure offering to the Lord.

For My name will be great among the nations, from where the sun rises to where it sets. In every place, incense [i.e. frankincense] and pure offerings will be presented in My name, because My name will be great among the nations," says the LORD of Hosts. Malachi 1:11

Frankincense was a required ingredient in the incense which the priests burned every morning and evening at the golden altar. It represents Jesus's priesthood as well as his life of prayer.[118] In many scriptures referring to prayer, frankincense is translated as incense.

Then another angel, who had a golden censer, came and stood at the altar. He was given much incense [frankincense] to offer, along with the prayers of all the saints, on the golden altar before the throne. And the smoke of the incense, together with the prayers of the saints, rose up before God from the hand of the angel. Revelation 8:3-4

Today, centuries later, the thought of frankincense beside the bread in the most holy place adds a mysterious sacredness to the entire table. It reminds me of God's invitation to us. He invites us to live before him just as the cakes of bread rested in his presence. Under the light of the lampstand, surrounded by the walls of his golden life, covered by his

---

[118] https://www.biblicalarchaeology.org/daily/people-cultures-in-the-bible/jesus-historical-jesus/why-did-the-magi-bring-gold-frankincense-and-myrrh/

protection, and soaking in the aromas of incense from the golden altar and frankincense from the table, the bread rested in his presence. That's what God wants for us. As the aroma of frankincense surrounded the unleavened cakes, God wants the preserving aroma of Christ to infuse every part of our own lives. From sunshine to sneezing, God calls us to live fully and practically in communion with Jesus, in the restful joy and peace of his holy love.

God is never discouraged. As the cakes of prophetic bread soaked before God's presence in the symbolic fragrance and light,[119] they pictured our need for his edification and encouragement from the bread of his word. as we read it, meditate on it and receive his nourishing, hopeful truth.

The bread is also a type of Jesus's body, given and broken for Israel and for us. The frankincense offering beside the bread reminds us that Jesus's life is sustained in us by prayerful connection with his living word.

I love the picture of Jesus and of us, his followers, prayerfully soaking in God's presence as living bread. It encourages me to restful trust. But before my imagination stretches too far, I recall that resting in Jesus is a simple gift of faith in him and that seeking to soak in a mystical experience or emotion as an end it itself can be dangerously misleading. Although the Holy Spirit wants us to experience Jesus's love as much as we might hunger for it, the safest way to know our Lord is to fasten our eyes on him and his word and do his will and not to seek a "feel-good" experience. At times, the better part for me and you is to emulate Mary of Bethany, to sit as Jesus's feet, rest in his presence and listen to all he would speak to our spirits in the quietness of our waiting, watching silence before his love.

---

[119] Once again the unanswerable question comes up, "Was the veil thick or thin?" Did emanations of God's glory shine through or not? It is no longer important. God meets us where we are with the degree of his love that we are ready to receive. See also footnote 35.

With that caution, standing beside the table and looking down on the bread and around at the inner court, there is a sense-explosion that's filled with reminders of one spiritual truth about God after another. The fragrance of frankincense and incense fills our nostrils. The veils with artistic cherubim in blue, purple and scarlet thread before the Holy of Holies and above our heads recall the cherubim around God's throne in heaven. The warm glowing light of the lamps' clean flames is reminiscent of the golden light of heaven.

If the Holy Spirit would lift us up in worship and adoration of our Lord, we might even sense the presence of real cherubim around us. They guarded the way to the tree of life (Jesus, our source of eternal life) in the Garden of Eden and now surround the throne of God. The pure golden walls surrounding us suggest the gold of heaven. Shining like mirrors in the flickering lamplight, they reflect glints of red, scarlet and blue from the veils at either end of the small holy enclosure. Surrendering to the impressions from tabernacle symbolism, the crown of gold, a raised edge or molding rimming the table, might even remind us of Jesus, our king.

I've heard (and once believed) that the golden crown was a safeguard to prevent the bread from slipping onto the ground, but that's unlikely. Some English translations of Leviticus 24:6 describe the bread as set out in "two rows—six per row" indicating two parallel rows of six cakes each. But in Hebrew, the language indicates "two stacks—six per stack." The bread would easily rise above the decorative rim or crown.[120] Fortunately, the bread didn't need a guard-rail. God left nothing to chance. Whenever the cloud above the tent lifted to signal that it was time to break camp and move, the priests knew how to pack up securely. God had given Moses careful instructions about how to cover and protect the bread of his presence.

---

[120] https://www.chabad.org/library/article_cdo/aid/2974301/jewish/The-Showbread-The-How-and-Why-of-the-Temple-Bread-Offering.htm

The Inner Court: The Table of Shewbread

Over the table of the Presence they [the priests] are to spread a blue cloth and place the plates and cups on it, along with the bowls and pitchers for the drink offering. The regular bread offering is to remain on it. And they shall spread a scarlet cloth [symbolic of Jesus' blood] over them, cover them with fine leather, and insert the poles. Numbers 4:7-8

The priests carried the well-covered bread as it rested on the table just as God wants us to rest in him and let him cover us and carry us from one place to another through times of fatigue, difficulty, transition and change.

It can be difficult to let God's spirit take us where he wants us to go. It might require change, prayer, intentional dialing down and stilling our souls, shutting our mouths and changing our plans. It's not automatic second nature to think of untimely or unwanted changes and interruptions as opportunities to make room for God's plans or to give and receive his love. It's natural to want to stick to our desires, plans and schedules and insist on going where we want to go under our own steam. Playing with watercolor paints makes me happy. It's absorbing fun. Last year, when the Holy Spirit said, "Put away your paints," I hesitated for a moment. I'm glad I listened. He knew more than I did. Soon, I entered into a busy season and didn't have time to paint. Then, I needed my painting space for my sewing machine. Now, the Holy Spirit is asking me to paint again. The turmoil in our world is so great that some of my abstract work makes no sense visually, but I know that it's preverbal/nonverbal expression and intercession of groans too deep to be uttered and hopes too unlikely and invisible to be voiced without the Holy Spirit's release.

It is supernatural to be available to others as broken bread. It's natural to want friendship; true friends are gifts from the Lord. Jesus loved his friends. He died for them, so they could receive the Holy Spirit and be with him forever. Jesus drew people to himself because he was loving, compassionate, pure and holy. He revealed God to men.

If we spend time with our Father and determine to follow his will, the Holy Spirit might draw people to Jesus in us. That happened to Frank Laubach. After only three months of his great experiment of seeking to live in the will of God and keep up a continual inner conversation with him, Frank Laubach began to draw people toward himself, too. There was something of Jesus about him. He wrote,

> *People are becoming friendly who had suspected or neglected me. I feel, I feel like one who has had his violin out of tune with the orchestra and is at last in harmony with the music of the universe.* [121]

As Laubach's relationship with God deepened, he developed the habit of "holding people, seen and unseen, before God."[122] He loved them like Jesus did, not for himself but for God and for their own holy benefit. Without the Holy Spirit's help, we often fail in that kind of pure and holy love. It's common human temptation to draw people to ourselves and feed them with our own thoughts and feelings. Healthy bondings are wonderful, God-given gifts, but need driven attachments can become controlling life-draining substitutes for God's love. Without God, it's natural to hold others too closely. It's supernatural to love one another as Jesus loves us. Unselfishly. Freely. With no control.

Can we be broken bread for our friends and family? Can the Holy Spirit use Jesus's life in us to feed others and to draw them into a closer communion with God? Only he can meet their needs and satisfy their longings. And, if we trust him and yield, if we get out of his way, he

---

[121] Frank C. Laubach, *Letters by a Modern Mystic*, Purposeful Design, Colorado Springs, © 2007 by Robert Laubach, p. 10

[122] Laubach, p. 76

can! And he will move sovereignly in the lives of those we love. And, oh my, what love we receive in return—from our friends and from Jesus.

Oh, Lord! Help us. May we, like Jesus, be ground up into fine flour, flavored with frankincense and baked in the heat of God's love to nourish others with Jesus, the bread of life.

To sum up, in the wilderness, God gave the children of Israel manna to eat. But he also gave his priests unleavened cakes of fine flour. Both the manna and the cakes of fine flour prefigure Jesus himself as the bread of life. After Jesus fed the five thousand, people followed him. When they wanted to be able to multiply food, Jesus told them to believe on him. Doubting, they asked for a sign, like the manna God sent to their forefathers. Although Jesus gave many miraculous signs that proved his identity as God's son, he did not live by signs, he lived by the word of God. He never ever performed signs and wonders to prove who he was; he went about doing the good he saw his Father doing in heaven because his heart was moved with love and compassion for people. When the Holy Spirit led Jesus into the wilderness,

> The tempter came to him and said, "If You are the Son of God, tell these stones to become bread." But Jesus answered, "It is written: Man shall not live on bread alone, but on every word that comes from the mouth of God." Matthew 4: 3-4

So when the crowds asked for a sign, he once again replied by God's written word.

> Our ancestors ate the manna in the wilderness; as it is written: "He gave them bread from heaven to eat." Jesus said to them, "Very truly I tell you, it is not Moses who has given you the bread from heaven, but it is my Father who gives you the true

bread from heaven. For the bread of God is the bread that comes down from heaven and gives life to the world." "Sir," they said, "always give us this bread." John 6:31-34 NIV

Then, Jesus, who lived, died and rose from the dead in fulfillment of God's word, answered them,

I am the living bread that came down from heaven. Whoever eats this bread will live forever. This bread is my flesh, which I will give for the life of the world. John 6:50-51 NIV

Two thousand years before Jesus voiced the words, "I am the living bread that came down from heaven" God put a prophetic symbol of that truth in twelve cakes of bread on a small golden table in a little tent in the Sinai wilderness. In centering our faith, hope and love on Jesus, let us also remember that those simple cakes of bread first represented the twelve tribes of Israel and were

a most holy part of the offerings made by fire to the LORD—his portion forever. Leviticus 24:9

Jesus's brother, James encourages us to

be patient and strengthen your hearts, because the Lord's coming is near. James 5:9

A day is coming when we shall join with Israel in the cry of "Maranatha!"

Come Lord Jesus! Revelation 22:20

Until then,

"Blessed is he who comes in the name of the Lord."
Matthew 23:39 [123]

Lord, be our bread of life. Help us live by your word.

THE GOLDEN ALTAR OF INCENSE

"You are also to make an altar of acacia wood for the burning of incense. It is to be square, a cubit long, a cubit wide, and two cubits high. Its horns must be of one piece. Overlay with pure gold the top and all the sides and horns, and make a molding of gold around it. And make two gold rings below the molding on opposite sides to hold the poles used to carry it. Make the poles of acacia wood and overlay them with gold.

"Place the altar in front of the veil that is before the ark of the Testimony—before the mercy seat that is over the Testimony—where I will meet with you. And Aaron is to burn fragrant incense on it every morning when he tends the lamps. When Aaron sets up the lamps at twilight, he must burn the incense perpetually before the LORD for the generations to come. On this altar you must not offer unauthorized incense or a burnt offering or grain offering; nor are you to pour a drink offering on it.

"Once a year Aaron shall make atonement on the horns of the altar. Throughout your generations he shall make atonement on it annually with the blood of the sin offering of atonement. The altar is most holy to the LORD." Exodus 30:1-10

---

123 The week of his death, knowing he was entering Jerusalem to be crucified, Jesus said,
  "Jerusalem, Jerusalem, you who kill the prophets and stone those sent to you, how often I have longed to gather your children together, as a hen gathers her chicks under her wings, and you were not willing. Look, your house is left to you desolate. For I tell you, you will not see me again until you say, 'Blessed is he who comes in the name of the Lord.'" Matthew 23:37-39 NIV

More than once while writing and revising this book I've stopped here, before this golden altar of incense that is most holy to the Lord. Can you join me? We're in a small room where all the walls and every piece of furniture glows of purest gold from the lampstand's seven steady flames of fire. The table of showbread and the lampstand are behind us. The veil to the holy of holies is before us directly behind the altar of incense. We're in a quiet, insulated space, filled with the aroma of frankincense and sweet spices, the scent of pure oil and the hush of holiness. Reverence is easy and appropriate. I sense the Holy Spirit. It is easy to look to Jesus and be still.

Do you sense the Lord too? When we get distracted by the world situation and the pressures in our lives, we need to be intentional about remembering him and recognizing his presence. What are your memories of his touch? At once particular season I'd get goose-bumps or a feeling of tingling energy when God drew near. My husband often knew God's touch as a sense of warm honey pouring over his limbs. Recalling moments of supernatural peace, times when my soul became centered in him and he lifted away my concerns, often helps me reestablish a missing sense of connection with him and awaken faith.

One of my most memorable experiences of mental clarity and supernatural peace from God came on a June day in 1971. As soon as I knew that all my children were to live with me, not with their father and stepmother, the Holy Spirit was there to confirm it. I walked down a familiar street in a bubble of palpable peace.

At times, when God draws near, I sense nothing until a wave of gratitude and adoration rises up within my heart. I might whisper, "Thank you, Father," or "I love you, Lord." At other times, it's just as likely that I might laugh, weep, or rest in silent worship and adoration—unable to speak. I've learned that when God is near, our conversations with him change. Our words come carefully; authentically; most likely through our minds, but not from them. They well up in wholeness from our innermost beings, from the same springs of living water that Jesus promised the Samaritan woman.

> *Jesus said to [the Samaritan woman], "Everyone who drinks this water [from Jacob's well] will be thirsty again. But whoever drinks the water I give him will never thirst. Indeed, the water I give him will become in him a fount of water springing up to eternal life." John 4:13-14*

At other times, those living springs of water from the Holy Spirit may bubble up in spontaneous song. At times the Holy Spirit lifts us in praise until it feels like we might even be joining the angels around the throne of God in praising Jesus. We sense in our bones that he is HOLY, HOLY, HOLY and respond to the Spirit's call to "Come, let us adore him."

THE TABERNACLE

There's often a staying power before the golden altar of incense. The Holy Spirit himself imparts grace to help us wait before God until his purposes are met. Whether we rest in silence or are swept up in prayer by his Spirit of grace and supplication, when the holy presence begins to fade and the grace for prayer lifts, and it will—for he does not keep us forever in focused intensity—we will find ourselves renewed, refreshed, certain of God's love, but once again back in the familiarity of more conversational prayer with our Lord and ordinary responsibilities. One way to describe this is to say that "the anointing lifted." Generally, we're left with new peace and certainty of God's loving reality and power. But at times, other thoughts and feelings may begin to intrude to divert us or even to challenge and battle against God's Spirit. At such times it helps to gently turn our thoughts to rest on Jesus. Often his presence ebbs and flows—new waves of his holy love may roll in to encourage us to wait upon him longer. If we wait quietly for his return, he may draw us closer to his heart and give us more tastes of his glory. But then again, with his song in our hearts, maybe it's time to wash the dishes, pay the bills, read a book, replace the lawnmower spark plugs or text a friend.

After such communion with God, it's easy to understand why the golden altar of incense is described as most holy. Some Bible translations capitalize both words, MOST HOLY. It's not by coincidence. Of all the furniture in the tabernacle, only the brazen altar and the altar of incense are named MOST HOLY. Both are life-transforming places. The parallels between them are many.

Both are square and have horns at all four corners. Both are places of daily morning and evening sacrifice. Every animal sacrificed at the brazen altar recalled Israel's history with God and anticipated

Jesus[124] who, on the night of Passover, became our Paschal Lamb, sacrificed to set us free from sin and send us his own Holy Spirit. At the cross, typified by the brazen altar, the Holy Spirit joins our earthly journeys, not as a spirit hovering over us or coming upon us, but as an ever-present indwelling teacher, comforter and guide. He helps us to do God's will by encouraging us and strengthening us in habits of loving-kindness, truth and devotion to God.

The altar of incense is also named the *place of slain offering*. Before the sacrifice of incense, we offer our redeemed souls to God in worshipful prayer. The indwelling Holy Spirit moves us into his own full, rich harmonic agreements with God's eternal plans. He rests upon us in greater measure to give us power to witness to Jesus Christ. As the priests stood before the golden altar to light the incense, they prefigured the the day when the fire that came down from heaven to consume the sacrifice

---

124 I'm keenly aware that this manuscript is incomplete. I've skipped any systematic description of the priest's garments as well as the offerings and the feasts and how they point to Jesus and the church. The major sacrificial offerings that Jesus's death fulfilled included the morning and evening sacrifices, the burnt offering, the peace offering, the sin offering and the guilt offering. The major feasts were:

1) Passover, Jesus is our Passover lamb. Leviticus 23:4-8

2) The feast of unleavened bread, coming seven days after Passover, points to Jesus's sinless life. Leviticus 23:6

3) The feast of first fruits, the third day after Passover points to Jesus as the first fruits from the dead. Leviticus 23:10

4) The feast of weeks, fifty days (seven weeks) after first fruits was the day of Pentecost, when the Holy Spirit came to believers and signifies the beginning of the church. Leviticus 23:16

5) Rosh Hashanah is the feast of trumpets, the beginning of the Jewish new year. It's a time of rest that commentators have linked to rapture and the wedding feast of the bride; it's a two-day feast that I personally associate with a time of grace and growing maturity in the church and a coming into the Sabbath rest of Jesus. Leviticus 23:24

6) Yom Kippur, the day of atonement, is a day repentance to God and restitution for our sins. It was the only day the priest entered the holy of holies and was the day when one scapegoat was slain and another was set free. Commentators link it to Christ's 2nd coming and a day of judgment. Leviticus 16, 23:26-32

7) The feast of Tabernacles or booths is a joyous celebration following the Day of Atonement that is set aside to give thanks to God for his protection and provision. Commentators suggest that it points toward Jesus dwelling or tabernacling among his people again. Leviticus 23:34

on the brazen altar would burn in Jesus and light the incense of continual, intercessory worship and prayer within our own hearts.

> *His divine power has given us everything we need for life and godliness through the knowledge of him who called us by His own glory and excellence. Through these He has given us His precious and magnificent promises [of the Holy Spirit], so that through them you may become partakers of the divine nature, now that you have escaped the corruption in the world caused by evil desires.*[125] *For this very reason, make every effort to add to your faith virtue; and to virtue, knowledge; and to knowledge, self-control; and to self-control, perseverance; and to perseverance, godliness; and to godliness, brotherly kindness; and to brotherly kindness, love. 2 Peter 1: 3-7*

God directed Moses to place the two altars described as Most Holy directly line with each another. Both burned with holy fire. Every morning and evening, near the time of the morning and evening sacrifice, a priest would wash at the laver and carry fire from the brazen altar into the holy place to light the incense on the golden altar. These priests followed the pattern established by God.

Last year, as I wrote about the inner court, it seemed like a good idea to follow a similar pattern for daily worship. Every morning after arising and every evening before bed I'd take time for the Lord. My morning and evening worship usually began something like this. I'd draw aside to the same chair and lamp, shut out distractions as best I could and turn to the Lord saying,

"Here I am, Lord. I offer myself to you as a living sacrifice—I give you all I am, all I have, all I think and all I do. What I'm holding onto

---

[125] Believers escape the corruption of the world caused by evil desires at the cross and in the Word, prefigured by the brazen altar and the laver.

and can't give you, please take or help me let go. What you don't like, please change. Bring me into agreement with you. Thank you, Father, for your Holy Spirit."

In the mornings I'd ask the Lord to please help me to yield to him through the day ahead. I'd pray "Draw me to Jesus. Dear Holy Spirit, please search my heart. Please show me if there's anything you want to change. Show me if there's any wickedness, any rebellion in me." If anything came up, I'd ask the Lord to forgive me. I'd repent and talk very honestly with the Lord about it. At that season, I was being bombarded by intense negative pressures, so I often asked the Lord to cleanse me of anything retaliatory or dark in my dreams. Then I'd ask the Holy Spirit about his plans for the day. In the evening, I'd give myself to the Lord once again, review the day and talk with him about what went wrong, where I'd fallen short of his love. I'd ask him to be with me through the night. Both morning and evening, I'd offer all those closest to me to the Lord and ask him to bless them and keep them. As thoughts came to mind, I'd pray for them specifically.

After that, I'd either open my Bible or a hymnal. Sometimes a specific text or portion of scripture would come to mind. If not, I'd continue on with a yearly read through the Bible. Either before or after reading the Bible, I'd worship the Lord in song. Sometimes I'd silently rest in the Lord, sometimes the Holy Spirit would give me words of praise and worship.

That simple practice of prayer became a very precious time between me and the Lord. On Saturday mornings and days without obligations to others, I lingered in Bible reading, prayer and worship for as long as the Holy Spirit's peace rested upon me. This routine was a pattern, not a rut or a ritual. Some mornings, the Holy Spirit led me to remember Jesus in communion; other mornings I journaled or waited on the Lord in silent watching. On mornings when I needed to be up-and-at-'em, God's presence was usually as real in one verse or phrase from scripture and a short song on-the-run as he was in extended times of waiting, reflection, prayer and worship.

My general pattern of daily worship during that season agreed with the priest's steps in tabernacle worship. I loved it. But God is not legalistic and the Holy Spirit will vary our worship routines to suit our health, personal bio-rhythms, schedules and learning styles. For various reasons, my pattern has changed, but I look forward to returning to a personal daily worship pattern that lines up with God's tabernacle plan. I sensed a harmony with divine order in it.

Not only did my daily worship agree with the pattern of tabernacle worship, so also does my journey from salvation toward maturity. Whether the Holy Spirit takes seconds, minutes, days, or years to move us from salvation and cleansing in the outer court into inner court worship, he wants to grow us up into the fullest union with Jesus possible. In the inner court, under the steady light of the Holy Spirit's lamps, God illuminates his word in our hearts and nurtures us through communion with Jesus in our fellowship with other believers around the bread of his presence. He draws us closer to our Lord's manifest presence in prayer and worship before the altar of incense.

To sum up, these comparisons and contrasts between the two most holy altars, the brazen altar and the altar of incense are significant. The brazen altar stood directly before the door to the outside world; the altar of incense stood directly before the veil protecting us from the intense glory of God's manifest presence in the holy of holies. Although we might want to hold our nose at the smell of charred meat coming from the brazen altar, both altars lifted sweet fragrance to the Lord.

Under the open skies at the brazen altar, the priests burned the sweet-smelling animal sacrifices that temporarily atoned for human sin and signified the death of sinful flesh. Under the tabernacle roof, the priests burned the fragrant incense at the golden altar that foreshadows the service of repentant, cleansed and forgiven believers who are drawing near to the holy of holies.

Stepping under the tabernacle roof into the light of the lampstand, we know that our old sin nature has fallen away. The brazen altar which foreshadowed the cross where Jesus atoned for our sin nature is behind us. There he was our Savior. Now, at the altar of incense, Jesus will be our Lord. Our new life in Christ is growing.

Upon the altar of incense, enclosed beneath the protective coverings of the inner court, the priests burned a sweet-smelling compound of frankincense, stacte, onycha, galbanum and salt. This fragrance pictures the beauty of harmony that is established between heaven and earth when we commune with God and come into agreement with him. At the altar of incense, the Holy Spirit gives us grace and faith to move in the humility, purity and beauty of worshipful prayer. The sweet aroma fills the room as it rises before the veil into the holy of holies, the place of God's mercy seat and his manifest presence.

Each day, as the priests lit the incense, they reenacted the truth that coming to faith in Jesus at the cross is not all that God has for us. What can we, as a royal priesthood and a holy nation learn from these tabernacle priests of old?

> *But you are a chosen people, a royal priesthood, a holy nation, a people for God's own possession, to proclaim the virtues of Him who called you out of darkness into His marvelous light.*
> *1 Peter 2:9*

Let's also review God's pattern for worship from perspective of the priesthood. First, as the priests walked from their personal family tents toward their daily responsibilities in the courts, they would pass before the standard of Judah in praise of the Lord.

THE TABERNACLE

Once in the Lord's courts, each priest would move into his own assigned responsibilities; most likely a lot was going on simultaneously. The rituals of morning and evening sacrifice and daily tabernacle worship took community co-ordination. Although their communal routine metaphorically pictures our individual journeys, the picture of one priest doing everything is most likely inaccurate. It's more realistic to picture some priests involved with the messy work of slaughtering and burning the morning and evening animal sacrifices at the brazen altar and others washing at the laver before carrying clean utensils, incense, fresh oil, new wicks and trimming tools into the inner court. Perhaps one priest would part the curtain and hold it open for another priest, who carefully carried fire from the brazen alter to light the incense. Before the bread of God's presence, the priests might stop and talk with each other before they filled the lamps with fresh oil and lit the incense. Their daily service together prefigures the corporate nature of the church as well as our own journeys into the courts of the Lord.

We begin by acknowledging Jesus with thanksgiving and praise, we offer ourselves to God, we seek the Holy Spirit's light on the bread of his word, we fellowship with one another and work together as Christ's body and we draw near to God by burning the incense of prayer at the golden altar.

When I ramble on, I don't know if I'm talking to you or myself, but as I write, I'm sensing a strength of longing in our Lord that I've never known before. He longs for us—for you and for me—to draw closer to the place of his presence and partake of his love. He longs for us to abide[126] in him and surrender to the Holy Spirit. He wants us to focus on him in our prayers, our worship and our lives. Jesus promised us that

---

126 See Appendix on Abiding

> *If you abide in Me, and My words abide in you, you will ask what you desire and it shall be done for you. John 15:7 NKJV*

God wants to talk with us just as he spoke with Moses, Abraham, David and the prophets. He wants to tell us about his plans and involve us in them. He wants us to find our fulfillment in union with him. He is the ultimate source of unending marvel, power, wisdom and love. We will never know God fully. We will never receive all the love he is able to give us. There will always be more to God than we can know or receive.

> *So let us know—let us press on to know the LORD. As surely as the sun rises, He will appear; He will come to us like the rain, like the spring showers that water the earth. Hosea 6:3*

Holy Spirit, will you please give us the heart of Saint Paul, who surely knew Jesus better than most of us, yet wrote,

> *I want to know Christ and the power of His resurrection . . . Philippians 3:10*

> *I press toward the goal of the prize of God's heavenly calling in Christ Jesus. Philippians 3:14*

In kindly, generous understanding of our weaknesses, God sustains our journeys toward his presence with his grace, wisdom and power. He is with us through challenges, adversities and temptations; he doesn't go away.

> *When you pass through the waters, I will be with you;*
> *And through the rivers, they shall not overflow you.*
> *When you walk through the fire, you shall not be burned.*
> *Isaiah 43:2 NKJV*

THE TABERNACLE

The golden altar of incense illustrates that through Jesus, God has already prepared the way for us to draw near to him and receive his love. He is there when we come to him. We don't need to labor for perfection and try to get good enough first—that's impossible! We can never approach God, let alone get close to him by our own methods.

Although the Holy Spirit will enable us to agree with God's ways and means, we must do our part and choose to agree with him (or at least be willing to be made willing to agree). In keeping our commitment to seek the Lord and obey his command to love him with all our hearts and minds and souls and love our neighbor as ourselves, we learn to keep short accounts with God. We repent quickly when we fail in love, we forgive quickly when others fail to love us, and we learn to open our hearts to gratefully receive God's forgiveness through the cleansing power of Jesus's blood. As we learn to keep our consciences clean and current with the Lord, the Holy Spirit fills us with more of himself.

> *But the fruit of the Spirit is love, joy, peace, patience, kindness, goodness, faithfulness, gentleness, and self-control.*
> *Galatians 5:22-23*

Then, we give the Lord our time. We may need put down the books we're reading and writing to look toward him to say, "I love you, Lord." We may need to ask, "What now, Lord?" This journey from the outer court of salvation to the inner court of living in God's presence is no heavy, religious task. It's a relationship of great love. And the cleaner we are, the closer we can get to God. The Holy Spirit won't fill the dark closets in our life with God's light. Fortunately, his conviction of sin is qualitatively different from our own feelings of guilt. When people and the destroyer bring up our sins, they are accusing and condemning.

We may feel criticized, guilty, helpless and unable to change. But when the Holy Spirit convicts us, he supplies grace to confess; he helps us to change our thinking and choices and quickly accept God's forgiveness. It may take time and focused willingness; some of us may need healing and deliverance; but God does not play games with us or ask us to do the impossible. He knows we can't change our own natures without divine help.[127] The process of changing us from children of Adam to children of God began when we were born again. Since faith comes by hearing, I repeat some truths again and again. It can take up to thirteen repetitions to truly hear an idea that runs counter to ingrained thinking. It's essential to fully realize and accept the truth that very second we came to heart-faith in Jesus, God freed us from our inborn Adamic sin nature, planted the Holy Spirit within our beings and gave us a new life in union with Jesus Christ. He is no ascended master or spirit guide. He is the living God who came to earth fully man and fully God. He is jealous to replace all counterfeits who would imitate him. We were born into this new life in his Holy Spirit as spirtual infants. The Holy Spirit is our helper, our comforter, our guide along our journeys to maturity. He teaches us and empowers us to exchange our flawed and incomplete thoughts, words, attitudes and actions for Jesus's very own.

So, when conviction comes, our part is humble agreement with God. We don't try harder, for our salvation is by grace through faith, not through doing better. We don't flagellate or condemn ourselves. We simply and willingly confess that we're sinners and that once again we've fallen short of God's holy love. We accept God's forgiveness. Every time

---

127 The Holy Spirit's help can be quite down-to-earth and practical. He embraces resources hyper-religious believers might reject as secular. When a man we know of was contemplating suicide, he prayed. That night, the Lord supernaturally delivered him from last stage alcoholism, instantly healed chronic oozing ulcers on his body and baptized him in the Holy Spirit. But after years of addiction this man needed more healing and deliverance. Before long, the Holy Spirit told him, "Go to AA." A couple of years later, he heard, "Be baptized and start going to church." God works through support groups, sponsors, counselors, mentors, teachers, pastors and friends in communities of faith.

we acknowledge our need for the Lord's transforming love in our lives, we weaken, change (or take off) lingering habits from our old nature and strengthen (or put on) our new nature in Christ Jesus. It's no big deal—just a sincere and honest, "Oh Father. I did it again. Forgive me, please. And help me. I can't change myself. Lord. Help me be more sensitive to your Holy Spirit." If God wants us to make restitution or amends, the Holy Spirit will show us. Our part is willingness to agree with God.

Because the altar of incense is a place of faith and relationship, we can always ask for God's help when prideful balkiness hinders our repentance. If our words and choices hurt others, we can pray for them and ask the Lord what to do about it. Hardening our hearts, resisting conviction and persisting in unloving choices that hurt us or others drains life, quenches the Holy Spirit and limits our relationship with God. Disobeying God's law of love will close the door to closeness and intimacy with Jesus and the Father.[128] Prayer and worship at the altar of incense is a place of reverent joy for those who humbly and willingly respond to God's correction and direction because their hearts are set on abiding in Jesus's love.

I'm not sure about this theologically, so this may be dangerous ground, but my relational experience with God suggests that he may only hold his willing children responsible for known sin, for what he shows us. I was reading one of Paul's letters in the New Testament one sunny afternoon in the 1980's, when the Holy Spirit spoke to me through the word. Suddenly, I saw a dark place buried deep within my soul. Repenting, I automatically knew that God had never blamed me or held me accountable for that darkness. It was a family pattern I'd lived with since childhood. Like

---

[128] Interestingly, spiritually abusive churches, cults, and dictatorships use accusation, guilt, confession, manipulation and humiliation (rather than humility) to break men and women and force compliance to dominating leadership and non-biblical ideologies. Brokenness, contrition and correction before God's truth leads to freedom and courage; brokenness, contrition and correction before demigods and lies leads to fear, victimization and servitude under a controlling person or system.

a small child, I didn't know the difference between right and wrong until Jesus opened my eyes. The Holy Spirit helped me understand that from that moment on, repeating that dark pattern would be wrong. Now, forty years later, I can't recall the sin. What remains is my memory of amazement at God's mercy and my gratitude for his complete forgiveness and lasting change. I recall his love, not my sin; I recall the light and freedom filling my soul that afternoon. His kind, fatherly attitude toward my accountability for that stain differed vastly from the critical standards I'd heard in church and the condemnation I often heaped on myself and others for our failures.

Although abiding in Jesus's love opens the way into inner-court communion and answered prayer, it's balancing to remember that abiding is not all about prayer and worship. At times the Holy Spirit draws us to the altar of incense. At other times not. He is intensely personal, concrete and practical. Right now, by a sense of inner peace and vitality, I know he is with me, encouraging me to write. Ours is a steady, quiet, pleasant, positive, smiling companionship. When I am unsure and ask, "Lord?" a scripture may come to mind or an intuitive knowing what to delete, add or change. I would break this peaceful sense of abiding in Jesus if "I" decided that "I" wanted to pray, worship, make a phone call or read a book right now. When I'm done writing, all peace and clarity about what to say next will lift. If the Holy Spirit is silent when I pray about pushing ahead, I know it's time to move on to something else.

So, whether the Holy Spirit's peace and direction for us is in prayer and worship, Bible meditation, reading, house and yard work, telling a joke, answering emails, calling friends or resting, every choice and activity that agrees with him gives life. Every choice and relationship that draws us away from any member of the trinity drains life. In seeking to live a Godly life, we exist on two planes simultaneously. As we follow the

Holy Spirit's peace-establishing lead in our daily tasks, we can sit with Jesus in the heavenlies and enjoy his companionship on earth.

> *But God, who is rich in mercy, because of His great love with which He loved us, even when we were dead in trespasses, made us alive together with Christ (by grace you have been saved), and raised us up together, and made us sit together in the heavenly places in Christ Jesus. Ephesians 2:4-6 NKJV*

In abiding in Jesus, our very lives—our choices and words—become our share in Jesus's own intercession for God's kingdom purposes on earth.

> *Therefore, He is also able to save to the uttermost those who come to God through him, since He always lives to make intercession for them. Hebrews 7:25 NKJV*

We are truly

> *...chosen by God and precious, [and] you also, as living stones, are being built up a spiritual house, a holy priesthood, to offer up spiritual sacrifices acceptable to God through Jesus Christ. 1 Peter 2:5 NKJV*

In the relational flow of the Holy Spirit, God usually always establishes some kind of order and encourages discipline. The priest faithfully dressed the lamps and burned sweet incense at the golden altar at the opening and close of every day. When the lamp wicks were trimmed and fresh oil was added, the flames rose and intensified. The golden walls and furniture glowed with fuller beauty. When fresh incense was burned on the altar, it filled the inner court with a fragrance symbolic of prayer and worship. So too, if we will consistently and intentionally position ourselves before God, the Holy Spirit's light will eventually intensify within us as the fragrance of our prayer and worship rises to our Lord. For those who think lightly of regular prayer times and say that New Testament grace frees us from Old Testament structures, remember that Peter and John regularly went to the temple to pray at three each afternoon.

Whatever pattern fits us, regular times of yielded attention to Jesus and the Holy Spirit are vital to knowing God. There's so much to divert us from prayer, so much global unrest and need, so much to pray about that it cuts through our flesh and human soul to realize that prayer at the golden altar is not about what we might want or think. It's about seeking what God wants. How we need that revelation!

Waiting before the Lord at the altar of incense encourages us to set our pride aside and seek God's will above our own will. It diminishes the big "I" by its simplicity and humility.

The altar was small, merely 18" square, just room for one single person to stand before it, space enough for the priest and God. This intimate place, hidden and set apart from the busy public eye of outer court activities, was designed to foster unassuming honesty before God. The kind of honesty behind Jesus's stern rebuke against insincerity and pretense in prayer when he said,

> *And when you pray, do not be like the hypocrites. For they love to pray standing in the synagogues and on the street corners to be seen by men. Truly I tell you, they already have their full reward. But when you pray, go into your inner room, shut your door, and pray to your Father, who is unseen. And your Father, who sees what is done in secret, will reward you. Matthew 6:5-6*

The small hidden space also reminds us that no one needs a cathedral, an audience, a group, a prayer partner or a walk in the woods to worship and pray. As Jesus said, his spirit dwells within us. About forty years ago I wrote a poem that reminds me of this place.

A Hidden Place[129]

Hidden deep within my heart
Safe from doubt and injury,
There's a place I do not enter
Carelessly.

A burning place of brilliant light
Filled with harmony,
It's a place I cannot enter
Unless love beckons me.

A place aflame with molten love,
Soaked with Majesty,
This place is only entered
In humility.

If Cherubim with flaming sword
Would guard the door from me,
The place is entered by Christ's blood
Most confidentially.

Yes, Jesus lives in our hearts! God's indwelling presence in you and me contrasts strongly with the altar of incense as an external, material thing. It was a picture, a type, a visual object lesson given by God that was pointing ahead toward our prayerful relationship with him and

---

[129] "A Hidden Place "by Ginny Emery. First published in *Meet Me at the Cross,* Ginny Emery and Joyce Long, eds., Given Word Publishers, p.132

illustrating the completed works of heaven. Because God loves us from spiritual infancy through maturity, because all of his callings are significant, we must think clearly about prayer, both from historical and personal perspectives. Despite all I've written about the importance of Holy Spirit prayer at the golden altar and vital as the altar of incense's prophetic meaning can be, we must be watchful not to elevate golden altar prayer to a higher or better place of prayer. We must never think it's the only kind of prayer God hears or favors.

Although I'm grateful whenever the Holy Spirit gives grace to pray out of his heart and mind, it is humbling and encouraging to remember that we don't need to sense God's presence and direction to pray. God receives every honest prayer from weak and powerless men, women and children. He might not listen to rote prayer, insincere prayer and unloving prayer that's inconsistent with his character. He turns away from prayers that we beam toward others rather than to him. But, because he hears our hearts as well as our words, every sincere word directed to him as God rises as fragrant incense before his throne. Our heavenly Father is ALL POWERFUL and ALL LOVING. He hears us when we are far from his tents and seeking to discover if he exists; he hears us when we begin to ask what his cross and life are all about, and he hears us as struggling, imperfect weak-faithed sons and daughters who seek to know him better. He hears the desires of our heart even when we don't know we're praying.

For two decades, I felt dissatisfied with an ugly, inefficient kitchen. From time to time, in outbursts of frustration, I'd say, "Father! What about this kitchen? Whatever can I do?" Of course, I had no money, no plans and no idea where to start. When it became possible to gut and remodel the kitchen, with funds earmarked especially for delayed maintenance on a needy home, the gift was so unexpected and naturally impossible that I knew God had received my frustrated words as a prayer. I don't recall asking him for a better kitchen. Maybe I did. But if so, I'm sure it was apologetically, for the request felt selfish and small. No matter, God heard my exasperation with an ugly and inefficient kitchen; he heard my longing for change and in generosity, grace and love, he helped remodel my kitchen.

Although God listened to my frustrations, my one-way conversations with him about the kitchen were radically different from Jesus's prayers. My words came from my soul; I did not expect him to listen or answer me. Jesus's prayers came from the Holy Spirit. He had expectant faith that God would hear and answer because Jesus said and did what he saw his Father saying and doing.

> *Truly, truly, I tell you, the Son can do nothing by himself, unless He sees the Father doing it. For whatever the Father does, the Son also does. John 5:19*

When we're filled with the Holy Spirit and in agreement with what God is doing, our prayers get answered too.

> *And I will do whatever you ask in My name, so that the Father may be glorified in the Son. If you ask Me for anything in My name, I will do it. . . . The word that you hear is not My own, but it is from the Father who sent me. John 14: 13-14, 24*

We all love golden altar prayers that come from the harmony of abiding in Jesus, but that shouldn't stop us from talking to God at any time. He listens when we're happy and grateful, when we're curious or tired, and when we're tempted, out of sorts, discombobulated, longing for a loving touch or needing the Holy Spirit's help, thoughts, direction and authority. Just the other night, feeling quite far from Jesus, God and everything spiritual, I needed to talk with God. I'd awakened around 3:30 AM with a horrible headache. Sleepless, I tossed, turned, wiggled, turned the light on, off and on again before finally asking, "Father, why? What's wrong? What should I do?" The thought came to read Psalm 47, so I did. Psalm 54 came to mind, and lastly Psalm 73. The Psalms turned into prayer and the prayer led to repentance for an ungodly attitude about a disagreeable situation. When I asked forgiveness, my headache broke. My conversation with the Lord had nothing of the beauty of holiness or certainty of agreement with God. It was a bothered human midnight need, but God heard. Sometimes I chatter to him, like a companion. Like right now—when I asked, "What now, Lord?" Like a flash, the impression came to get up and walk around. I've been sitting at this computer far too long.

While we seek and value Spirit-birthed prayers, it's reassuring to know that every honestly motivated prayer is as sweet-smelling incense to our Father in heaven. He hears the wordless prayers hidden in the depths of our souls, he hears prayers born in searching darkness, in fox hole terror, emergency room trauma and desperate need. All are sweet to his ears. Although God may turn away from selfish and unwise petitions, he answers more prayers than we may remember making.

As a single mom, when my children were teens, I stuffed quart mason jars with tiny scraps of folded paper. Each one held a concern that was impossible resolve on my own—so I wrote it down, put it in the jar and gave it to God as a prayer. Rarely did I feel any sense of God, Jesus or the Holy Spirit. But years later, when I reread those scribbled notes, almost every concern had been resolved. This convinced me that whether we sense God or not, his Father heart leaps in loving response to both our slightest and our weightiest requests.

If Jesus seems distant, if talking to God is hard and prayer falters, it helps to consciously remind ourselves that God hears us. He knows what is going on in every corner of the universe and in every hidden corner of our hearts. Whatever he wants us to know, he will show us.

If it's a matter of obedience, God will make it clear. If we hear nothing, he may be teaching us to trust him in the dark. He asks us to peacefully, quietly continue in prayer and accept the wisdom of his silence without fretfulness, anxiety or self-condemnation. We may need to ask the Holy Spirit to help us persevere, but if we don't get all bent out of shape, if we keep on talking with God and believing his word, we can trust that we're not alone.

For we live by faith, not sight. 2 Corinthians 5:7 NIV

God never plays games of push and pull. His invitation to seek a closer deeper relationship is always open. We respond by keeping our lamps trimmed, meditating his on his word, doing all he asks of us, turning our thoughts toward him and keeping in touch with other believers. Learning to abide by faith, not by sight and experiences, is part of our journey. We grow by trusting God when he seems far away. We learn steadfastness, perseverance and faithfulness. Missing him creates a hunger for more of his love. His apparent distance can spur us to prayer. It often provides just the opportunity and motivation we need to learn to set our hearts and minds upon him and practice his presence.

Set your minds on things above, not on earthly things. For you died, and your life is now hidden with Christ in God. Colossians 3:2-3

Although the Holy Spirit will withdraw when quenched, we have God's word that unless we blaspheme against the Holy Spirit, he will never, never, never leave us or forsake us.

Never will I leave you, never will I forsake you. Hebrews 13:5b NIV

The Golden Altar of Incense

As we worship and pray at the golden altar of incense, our spirits always soak in more knowledge of God than our minds can process. When we're near to our Father God, his very presence imparts wordless truth. His impartations in this wonderful place of the Holy Spirit's light are inexhaustible. And after three thousand years, God's tabernacle illustrations of his ways hold true and continue to apply to us.

Consider the altar of incense as a piece of furniture. Like the table of showbread, it was built of acacia wood and then overlaid with gold. As believers put on Jesus today, we fulfill the prophetic symbol of the altar's wooden frame being covered with gold. The Holy Spirit clothes us in Jesus's righteousness, his purity and value. Our spirits and souls become the altar from which the incense of prayer arises to God. The beautiful fragrance of Jesus is revealed and released in and through us.

The altar's measurements also illustrate his ways; they are full of metaphorical possibilities.[130]

- A biblical cubit is approximately eighteen inches, about the distance from a man's elbow to his fingertip. At two cubits high, the top of the ark would stand about thirty-six inches from the ground. That's low for most of us, but fortunately, the average height for men in Moses's time was 5' 6." Bowing before God denotes our humility, but standing before God (or any ruler) to serve him suggests both a legal right to stand and confidence in our relationship. When Jesus said,

  And when you stand to pray, if you hold anything against another, forgive it, so that your Father in heaven will forgive your trespasses as well. Mark 11:25

---

[130] Although not all of these illustrations are supported in scripture, and some stretch credibility, each one illustrates Biblical values and principles.

His words suggest a divine order and protocol. When we're washed by Jesus' blood and cleansed by his word, we have a legal right to stand before God as our Father. Unforgiveness is a sin that blocks our relationship with God and others. Based on that, standing before God in prayer might be fruitless if we're in known rebellion and sin (unless it's to admit our sin and ask forgiveness).

- The ark was 2 ½ x 1½ x 1½ cubits. The number one for each side of the ark is unique. It is neither prime nor composite. The number one stands alone, with nothing added to it. God is one. There is one God. The Trinity is one. Listing and discussing all of Jesus's singularities would fill pages. He is the only Son of God. Both Jesus's life and work stand alone; he stands alone. He lived and died once. Repetition is not necessary. (You and me, on the other hand, oh my, how often we need second chances!)

- One by one is a perfect square; it's the same in all directions. Christ's love reaches out in all directions.

- And finally, for those Bible readers interested in numbers one by one by two cubits might possibly suggest a finality, a unity, and a simplicity.

THE HORNS OF THE ALTAR

A golden horn rose from each corner of the altar. Once each year, the horns were cleansed by blood from the sin offering, another symbolic reminder that we draw near to God only by the blood of Jesus. Even when the Holy Spirit helps us agree with God, our human prayers and praises can be imperfect, mixed and faulty—all that draws near to God must be cleansed by the blood of Jesus.

These horns are significant. Throughout the Bible, horns are a symbol of strength and power; they're a visual reminder of God's ability to conquer every foe. They symbolize God's power, protection and government. In the books of Daniel and Revelation, horns are the Holy Spirit's metaphor for kingdoms and governments. Prayer at the altar of incense releases God's authority, his governing strength and his Holy Spirit's power for all who bow low in surrender to him.

David must have been thinking of this when he sang,

> *The LORD is my rock, my fortress, and my deliverer.*
> *My God is my rock, in whom I take refuge,*
> *my shield, and the horn of my salvation, my stronghold.*
> *I will call upon the LORD, who is worthy to be praised;*
> *so shall I be saved from my enemies. Psalm 18:2-3*

When John the Baptist was born, his father, Zacharias, prophesied that Jesus would be a horn of salvation. That is, Jesus would have all of God's power, strength and authority to save us and establish justice.

> *Blessed be the Lord, the God of Israel, because He has visited*
> *   and redeemed His people.*
> *He has raised up a horn of salvation for us in the house*
> *   of His servant David,*
> *as He spoke through His holy prophets, those of ages past.*
> *   Luke 1:68-70*

THE GOLDEN CROWN

Most likely, the crown of gold around the altar looked just like the crown guarding the table of showbread and the ark of the covenant. Taken together they visually illustrate a joining of the priestly and the kingly position, function and authority of Jesus. By extension, they suggest the unity in the function and authority of believers as kings and priest.

> *[He] has made us kings and priests to His God and Father, to him be glory and dominion forever and ever. Amen.*
> Revelation 1:6 NKJV

THE INNER COURT: A FEW MORE THOUGHTS

The inner court is not about work; it's all about agreeing with the Holy Spirit in the disciplines of holy living. It's about replenishing the oil of the Holy Spirit and keeping the flame burning; it's about being bread, soaking in the aroma of frankincense and resting on the table before the presence of God; it's about fellowshipping with others around God's word and lighting the daily incense of prayer at the golden altar.

The priest's fellowship around the table of bread foreshadows the koinonia, or fellowship of Christians who are united in Jesus. As Bonhoeffer wrote, "The physical presence of other Christians is a source of incomparable joy and strength to the believer. . . . Their fellowship is founded solely upon Jesus Christ." [131]

Serving Jesus in the Holy Spirit's light, our own self-efforts and strivings fall away. We move in his strength and peace. That said, work in concert with Jesus is still work, it takes initiative, focus, energy and preparation. The grain had to be ground, the bread required baking, the oil was purified and carried in to fill the lamps, the wicks trimmed and the incense prepared and offered. When Jesus sent out his disciples, they had to walk the dusty roads from town to town to preach the good

---

[131] *Life Together* by Dietrich Bonhoeffer, © 1954 by Harper and Row Publishers, pages 19 and 23

news that the Kingdom of God was at hand. But trusting upon Jesus's directions, they moved with confident rest in his authority and threw themselves into following his plans.

Today, all Kingdom work is by the Holy Spirit and we do no more than he wants done. Some very few, he calls to remain in the inner court, their worship and intersession hidden from the world. Others, he sends out to serve others in his strength and wisdom, not their own powers and abilities.

Allowing God to equip us for Kingdom work takes willingness. Some of us feel growing pains. Dying to ourselves, we often die hard. When I was fifty-four years old, Jesus stood in front of me and said, "I want you to go back to school." My answered "Yes" was immediate. But I wept and wept with grief at the change. He dried my tears, went before me, helped me through a rigorous academic program and linked me with others in Kingdom building relationships. At the University I gained the computer skills and confidence to write this book. Surrender to the Holy Spirit takes following Jesus in his plans for our lives and emptying ourselves of all that is not his compassionate holy love.

> *Let this mind be in you which was also in Christ Jesus:*
> *Who, existing in the form of God, did not consider*
> *equality with God something to be grasped,*
> *but emptied Himself, taking the form of a servant,*
> *being made in human likeness.*
> *And being found in appearance as a man, He humbled*
> *Himself and became obedient to death—*
> *even death on a cross. Philippians 2:5-8*

Our willingness to agree with Jesus in our big choices (like going back to school, changing jobs or moving across the country) is strengthened or weakened by our smaller, ordinary day to day decisions. I'm trying to maintain a habit of God-consciousness by giving all my busy interrupting thoughts and distracting feelings to him. It helps to write them down. I often need to consciously dial down, moment by moment. I want to learn to get out the way, to still my soul and not get in God's way. I know that as we quietly, gently and intentionally empty ourselves of all but love for Jesus, the Father and others, his peace will begin to guide us through our daily activities. If he shows us sin or judgments, we repent. We determine

> ... to know nothing but Jesus, and him crucified.
> 1 Corinthians 2:2

If the Holy Spirit brings something to mind, we don't fight it; we speak it, sing it, write it down or pray about it, trusting that God is in charge. We want to get out of his way, let him call all the shots if you will. Whether you call the process surrender, yielding, centering, dying to self, crucifixion, presenting your body as a sacrifice, taking the cross or turning your eyes upon Jesus, the result is similar. Simply and quietly, it's a turning to God (remembering that his kingdom is within) and inviting Jesus to live out his life in us by the power of the Holy Spirit. It's what Paul described when he wrote,

> *I have been crucified with Christ; and it is no longer I who live, but Christ lives in me; and the life which I now live in the flesh I live by faith in the Son of God, who loved me and gave himself up for me. Galatians 2:20 NKJV*

When we truly look upon Jesus as

> *The Lamb of God who takes away the sin of the world. John 1:29*

we worship him.

We can't fake true worship or Holy Spirit-led prayer before God. Anointed worship and prayer are God-given gifts, not emotional moods, outpourings or highs. Trying to drag the lampstand back to the outer court, hungrily and unnaturally seeking to replicate in the flesh what God gives in the Spirit, is pretending to have a light we don't have. We might fool some people, but our imitation worship won't fool God. Carnal believers might be entertained, informed and persuaded. They might believe religious words,[132] join religious social communities, participate in pleasing ego-satisfying meetings full of unity of mind and emotions and think they've felt God.

But they're deceived. Think of the ecstatic highs we can feel when a unified crowd rises to its feet cheering a tremendous football play or when an audience claps until their hands hurt and calls out "Bravo! Bravo!" after an outstanding musical performance. I rise to my feet and applaud a fine performance longer than most. It's good to recognize and honor extraordinary achievement. But hopefully, the athletes and performers will not take kudos to themselves but hand their bouquets to God in gratitude. Quite often threads of divine truth weave through great performances. But, bottom line, centering on a performer, athlete, leader, worship team or an enthusiastic emotion rather than on Jesus, can turn into idolatry. God does not like worship at the pagan altars evoked by rock stars and performance. Entertainers and performers in the pulpit will not bring the presence of the Lord.

We can never fake the truth or power of God's word either. The Holy Spirit alone can give life to preaching, teaching, speaking, reading and

---

132 But! God's word does not go forth void. Many people met Jesus and came to authentic faith through the meetings of a man called Marjo. Marjo was trained and forced by his parents to be a child evangelist. He did not believe what he taught and preached and later exposed the false tactics of many evangelists. You can read about him on Wikipedia and IMbd sites. Unbelieving counterfeits may lead many to doubt the reality of God's good news to us in Jesus Christ but they cannot ever negate the authentic power of God's love and the truth of his word.

writing about God and his word. Trying to communicate what God actually wrote, meant and wants us to say about his holy word is serious business. Our mistakes may fool people. We may even fool ourselves for a while. The Holy Spirit is a patient, kind and loving teacher to God's well-meaning children. But the God-head will never endorse error, even unintentional error. Mentally building on, fantasizing about, embellishing or adding to the truth God wrote and gives by his Spirit is pretending to have a light and authority that we just don't have.

I should know, because I've unintentionally done it. My first drafts of this manuscript were full of errors. I didn't check-out all my facts. If I'd read it, heard it or thought it and it didn't violate scriptural principles, I assumed it was right. While writing, the Holy Spirit has repeatedly challenged and humbled me. In fact checking, I've often been wrong and so have some of the respected teachers, pastors and resources I've consulted. I'm not a Bible scholar. I'm an elderly woman who loves Jesus. When I started writing this book, I thought the Holy Spirit and my forty-year-old class notes would be enough. I felt so inspired that I didn't even go back and re-read Exodus.

God watches over both his children and his word with jealous care. He wants us to preach, teach, write and speak with Holy Spirit inspiration and accurate information. He cares about his word, *and* he cares about us. By privately humbling me and helping me correct errors and omissions, he's saved me from publicly publishing many of the mistakes in early drafts. I'm grateful to every brother and sister in Christ who has read my manuscript and said, things like, "Really?" or "You misapplied that verse; it's out of context." or "That's not logical!" or "Your typology isn't Biblically credible." None of us want to misapply God's word in ways that violate his truth and love. It's important to do our best to get God's word right. It matters.

If the Holy Spirit chooses to shine his light on my experiences, facts and understandings, they will be alive and helpful; if not, the text will be lifeless. I'm doing my best in trust that the same Spirit of Truth who has guided me will also give readers discernment and cover my limitations with his mercy. I trust him to help readers to check out God's word for themselves and fill in the gaps if they spot any omissions,[133] opinions and mistakes, so that no one will be led astray by my witness to God's revelation of himself to me.

That said, all of us who aspire to be among God's faithful servants must sow the seed we're given as God guides us, fully knowing the fruit and harvest will never be our own. There's a mystery about God's anointing. D.L. Moody reported preaching the same sermons in the USA and in England. Stateside, nothing happened; in England the Holy Spirit breathed life and conviction over those who heard and many came to believe in Jesus.

The Holy Spirit is within us; yet paradoxically, he is also (as Jesus told Nicodemus in John 4) like the wind. He blows when and where he chooses and we can't see his comings and goings. We can stir up the gift of God within us by asking his help, by praying in tongues, reading his word, and singing hymns, psalms and spiritual songs, but we must do as he chooses, not vice versa. That said, positioning ourselves to receive from him is not a big deal. It's no more than a simple matter of willingly setting our eyes on Jesus, shutting our mouths until we believe God gives us something to say and then taking the risk of saying it. He is ready to join us.

I love how the Holy Spirit visits our ladies' Bible study. At each meeting we sit around a table visiting over tea, coffee and sweet treats. After a bit of catching up with each other, we always share our prayer requests

---

[133] Two huge omissions are God's directions for the priest's garments and the feasts and sacrifices.

for family, friends and neighbors. Many of the women have lived in this community for seventy or eighty years. Their roots are deep. They know and care about families all over the area. I get tears in my eyes thinking of how these dear elderly saints continue to build on their parent's and grandparent's foundations of faith. Before the world, they continue their church traditions of quilting, church suppers and ice cream socials. They keep alive family traditions of lebkuchen, krumkake, nifflies (spaetzles to some) and German pretzels. But behind closed doors they quietly continue to cover their families, churches and community in prayer. As soon as we turn to look toward God in silent prayer, the atmosphere in the room changes. We know that God is with us.

Emmanuel. God with us! His recognizable presence has joined us on telephone calls and surprised us in the car, at the grocery store and on the beach. The Holy Spirit is full of surprises. He will bubble up inside of us with words of worship and gratitude for the beauty of God's creation. He comes in the quiet moments of reading his written word. He often lifts me into awareness of heavenly majesty when anointed musicians follow the Holy Spirit with instruments and song.[134] I've heard strains of God's voice in Leadbelly's authenticity and in the creative humility of Bill Monroe's bluegrass, he speaks hope through Doc Watson's guitar and Johnny Cash's gospel songs. I glimpse a natural example of his supernatural perfection in Jussi Bjorling's perfect voice and many have recognized his harmony in the blending voices of Josh Grogan and Celine Dion as they sing "The Prayer." Others may be reminded of the

---

[134] I'm still learning about distractions to worship. I can't worship if I'm anxious, fretful or worried. I've got to take all my inner distractions to the Lord in prayer. I can't worship if I hold anything against anyone at the time. I can't worship if I judge the musicians. I can't worship easily in circumstances where others are suffering. I can't worship when a sound technician turns-up the volume so loudly that little children cover their ears in pain while their mommies and daddies close their eyes, sway, lift their hands high in the air and jump around in emotional ecstasies described as worship. The sound hurts my ears too; it has little to do with the love of Jesus. All this may be my flesh. I recall Judson Cornwall saying that he had learned to worship despite carnal worship teams, bad music, distractions and disinterested congregations.

fine tuning of his inexhaustible vitality as Hilary Hahn's energy moves through her violin to understand a Bach partita. The Holy Spirit is not limited to Handel's Hallelujah chorus or our musical tastes. He can lift us into worship at a church where the pianist pounds out one old hymn[135] after the other with the distressing mechanical rhythms of a marching band. And when God is near, we can worship while singing the same, ordinarily boring, repetitive simple chorus over and over again because the Holy Spirit is resting on the words and music.

At times, Jesus visits us with an anointing for another person. When that happens to me, I might feel an intense sitting-on-the-edge-of my chair focus, a fresh alertness and clarity or a warm burning love in my heart that reaches far beyond my own capacity for love. An anointing from the Holy Spirit that connects me and others with God in any way at all—be it through prayer, words or simple acts of love is not usually like personal worship or prayer.

At these times, the Holy Spirit usually has a very specific purpose. He may want to release divine power to heal or he may give words that carry his own compassion and authority. For a young believer, unused to moving with the Holy Spirit, it may be natural to question or resist the outward flow of his love. It's natural to protect ourselves and others from foolishness or error. It can be risky to step out in faith. But if we surrender and agree, God's kingdom breaks in and the Holy Spirit carries us through until his purpose is complete. [136]

---

[135] A friend noted that many of our old hymns of faith remind us of our history and the faith commitments of those who have gone before us. They were birthed in powerful, life-changing revival movements. God gave different priorities and emphases to fit the historical circumstances and needs of his people, and if we are open to hear, these reminders are as powerful today as when they were written.

[136] One of the most heart touching and realistic descriptions I've read recently about stepping into God's Kingdom breakthroughs is by Steven R. Musick, in *Life After Heaven*. Musick describes Kingdom breakthroughs as "Kingdom of Heaven Bubbles." His faith building autobiography is a true witness to God's miracles of love. *Life After Heaven* by Steven R. Musick, Waterbrook, 2017 © Steven R. Musick

The Holy Spirit prepares us for those moments of ministry to others in the inner court, as we spend time with Jesus, eat the bread of God's word, pray at the golden altar of incense and draw close to worshipping the Lord in the holy of holies. There, we learn to surrender to God. We get to know holy love. We follow him through the spiritual disciplines of loving service, the obedience of faith and life together with other believers. We open ourselves to personal worship and learn the Holy Spirit's voice and emotional vocabulary through his words, songs, silence, tears, travail, groans, laughter and hallelujahs. Bit by bit, he establishes Jesus's rule in the throne room of our very own hearts.

THE HOLY OF HOLIES

Every Christian's journey toward knowing God includes the holy of holies. Whether we know it or not, whenever grace opens our eyes and brings us to pray, "God, be merciful to me, a sinner," we're centering ourselves before God's mercy seat. In paradoxical tension, at the very same time, almost all of us are standing outside the veil between the inner court and the holy of holies. Oh, I know the scriptures, that the veil has been torn away—as the writer of Hebrews says, we can

> . . . come boldly unto the throne of grace, that we may obtain mercy, and find grace to help in time of need.
> Hebrews 4:16, NKJV

And I believe it, and live it and do pray boldly for mercy and grace. And I know God hears and answers—yet, experientially, apart from visionary glimpses and faith, I've not been in God's throne room. Like the kingdom of God, the holy of holies is both a present and a future place, a here-but-not-here, a now-but-not-yet place.[137]

The throne room is nothing like the reports of those who return to earth after near-death experiences and tell of the beauty, the joy of seeing Jesus and of meeting friends and family. Isaiah's report is a far clearer

---

[137] A friend emailed this comment: "Can any mortal, clothed in sinful flesh, enter that holiest of places and live? A veil of flesh—our own flesh—would forbid it. We enter the holy of holies by faith in Christ Jesus, our Great High Priest, who intercedes for us. (Romans 8:34, Hebrews 7:25-28)."

description. On seeing the Seraphim, hearing them cry out "Holy, Holy, is the LORD of hosts" and feeling the foundations tremble and the temple filling with smoke, he cried out,

> *Woe is me, for I am undone!*
> *Because I am a man of unclean lips,*
> *And I dwell in the midst of a people of unclean lips;*
> *For my eyes have seen the King, the Lord of hosts.*
> *Isaiah 6:5 NKJV*

What happened to Isaiah hast happened to very few others. Lots of people talk and write about God's manifest presence, but in my eighty-plus years, I've only heard four first-hand testimonies of throne room visits. One man said he felt uncovered and filthy. He fumbled to button the top button of his sports shirt. He said no more. Another, like Paul in the Bible, reported seeing and hearing things he could not speak of. The third, a close friend said, "You don't want to go there. It is terrifying. Everything within me trembled." When God asked her, "What do you want?" all she could say was, "Revival." Later, she told me that it would have been impossible to ask for anything that God didn't want to give her.

The fourth person who'd been to the throne room brought trails of glory into the room as he spoke humbly of sensing God's omniscience. He actually experienced a tiny fraction of God's constant complete awareness of the minutest details of everything. My mind was stretched by his concrete witness to a truth I'd accepted abstractly. By the time he finished speaking I was convinced that God really does know everything, everywhere—from the most miniscule movement of each particle of heat-energy that has ever been or will be generated in undiscovered galaxies to the configuration and movement of every sub-atomic particle in every snowflake on the Himalayas. It's impossible for me to humanly identify with the vastness of God's knowing. God simultaneously knows all history, past and present, including every hair on every head of every person who ever lived, every feather on every bird and all the thoughts and feelings that are buried so deeply within in our own hearts that we don't even know them ourselves.

So, although by the blood of Jesus, I can approach God's throne of grace in confidence and talk with my heavenly Father more easily and openly than daughters might usually talk with the most wise and understanding earthly dad, and although at times I've sensed the warmth of God's love in my heart and felt the electricity of his power in my mortal body, I know there is more. It scares me, but at the same time, I've a hunger, a longing, to visit the throne room. I want to know more of the immeasurable glory and power of our Creator, our Father-God, my merciful Abba, whom I've grown to know and love through Jesus. I think he'd like to show all of us more of his love, our longings to know him must come from him. So many of us have sensed God's presence and drawing power. But for now, like most of my brothers and sisters in Christ, I must write about the holy of holies from the outside, from the human side, from the Holy Spirit's revelation of Jesus to a twenty-first century woman. So, I draw on my own paltry thoughts and ramble on about my experiences. I share the testimony of others and Bible texts, including those about the tabernacle. Putting it all together, writing about the holy of holies inspires reverence and awakens a holy fear. It is a place of holy worship and reminds me of shivers I sometimes feel when I sing

> *Take me into the holy of holies,*
> *Take me in by the blood of the Lamb,*
> *Take me in to the holy of holies,*
> *Take the coal, cleanse my lips,*
> *Here I am.*

I can't sing it casually. Everything about the holy of holies is set apart for God. It pictures the throne room, God's eternal home, and it reveals God's mercy, glory and majesty. Until Jesus came to earth, the holy of holies, the space reserved for the ark of the covenant in the tabernacle and Jerusalem temples, was God's one and only holy throne room on earth. The high priest never entered it casually. On the Day of Atonement, after thorough cleansing and preparation, he alone, and no other, was allowed entry. Only then, fully prepared, would he dare pass through the veil and approach God's mercy seat, the place of his manifest presence.

THE VEIL OF CHERUBIM

You shall make a veil [to divide the two rooms] of blue, purple, and scarlet fabric and fine twisted linen, skillfully worked with cherubim on it. Exodus 26:31 AMP

When the Day of Atonement came and the high priest was readied, he carefully carried a vessel filled with sacrificial blood from animals slain at the brazen altar into the holy place. He walked past the lampstand and the table holding the bread of God's presence. What were his thoughts and feelings as he stood before the final veil and reached out his hand to touch the fabric and part the veil behind the golden altar of incense?

The veil was intricately lovely, embroidered with cherubim, those supernatural beings around God's heavenly throne who were also chosen to guard the way to the tree of life.

He [God] drove out the man, and at the east of the garden of Eden he placed the cherubim and a flaming sword that turned every way to guard the way to the tree of life. Genesis 3:24 ESV

I've wondered if any high priests ever thought of the cherubim that we know about from Genesis 3. Did they recall those heavenly angels God placed at Eden's entrance to keep Adam and Eve away from the tree of life? Mercifully, God protected Adam and Eve from eating of that tree and living forever in disobedient flesh. Also in great mercy, God didn't curse our disobedient love-refusing species to eternal existence apart from his love.

When the high priest passed through the veil embroidered with cherubim and set his feet within the holy of holies, he prefigured our complete redemption from the consequences of sin and the fullest possible restoration of our broken relationship with God. His action looked forward to the day when the Holy Spirit would return to Adam's offspring with the offer of eternal life because, by the blood of Jesus and the power of the Holy Spirit, forgiveness and cleansing would be available to our human race. Today, when believers partake of Jesus, the tree of eternal life, the communion and peace that Adam once knew with God, woman, himself and the created world is restored to Adam's descendants. God himself made a way for us, Adam's sons and daughters, to enter into Holy Place.

Most likely the ground cloth of the veil was firmly woven from finely spun white linen threads that had been heavily embroidered into a dense tapestry-like fabric. God had directed Moses to use colors that were rich with symbolic meaning: purple for the royalty of kings, scarlet for blood sacrifice and white for righteousness. The veil was hung from golden hooks and clasps attached to supportive acacia pillars that were covered with gold and set within silver bases. The colors and materials of the veil symbolically represented Jesus as prophet, priest and king. God knew that when Jesus died, the veil would split open. God knew that Jesus's flesh, rent by death, would open the way into the holy of holies for all. The writer of Hebrews confirms Christ as the veil.

> *Therefore, brethren, since we have full freedom and confidence to enter into the [Holy of] Holies [by the power and virtue] in the blood of Jesus, By this fresh (new) and living way which He initiated and dedicated and opened for us through the separating curtain (veil of the Holy of Holies), that is, through His flesh.* Hebrews 10:19-20 AMPC

Matthew records that the veil in Herod's temple was torn open at the moment Jesus died.

> *When Jesus had cried out again in a loud voice, He yielded up His spirit. At that moment the veil of the temple was torn in two from top to bottom. The earth quaked and the rocks were split. The tombs broke open, and the bodies of many saints who had fallen asleep were raised....* Matthew 27:50-52

That history-changing moment indicated that Christ's sacrificial death was perfect; his work on earth was complete. His death had reconciled God's wrathful justice with God's merciful loving kindness. The split veil was a visible sign that Jesus's obedience unto death had defeated the legal power that sin and death had held over mankind. He had finally overcome the sin nature in man and canceled the consequences of Adam's rebellion. Before Adam disobeyed God, the Holy Spirit was in him and with him. When Adam ignored God's command, the Holy Spirit left him. Jesus's obedience unto death opened the way for the Holy Spirit to return to indwell men.

Jesus's death also did away with the need for a material brick-and-mortar, wood-and-nail earthly temple. He established worship in spirit and truth. Joined by faith to Jesus Christ, our mediator and advocate, men and women can now approach God in a "new and living way."

Therefore, brothers, since we have confidence to enter the Most Holy Place by the blood of Jesus, by the new and living way opened for us through the curtain of His body, and since we have a great priest over the house of God, let us draw near with a sincere heart in full assurance of faith, having our hearts sprinkled to cleanse us from a guilty conscience and our bodies washed with pure water. Hebrews 10:19-22

Once we enter into the holy of holies through the veil of Jesus's flesh, we will no longer *choose* to bow before him of our own volition. On meeting the humility and the purity of his consuming love, we not only *want* to bow before him, we *must* bow before him and surrender to his will. We will either agree or die. The holy of holies symbolizes the place of completest union with God, the place of living, moving and having our entire being in him. It is not absorption into him, it is yielding to his true all-powerful holiness; it is surrender to his majesty and supreme authority over all.

How do we get there? Positionally, we're there by faith. That's fairly easy for most of us to accept. It's harder for some of us to realize that our actual experience of ongoing union with Jesus is simply by faith too. Despite our human tendencies to earn God's favor by good works, from what I've read in God's word and seen confirmed the biographies of men and women who have lived in close union with God, that's it. Faith. It's all very simple. Look to Jesus, trust and obey. Digging deeper, getting down to the practical nitty-gritty of it, both the Bible and the life histories of godly men and women, indicate that most of us, including the greatest saints, begin our Christian life as babes in Christ. Then, depending on many variables, including our calling, desire, character and personality, the Holy Spirit teaches us and guides us. We grow-up in Christ along individual learning curves designed to draw each one of us nearer to

God. But even then, we can't enter into all the fullness of God's presence by our own volition. There's reciprocity.

Draw near to God and He will draw near to you.
James 4:8 NKJV

Our part is choosing to believe. Determining to believe. Fighting to believe. Anti-Christ spirits take many forms. They may try to poke drain-holes in our faith through well-meaning unbelieving friends and family. The spirits of the age and local principalities and powers cloud the air we breathe. They attack our weak spots by turning our eyes from Jesus and dropping distractions, doubts and unbelief into our unguard hearts and minds. When I lived in a Chicago suburb, I felt my faith being drained and pulled on by an overwhelming, too-much-to-do-busyness, a critical pecking-order-pride and the engaging allurement of getting away from it all in shopping mall consumerism. While living in a secular Big Ten university town, my faith was challenged by competitive intellectual pride and control issues of academic hoop-jumping. Living near another secular Big Ten university, I felt buffeted in an atmosphere of self-confident prideful superiority, triumphalism and an analytical devil's advocate. I'd stumbled into joining the we're-better-than-you crowd by my super-hot critical attitude toward those breathing in the same air of superiority that had triggered and fed my own attitude.

Principalities, powers and prevailing winds are real. We weaken them and overcome them personally by shining the light of God's truth upon them. Not by proclamations, declarations and prayers as much as by our lives. Today, our nation's faith is being tested by relativism, materialism, fear, unbelief, media-fed divisiveness, accusations about attempts at mass mind control and more. God's light beams from our hearts when we affirm his unchanging nature, choose spiritual values over materialistic once, courage over fear, faith over doubt and unity in Jesus over divisiveness. We overcome accusations by recognizing that God does not accuse us or others—he convicts us of the truth and we defeat control by finding freedom in the truth of God's word.

> *It is for freedom that Christ has set us free. Stand firm, then, and do not be encumbered once more by a yoke of slavery. Galatians 5:1*

Lord, please give us discernment to know when our faith in you and your word is being challenged, eroded and drained. We are not to conform to the spirit of the age. Paul reminded the Romans

> *Do not be conformed to this world, but be transformed by the renewing of your mind. Then you will be able to test and approve what is the good, pleasing, and perfect will of God. Romans 12:2*

And Paul admonished Timothy to

> *Pursue righteousness, godliness, faith, love, perseverance, and gentleness. Fight the good fight, holding on to faith and a good conscience, which some have rejected and thereby shipwrecked their faith. Take hold of the eternal life to which you were called. 1 Timothy 1:18b-19 and 6:11-12 [adpt.]*

We do all this, we fight the good fight of faith and overcome hindrances to living in the vibrant reality of God's eternal life by leaning into the Holy Spirit. Without him, it's as impossible as pulling ourselves up by our own bootstraps. Jesus is our example of living by faith. He held onto the Father's life in moment-by-moment love and dependance on the Holy Spirit.

THE TABERNACLE

Following in Jesus's footsteps is no narrow-minded, grievous, dutifully hard, hair-shirt religious thing. It's a life of contentment that's filled with love, joy and meaning. All it takes is keeping our hearts open to Jesus's love as Jesus kept his heart open to our heavenly Father's love. Some of us might need a bit of healing and deliverance at first. Our brains might need rewiring to contain all the light of God's creative love. Fortunately, he is our healer, our deliverer and a constant source of light and life. But trying to follow Jesus under our own steam won't take us into the Holy of Holies or a throne room experience of his glory. If your road is anything like mine, at various seasons, you'll fall into ruts or potholes of legalism, pride, doubt, vain imaginations, hypocrisy, delusions, self-deceptions, complacencies, inertia and other weaknesses. We need the constant companionship of the Holy Spirit to walk in untarnished love and authentic freedom, humility, faith and truth.

As we agree with the Holy Spirit and learn to live in God's word, we grow to experience more of Jesus's love. The more we know of his love, the more we want. It becomes a joy to run after him. And it's so easy, all it takes is making him the center of our thoughts. But sometimes that takes a transfer of affections.

Did you ever center your thoughts on another person? Or idolize a relationship? Or pursue your own idealistic fantasies of romantic love? Or success? If so, you know what it's like to chase after disappointments. The devil has dozens of unsatisfactory substitutes for the gives and takes of real love and satisfaction. I've done it. It's wanting a counterfeit. It's like reaching out for a beautiful sparkling scrumptious looking ice cream cone and finding it full of broken glass. Our false expectations can open us up to hurt and disappointment. God's ice cream cones may not sparkle and look as good on the outside, but they're smooth, creamy rich and delicious on the inside.

I've centered my life around idealized goals and imaginary perfect relationships more than once. My first fall into unreality was not over Frank Sinatra or Elvis, but over a skinny fourteen-year-old neighbor boy. I was an insecure naïve just-turned-fourteen-year-old high school freshman. In 1953, we called it *a crush*. In every study hall, in every passage between classes, I automatically scanned the corridors for a sight of my secret-love. I watched for him as I walked home from school and searched for him at school events. Although I never spoke with him and I dated other boys, my secret-love never waned. Our eyes met often, but he never sought me out and I never got up enough courage to talk with him. It was enough to know that he was around. Decades later, when I saw him and his wife looking at plastic refrigerator dishes at Big Lots, our eyes met again and we both turned the other way. I was still tongue-tied before my idol. How unlike Jesus's love. Oh, Father! Help!

We love because he first loved us. 1 John 4:19

Jesus returns our love. He also centers us in realities. As we center our thoughts on him and seek God's will for our lives, he replaces our idolatries with real relationships and leads us in love. Whether we get God's love directly from him or learn about love from people who love us, we all need love before we can love others. The truth that not one of us can give what we don't have is so simple and self-evident that it's almost silly. Just saying it smacks of being patronizing or condescending. Truth can be like that. God is love. The whole idea of love is his. Recognized or not, he is the source of love. He is the love that we all long for. We need to meet with him.

Meeting with God, spirit to Spirit, is as real as my first meeting and conversation with the man who eventually became my husband. As we stood outside a college classroom and talked about our work, I'd no idea he would be my husband. It was a rather ordinary conversation. I didn't know who God was in my earliest childhood glimpses of him either. [138]

One, early God-encounter stands out particularly. I was nine years old. I think it was July 31, 1948. That day Frank Casey, my father's best friend, unexpectedly died at the age of thirty-eight. When the phone call came, my family mobilized. Dad and grandma took off work. Grandma took the next El train home to stay with me and my younger sisters. My parents packed a suitcase and sped from Chicago to Flint, Michigan to comfort, help and support Frank's widow. Everything Frank owned was being held in probate. His bank account was frozen, his car was held, and his widow didn't have money or transportation to get to the store and buy milk or food for their two tiny children.

We loved Frank. My dad said that when Frank moved into a neighborhood or apartment building, neighbors who had been strangers for years would suddenly all become friends, knit together by Frank's love. That day, after my parents left, I sat alone on the front steps under the arching canopy of two gigantic Dutch elm trees and God came. I had no idea it was him. It was the same presence within and without that fills me today when Jesus draws near and stills my soul with supernatural peace.

As anyone who has read thus far knows that I'm all for experiencing God. I love to feel his presence and I'm learning to live in a steadier communion with him. But once again, it's worth repeating that seeking goosebumps and believing in them or trying to conjure up spiritual experiences has pitfalls. Counterfeit peace can be God's withdrawal, not his approval. Enthusiasm is not always God's energizing presence. Counterfeit love is often seductive and manipulative, not holy. Experiences that are not grounded on faith in Jesus Christ and consistent with the whole of God's written word can lead to divisiveness with our

---

138 I'm not dismissing love at first sight. It must be wonderful when it turns out right.

brothers and sisters in Christ. They can feed self-deception, demonic deception, unclean emotions and a dependence upon our experiences (and our interpretations of them). God's love is pure and holy.

> *Do not arouse or awaken love until the time is right.*
> Song of Solomon 2:7b

If your journey into a life that's awakened by and filled with God's holy love is anything like mine, it began on the inside. While an outside event, like hearing a message that awakens us to Jesus's love may be a turning point for us, most likely God has been at work on the inside of us, drawing us to Jesus and preparing us to hear his word. Jesus said,

> *No one can come to Me unless the Father who sent Me draws him, and I will raise him up at the last day John 6:44*

No wonder the Schulamite in Solomon's Song cried out to her beloved,

> *Draw me after you and let's run together!*
> Song of Solomon 1:4a NASB

Standing apart from Jesus and looking at his courts from afar works like a love relationship. So is beginning to get to know him in his outer court and wanting to get closer. In most healthy love affairs, attraction leads to friendship, conversation and doing things together before growing into more intimate courtship. Jesus, our heavenly bridegroom, is already in love with us. He waits to know if we will love him in return. The Holy Spirit, like a marriage broker, draws us to Jesus, works to put us together and prepares us for greater intimacy with our Lord.

The Holy Spirit has attracted me to Jesus by inner stirrings, by my own need, by God's word, by Jesus's presence on others, by beautiful music and art work, by more books than I can recall and the glories of his creation. Reasonable, objective evidence, like the apologetic works of Josh MacDowell,[139] that clarify who Jesus is and what he has done have added weighty drawing power and convincing truth to my journey.

On entering the courts of the Lord, we transition from unbeliever to believer. Drawn to know more of Jesus, we enter a time of discipleship and follow him more closely to do his bidding and learn his ways. As the Holy Spirit draws us closer to our Lord, our discipleship turns into friendship and family intimacy. The Holy Spirit draws us one step at a time, until we can confidently say,

My beloved is mine and I am his. Song of Solomon 2:16a

To restate it in other words, the Father draws us to Jesus. The Holy Spirit shows us how far we are from God's love and how much we need a relationship with Jesus. He first invites us to give ourselves to God at the cross (prefigured by the brazen altar). The moment that we identify with Jesus's death and receive God's forgiveness for all that has estranged us from his holy love, we are born again or regenerated. God plants a seed of his very own life within us through the power of the Holy Spirit.

After rebirth, our journey toward God accelerates; the Holy Spirit pulls us toward God. We begin to grow inside, to recognize God's goodness, to think his thoughts and feel his feelings. The Holy Spirit takes us into God's word (the laver), and helps us align our thoughts and actions with God's word and character. Cleansed by the water of his word, the Holy Spirit begins to move us into inner court experiences.

As we spend time in the inner court under the light of the Holy Spirit, we learn to discern. We begin to recognize spiritual counterfeits and see the salt and light of God's creative energies in unexpected places.

---

[139] Two of MacDowell's books that answer questions raised by skeptic are *More than a Carpenter* and *Evidence that Demands a Verdict*.

Lately, I've seen God working in a local food truck, a friend turned film director, a sporting goods store, a very secular hospital, a water conditioning business and a professional printer. Growing discernment is only a fraction of the rich spiritual inheritance God begins to download to us as we surrender to the guidance of the Holy Spirit. In the inner court we're nourished by eating the bread of God's word in fellowship with other believers and we build our relationship with God by conversations together at the golden alter of incense. There, the Holy Spirit seals the loving bonds between us and our heavenly Father. Prayer, praise and worship become part of our normal lives—not Sunday-only events.

Choice by choice, our love for Jesus matures. It will never match his love for us, but as our thinking comes into fuller agreement with God's, our spirits grow stronger. We become keenly aware of the vast difference between God's Holy Spirit and our own souls and spirits. We begin to draw away from the spirit of the age. We receive grace to overcome doubt and fear; our motivations and goals change. As we step out in the obedience faith, God gives us resources, strength and power to do his will. Grandiose ideas and vain imaginations fall away. With holy ground under our feet, we love and worship God in Spirit and in truth. As our roots go deeper into God's word and our souls surrender more fully to the Holy Spirit, he works within us to establish the reality of a deepening, trusting moment by moment spirit-to Spirit union with Jesus. It is enough. More than enough.

God knows our hearts and longs to draw all of us into the holiness of loving union with himself, with Jesus and with one another. It's our spiritual birthright. Positionally, all believers are one body and one Spirit in Jesus. How I long for that reality to mature among believers. Have you ever looked at the inspiring unity and disciplined self-less team play of John Wooden's and Morgan Wootten's championship teams on the basketball court, only to feel your heart stabbed with Holy Spirit discontent when brothers and sisters in Christ can't work together and accept their positions on the team? I have. And asked, "Lord, is it me?" Am I the one out of synch? Am I a burr under some brother's or sister's saddle? Help me to love like Jesus did. Search me, Oh Lord."

> *Let the peace of Christ rule in your hearts, for to this you were called as members of one body. Colossians 2:15*

> *So in Christ we who are many are one body, and each member belongs to one another. Romans 12:5*

Our unity with one another grows as we join up more consistently with Jesus. As *we live and move and have our being* in him (Acts 17:28), Jesus's humility in us will rise up within us to put others before ourselves. His compassion will move us to pray for others and care for them as he does. His faith in our hearts will receive the word of God and act upon it. Accepting our union with Jesus and one another is not an impractical, unattainable place. As we yield to the Holy Spirit in the obedience of faith, he begins to heal the wounds of sin (our own and the sins of others against us) that separate us. We must trust our Heavenly Father, Jesus and the Holy Spirit because only they know how to apply the pressures and rewards that will build our relationship with them. Only they know how we need to be loved; only they have the wisdom and capacity to lead us into the resources, situations, relationships and opportunities designed to mature us. Trusting in God's power to fulfill his word we will, we really truly will "grow up into Christ himself."

> *Speaking the truth in love, we will in all things grow up into Christ Himself, who is the head. From Him the whole body, fitted and held together by every supporting ligament, grows and builds itself up in love through the work of each individual part. Ephesians 4:15-16*

This is not pie in the sky someday. It's what God wants for you and me right now. Searching our own hearts and looking at the dissonance between believers, it may take a good fight of faith for those with a half-empty glass to hold onto the truth in God's word and believe that this kind of mature love is possible. Lord, forgive our unbelief and help us stand in your truth. Help us to trust your life within us. Help us to hold onto all that the Holy of Holies prefigures for us. Please open our eyes to see what form that will take.

Unless you show us, we don't even know our rightful places in Jesus's body. We don't know what you've called us to be and do. For some of us, it might mean changing directions and getting in touch with our childhood dreams, for others it might even mean an actual equipping visit to the throne room, one like Isaiah's. We don't know if St. Paul visited the throne room or not, and we don't know if throne room experiences are "in the body or out of it." But Lord, we want to be open to you and to whatever the Holy of Holies might point toward. St. Paul didn't know exactly how he visited heaven. In in discussing visions and revelations from the Lord, he wrote,

> *I know a man in Christ who . . . was caught up to the third heaven. Whether it was in the body or out of it I do not know, but God knows. And I know that this man—whether in the body or out of it I do not know, but God knows—was caught up to Paradise. The things he heard were too sacred for words, things that man is not permitted to tell. 2 Corinthians 12:1-4*

I'm coming to believe that in this season God is calling many of us, if not to literal actual throne room experiences, then surely to the joy of a loving total surrender to God's sovereignty which the throne room represents. Just as God once used Martin Luther to release the truth that we are saved by grace through faith, God is now speaking through many believers to release the truth that we can live in union with Jesus by grace through faith. A relationship with Jesus that once seemed reserved for God's chosen few saints and forerunners is our inheritance. Theresa of Avila writes of how, in our humanness, the innermost room of our heart corresponds to the holy of holies.

The throne on which he sits—a throne of immense value—is your very heart...

> *Do you see the wonderful mystery of it all? —That He, who could fill a thousand worlds and more by His greatness, is so great that he can confine himself in such small space ... that he, being the sovereign Lord, longs to bring us liberty. And that he, whose love for us is so high, has lowered himself to enter our nature.*[140]

As we surrender to God, he enthrones his mercy within our very own hearts. Can you picture Jesus Christ, prefigured by the mercy seat in the holy of holies, enthroned within your heart? (I have to stop writing to do it.) As we yield to who Jesus is and bow before him in awe and love, we pass through the veils from the outer court toward the holy of holies. As the Holy Spirit opens our eyes to see the face of God in Jesus Christ, our awareness of God increases. A reverent and fulfilling God-consciousness begins to replaces all insecurity, self-consciousness and doubt.

> *For God who made the world and everything in it and has made from one blood every nation ... so that they should seek the Lord, in the hope that they might grope for him and find him,*

---

[140] From *The Way of Perfection* by Theresa of Avila, an e-book by Allison Peers, trans. public domain. I first read this in David Hazard's book, *Majestic is Your Name, A 40-Day Journey in the Company of Theresa of Avila*. I love Hazard's series of devotional booklets, *Rekindling the Inner Fire* and recommend them to all.

> *though He is not far from each one of us; for in him we live and move and have our being. Acts 17: 24-28 NKJV*

As we "live and move and have our being" in him, he lives and moves and has his being in us, not theoretically, not positionally, but in loving, present-time authenticity.

> *And we all having been unveiled in face, beholding as in a mirror the glory of the Lord, are being transformed into the same image, from glory to glory, even as from the Lord, the Spirit. 2 Corinthians 3:18 BLB*

When we begin to see more of Jesus, all human pride and pretension unravels before our glimpses of his infinite power and unfailing love. We become thoroughly dissatisfied with our human powerlessness and failures to love. We no longer want to serve him with merely head knowledge and natural abilities. We want to follow him. We want to be vessels for his spirit. We want to abide in him fully, so that his gentle humility and healing compassion, his comfort, wisdom, goodness and power will flow out through us to others. We want his wise discernment and strength to rise up, confront and unswervingly reject evil. We want to recognize deception and overcome it. We begin to understand why Jesus hated merciless hypocrisy and repeatedly upbraided his disciple for their fear.

God's people want others to know Jesus's love. It's the Holy Spirit's yearning within us. We know that we can offer others nothing of eternal value without the Holy Spirit. We realize that all Jesus did was by the power of the Holy Spirit. As we sense our Lord's compassion for the lost and suffering, our dissatisfaction with our own powerlessness increases. We want all our friends, family and neighbors to know the love of Jesus. We hunger to move with Jesus in same obedience of faith and power of the Holy Spirit that moved through him.

I've a fear of the Lord as I write. The words are true, I've tasted them and know them to be sound, but I know myself too. In some ways, I'm writing beyond my experience, but I continue on in faith and hope that others who read these pages will go beyond me.

As God draws us to himself and we purse his love in return, the Holy Spirit begins to transform any white-knuckled determination to obey God into grateful trusting obedience for all he asks. He changes our independent I-can-do-it-myself attitudes into gratitude that we no longer have to go it alone. We can ask for his help and receive his wisdom and love. We can receive his abilities for all he asks us to do. When others speak harshly or shower us with perturbing words, he turns our tongue biting challenges into softer answers that turn away wrath; he teaches us to refuse the hooks of manipulation and intimidation and reject agreement with any plans for us but God's.

Not wanting to quench his love, we seek grace to stop judging others. Forgiveness and the obedience of faith become priorities. We want to guard our hearts from all that quenches God's spirit. We begin to talk to God about our feelings and opinions as soon as we become aware of them. Eventually, seeking God's mind begins to become a habit. We don't want to forfeit Jesus's peace in our hearts by pursuing worldly values, feeding self-pity, nursing wounds and building self-defensive identities that limit his love.

Ahh—big or small, visible or hidden, only what God does in and through us by the Holy Spirit will endure the fires of holy judgment against all hard-hearted prideful refusals to love. Lord, judge us mercifully. I'm so thankful that you look at Jesus, not us.

> *For no one can lay a foundation other than the one already laid, which is Jesus Christ. If anyone builds on this foundation using gold, silver, precious stones, wood, hay, or straw, his*

workmanship will be evident, because the Day will bring it to light. It will be revealed with fire, and the fire will prove the quality of each man's work. . . . 1 Corinthians 3:11-13

The Holy Spirit works within us carefully. Unless we refuse him completely, he gives us many chances. He is a patient teacher. He is not as hard on us as we can be on ourselves. He doesn't set the bar higher than he will help us reach. His lessons and revelations of Jesus are usually uniquely personal, as if tailor-made for us alone. He chooses the wheres, whens, whys and how-to's of opening our eyes to see our Lord. He knows that we could not see the full manifestation of God and live. So, we wait, we trust and we live by faith, knowing that the Holy Spirit will show us all that he chooses to show us, no more. Again and again, we're reminded that in his light alone do we see light.[141] The veil screened the ark, the place of God's unveiled, blinding presence. In Jesus's human body and soul, the veil of his flesh concealed his glory from the crowds. His hiddenness is merciful; it protects us from his judgment.

Until recently, I shrunk from the idea of wanting or asking for more than the Lord had already given me. Then a difficulty came. I needed God's strength and direction. I asked, and he answered. The difficulty intensified. His next answer came in the form of brokenness and repentance. Week after week, I cried and forgave until his peaceful presence followed my tears. I grew to want more of his presence. The difficulty did not resolve, but his peace calmed my troubled feelings and his presence and joy began to fill my days.

During this time, I continued to write about the tabernacle. While reflecting on the tabernacle message God entrusted to Moses and fulfilled in Jesus, I came to see that throughout scripture God entreats his children to ask for more than he's given us. He wants us know him

---

141 *For with You is the fountain of life; in Your light we see light. Psalm 36:9*

more fully and be intentional about seeking him. He wants us to be as intentional about entering the holy of holies by the blood of Jesus as the high priest was with the blood of animals. We must, like the high priest, prepare ourselves and enter humbly, carefully and reverently, with cleansed hands and heart. Human flesh cannot live before the revelation of God's glory. When Moses asked God,

> *"Please show me Your glory." God replied, "I will cause all My goodness to pass before you, . . . and I will proclaim My name—the LORD—in your presence. I will have mercy on whom I have mercy, and I will have compassion on whom I have compassion." But He added, "You cannot see My face, for no one can see Me and live." The Lord continued, "There is a place near Me where you are to stand upon a rock, and when My glory passes by, I will put you in a cleft of the rock and cover you with My hand until I have passed by. Then I will take My hand away, and you will see My back; but My face must not be seen." Exodus 33:18-23*

Lord, help us! We would seek your face and see your glory in the face of Jesus. [142]

---

[142] A friend commented: "Jesus, as we know him through God's word, is the only safe place for us to see God! Jesus, God in human flesh, is the fullest revelation of God's glory that is available to us. God provided Him for us and invites us to come to Him, believe in Him, abide in Him and walk with Him. Jesus alone entered the true, heavenly Holy of Holies, which He did once on our behalf, to offer His innocent, pure, shed blood to the Almighty. To see the Risen and Ascended Christ's face is possible; it happened to St. Paul on the Damascus road (when it blinded him). Almighty God Himself said that no one can look on His face and live. To seek God's face means to seek God's favor, not to look at Him." Kathryn Riss, in an email conversation, 2021.

THE ARK
OF THE COVENANT

The ark, was the only piece of furniture in the holy of holies. It was a small, rectangular box that measured 2 ½ x 1 ½ x 1 ½ cubits. Although most of us could pick it up and carry it ourselves, touching it was sternly forbidden by God. Although God invites us to seek his glory and lets us carry it, it is not ours. God's glory belongs to God alone. Woe to the man or woman who touches God's glory for his or her own purposes, who takes credit for something God has done. God's instructions on who could carry the ark and how they were to do it were exact. The designated priests lifted the ark on permanently-placed, long, gold-covered poles that went through rings on two sides. The poles carrying the ark, the place from which God ruled, rested upon their shoulders. Centuries later, Isaiah prophesied that the government would be upon Jesus's shoulders.

> *For to us a child is born, to us a son is given, and the government will be on his shoulders. And he will be called Wonderful Counselor, Mighty God, Everlasting Father, Prince of Peace. Of the increase of his government and peace there will be no end. Isaiah 9:6-7 NIV*

Worshipping Jesus, our ruler and Lord, meeting him in the place of God's presence between the cherubim is the goal of our tabernacle journey.

Each step brings us closer to all the glory of Jesus that is prefigured by the ark of the covenant and the mercy seat.[143] What does the ark itself tell us about that?

- The ark was a partial revelation of the Godhead. We cannot see Jesus's full manifest glory on earth; we see only earth's half of the manifestation of Father God though His Son.

- The ark, the place of God's authority, symbolized Jesus as our ruling king. By contrast, the altar of incense, as the place of continual prayer, symbolized Jesus who lives to intercede for us. But because prayer and worship belong close together, the altar of incense was placed on one side of the veil and the ark was positioned directly

---

[143] Scripture supports many of comparisons between Jesus and the ark; others, not found explicitly in the Bible suggest biblically sound, devotional truth about God and his Son.

The Ark of the Covenant

opposite, on the other side. [144] When we speak to God with authentic reverence for his holiness, power and love, even our requests become worshipful. On earth, all that the altar of incense and the holy of holies symbolized were perfectly united in Christ Jesus. Because Jesus held (and holds) divine authority as God's incarnate Son on earth, he not only worshipped his Father in heaven, but he himself is worthy of the eternal worship which he now receives in heaven with the Father and the Holy Spirit. God is calling us, individually and together, to find that unity of authority, prayer and worship in Jesus.

- Every other piece of tabernacle furniture (the brazen altar, laver, lampstand, table of showbread, and altar of incense) speaks of Christ's ministry and his work on earth, but the ark of the covenant speaks of heaven. Following his crucifixion, Jesus returned to his Father in Heaven to offer his blood on God's heavenly altar, the true mercy seat in heaven itself.

Our Father in Heaven accepted his Son's offering as the Passover lamb. Thus, the eternal, totally effective and sufficient, atoning, sacrificial blood of Jesus Christ, God's Son, ended the need for earthly blood sacrifice. Jesus's act once and for all established his unshakable place and function as mediator between God and all of mankind. He is our mercy seat.

---

144 The writer of Hebrews, saw the altar of incense behind the veil, in the holy of holies, not outside of it. They may have started out together, or they may, in Heaven, have ended up together. I once heard a pastor assert in a sermon that after Aaron's sons, Nadab and Abihu, offered false fire to God, the altar of incense was moved outside of the veil. But that is speculation. We don't know. *Behind the second curtain was a room called the Most Holy Place, containing the golden altar of incense and the gold-covered ark of the covenant. Inside the ark were the gold jar of manna, Aaron's staff that had budded, and the stone tablets of the covenant. Above the ark were the cherubim of glory, overshadowing the mercy seat. Hebrews 9:3-5* According to Exodus 31:6-9 and Exodus 40, the ark and the altar are on opposite sides of the veil—where most scholars place them today. *Moses placed the gold altar in the Tent of Meeting, in front of the veil, and he burned fragrant incense on it, just as the LORD had commanded him. Exodus 40:26-27*

Jesus, the living word of God, fulfilled every prophetic word that had been symbolically represented by the ark and mercy seat.

> *In the beginning was the Word, and the Word was with God, and the Word was God. . . . In him was life. . . . And the Word became flesh and dwelt among us, and we have seen his glory, glory as of the only Son from the Father, full of grace and truth. John 1:1, 4, 14 ESV*

Jesus's fulfillment of tabernacle prophecy seals the Heavenly wisdom and truth of God's eternal plan. His fulfillment of tabernacle prophecy confirms the holy and ultimate authority of God's word.

> *But when Christ came as high priest of the good things that have come, He went through the greater and more perfect tabernacle that is not made by hands and is not a part of this creation. He did not enter by the blood of goats and calves, but He entered the Most Holy Place once for all by His own blood, thus securing eternal redemption.*
>
> *For if the blood of goats and bulls and the ashes of a heifer sprinkled on those who are ceremonially unclean sanctify them so that their bodies are clean, how much more will the blood of Christ, who through the eternal Spirit offered Himself unblemished to God, purify our consciences from works of death, so that we may serve the living God! Therefore Christ is the mediator of a new covenant, so that those who are called may receive the promised eternal inheritance, now that He has died to redeem them from the transgressions committed under the first covenant. Hebrews 9:11-15*

- The instructions for carrying the ark and the ark's half dimensions might both illustrate the truth that no one but Jesus can touch or carry the full revelation of God's glory.

  For the One whom God has sent speaks the words of God, for God gives the Spirit without limit. The Father loves the Son and has placed all things in His hands. John 3:34-35

- Because our earthly view of Jesus is incomplete, the very existence of the holy of holies is prophetic. God wants us to enter the worshipful glory of heaven's throne room. He wants us to see Jesus, sitting at the right hand of God the Father. He wants to show us his glory.

  But we see Jesus, who was made a little lower than the angels for the suffering of death, crowned with glory and honor, that He by the grace of God should taste death for every man. Hebrews 2:9 NKJV

- The ark of the covenant also pictures the security of abiding IN union with Christ Jesus. Noah and his family were safe in the ark that God told Noah to build. Moses safely met with God IN the Holy Place. IN Jesus, covered by His blood, identified with his death and resurrection, we can safely come before God's throne of grace today. As Paul warned and exhorted the Corinthian believers about sin, he said,

  Test yourselves to see if you are in the faith; examine yourselves! Or do you not recognize this about yourselves, that Jesus Christ is in you—unless indeed you fail the test? 2 Corinthians 13:5

Reflecting on the symbolism of that small box in a little gold-paneled room in a tent built by former slaves over 3,000 years ago lets me know that God has far more for us today than we have seen or imagined. If God didn't want more for me and you, he wouldn't have symbolized that possibility in the tabernacle.

> *Lord Jesus, open the eyes of our heart to see you. Enlighten us to know the hope of Your calling, the riches of Your glorious inheritance in the saints, and the surpassing greatness of Your power to us who believe.*
>
> *And Lord, since God put everything under Your feet and made You head over everything for the church, which is Your body, strengthen us to work together under Your headship, to be the fullness of You—who fills all in all.*
> *Ephesians 1: 18, 19, 22, 23 adapted*

INSIDE THE ARK

If we could lift the lid of the ark and look inside, we'd see three items, the golden pot of manna, Aaron's rod, and the tablets of the law. Each one is another prophetic symbol of Jesus Christ.

THE MANNA

The manna was food given from heaven to the Israelites in the wilderness.

> *In the morning there was a layer of dew around the camp. When the layer of dew had evaporated, there were thin flakes on the desert floor, as fine as frost on the ground. When the Israelites saw it, they asked one another, "What is it?" For they did not know what it was. So Moses told them, "It is the bread that the*

> LORD has given you to eat. . . . Now the house of Israel called the bread manna. It was white like coriander seed and tasted like wafers made with honey. . . . Moses told Aaron, "Take a jar and fill it with an omer [about 2 dry quarts or 2.2 liters] of manna. Then place it before the LORD to be preserved for the generations to come." Exodus 13b-15, 16: 31, 33

The Israelites didn't appreciate the significance of God's provision for them. Eating manna for seven days a week soon became boring; the nutrition sustained them, but they missed the flavor of leeks and onions. Our human appetites can be a gift from God. There's comfort in mashed potatoes and gravy and delight in the yummy taste of butter and honey melting into warm freshly baked bread. On the day I first wrote this paragraph, I had a once-in-a-lifetime gift slice of lasagna with nine layers of tender, melt-in-your-mouth homemade paper-thin pasta and the best combination of sauce, meat and cheese I'd ever tasted. My mouth waters to write about it. I thank God for healthy foods and appreciative taste buds. But when my appetite gets out of control and my physical tastes drive me, they turn into the devil's helpers. Now nothing is wrong with leeks and onions or appreciating God's gift of tasty food. In the 1950's my grandmother sent me a poem she'd cut out from the editorial page of the Chicago Tribune that started, "I know there are onions in heaven. They have such a heavenly smell." The Israelites problem was not in wanting the old familiar flavors. Their sin came in lusting to fulfill their tastes. Their thoughts toward God centered on ingratitude and deprivation rather than on grateful thanksgiving for his provision. So, when they grumbled, complained and whined for other food, God gave it to them. They were gluttonous, and they got sick.

God might treat us the same way if we persist in longing for the tastes of Egypt and grumble and complain about his provisions. More than once, the Lord has given me what I asked for—until I sickened of it. In the first semester of my freshman year at college, I longed for acceptance by particular social clubs. God gave me all I wanted and more. Once initiated into an outwardly glamorous group, I was surprised to find that many obligatory contacts were boring and time-consuming, the group-requirements and social expectations limited my freedom and study-time and the group-values compromised integrity. The heart-conflict was unsettling; I wanted out. Fortunately, God graciously led me out (without losing respect or friends) and inner peace returned. My example may seem a bit far from Jesus being our bread of life, but it's not. Continued association with compromise or unhealthy relationships drains life. And although I wasn't as aware of it at eighteen as I am at eighty, back then, despite my agnostic-getting-educated head, when Jesus had come into my believing twelve-year-old heart, he'd come to stay. He was and is my source of life. If we listen, the Holy Spirit will oppose all appetites that turn us from God. He is our bread of life. Jesus said,

> *I am the living bread that came down from heaven. If anyone eats of this bread, he will live forever; and the bread which I will give is my flesh, which I will give for the life of the world.*
> John 6: 51

Taken literally, that's a hard scripture to swallow. Many of Jesus's followers misunderstood him. The very mention of putting blood into their mouths, forbidden under Kosher law, was intolerably offensive. Those who took his words literally or were offended by his metaphor argued and complained about eating his flesh and stopped following him. They didn't realize how far-removed Jesus was from talking about human life or literal blood. He wasn't suggesting that physical life in our material bodies will exist forever either. He was talking about spiritual realities, about receiving himself as the living word of God. He was looking ahead to the day when believers would find eternal life by receiving his life-giving sacrifice by faith. He was talking about getting to know God and coming to worship God in spirit and truth through his indwelling presence and his word.

> *Now this is eternal life, that they may know You, the only true God, and Jesus Christ, whom You have sent. John 17:3*

Our choices draw us closer to knowing God or turn us away from him. Adam and Eve knew God. Eternal life was theirs until they listened to Satan, mistrusted God's word and disobeyed his command. Satan's temptations did not stop with Adam and Eve or Jesus. God's enemies do not want us to know God's love and receive his glorious eternal life. Our choices matter. We are free to agree with Adam's and Eve's choices in the Garden of Eden or to agree with Jesus's choices throughout his life and death on the cross.

In the Garden of Eden, life was all good. Adam's relationship with God was sure until Satan came along to disrupt the status quo. He deceived Eve and tempted her with the desire to be like God and experience the difference between good and evil. When she and Adam agreed to disobey God, they were cut off from God's presence. Their life was no longer all good. We're their children.

We start out with lives that aren't all good. Our world is imperfect, our capacity to love is imperfect and our relationship with God is not sure. We don't live in the close communion with God that Adam knew in Eden. We live in the curse of separation from God. The only way to reverse the curse of separation from God is by choosing to believe in and identify with Jesus.

Whenever we are tempted to doubt God and disobey his word, we have another choice. We can be like Eve and succumb to seductive lies. Or, we can be like Jesus and reject the tempter's enticements. He chose to trust in God's word. When we choose to trust in God's word, we regain territory that Adam and Eve ceded to Satan by their disobedience. We affirm and establish the relationship with God that Jesus bought for us when he reversed the curse of our separation from God.

Fortunately for us, Jesus went ahead of us to show us how to handle temptations. Hallelujah! And thank goodness! We need his example. Jesus's temptations and responses are significant to us today. Immediately after he was filled with the Holy Spirit, Satan tried to defeat him with the same tactics that worked on Eve. When we've been close to God, and yielded to the Holy Spirit, we too can be vulnerable to temptations. We need to recognize them and be ready with Jesus's strategy to reverse the curse. He overcame every challenge the destroyer threw at him by answering, "It is written" in God's word. Because Jesus showed us how to reject and overcome our temptations today, it's worth the time to look more closely at what happened.

> *[When] Jesus was led by the Spirit into the wilderness to be tempted by the devil. After fasting forty days and forty nights, He was hungry.*
>
> *The tempter came to him and said, "If You are the Son of God, tell these stones to become bread."*
>
> *But Jesus answered, "It is written: 'Man shall not live on bread alone, but on every word that comes from the mouth of God.'*
>
> *Then the devil took him to the holy city and set him on the pinnacle of the temple. "If You are the Son of God," he said, 'throw Yourself down. For it is written: 'He will command His*

angels concerning You, and they will lift You up in their hands, so that You will not strike Your foot against a stone.'

Jesus replied, "It is also written: 'Do not put the Lord your God to the test.'"

Again, the devil took him to a very high mountain and showed him all the kingdoms of the world and their glory. "All this I will give You," he said, "if You will fall down and worship me."

"Away from Me, Satan!" Jesus declared. "For it is written: 'Worship the Lord your God and serve him only.'"

Then the devil left him, and angels came and ministered to him. Matthew 4:1-11

Jesus *was* and *is* the living word of God, but he also *became* the living word of God as he lived it. When we refuse the devil's temptations to serve ourselves, our appetites or the world's riches, power and fame and we choose to live in Jesus's word, we make space for the living word of God to live in us. Lord, help us to remember Jesus's words,

> *"Moses did not give you the bread from heaven, but My Father gives you the true bread from heaven. For the bread of God is He who comes down from heaven and gives life to the world."*
> *Then they said to him, "Lord, give us this bread always."*
> *And Jesus said to them, "I am the bread of life. He who comes to Me shall never hunger, and he who believes in Me shall never thirst. John 6:32-35 NKJV*

Manna represented God's word. We need to feed on God's word, to draw life from Jesus daily. Six days a week, the children of Israel gathered enough manna for one day. If they kept it overnight, it got wormy. On the sixth day, they gathered enough for two days. It did not spoil, but nourished them on the seventh day of rest. Similarly, we can't put our experiences with God into freezer bags, preserve them in boiling water baths or dehydrate them for future use. Fortunately, we can build on our history with God. We can draw close to God by remembering times of his presence and stir up the spirit within us by reading anointed books and listening to and watching recordings of anointed worship and teaching. But we can't live on the right choices we made last week or last year or forty years ago. We must live his word in the choices before us today. Like the Israelites in the wilderness, we need fresh manna from God's living word each and every day.

AARON'S ROD THAT BUDDED

Aaron's rod, the second item in the ark, is a prophetic symbol of Jesus's priestly authority. God's chosen leaders function in his authority; their ideas come from Heaven and, like Joseph, Samuel, David and Daniel, they depend on God and seek his direction. Humbly recognizing and honoring God's authority on his servant-leaders (in every field, not just in the church) is vital. They are God's servants. They follow the Holy Spirit's directions to establish divine order and fulfill his eternal purposes by inviting Jesus into human life. After God had chosen Aaron and the Levites to serve as tabernacle priests, the tribal leaders pridefully and jealously asked, "Why them? Why not us?" They rebelled against God's choice. Moses squelched their insurrection by asking the leader of every tribe to bring him a rod. Eleven rods withered, but Aaron's rod budded, blossomed and bore almonds overnight.[145]

Aaron's rod brought forth almonds, good fruit. God's chosen leaders receive the seeds, nurture and mature the good fruit of God's Holy Spirit in themselves and others.

> *But the fruit of the [Holy] Spirit [the work which His presence within accomplishes] is love, joy (gladness), peace, patience (an even temper, forbearance), kindness, goodness (benevolence), faithfulness, gentleness (meekness, humility), self-control (self-restraint, continence). Against such things there is no law [that can bring a charge]. Galatians 5:22-23 AMP*

They release others into their God-given callings. False leaders, who rule with their own authority and pretend it's from God, use others to establish themselves, stunt growth and hurt their followers. I learned that the hard way.

In the mid 1970's, I was so hungry for more of God that I let myself be drawn into a controlling church. God inhabits the praises of his people and this group knew how to praise. Many members were sincere, persistent God seeking believers. Their praise and worship was wonderful, at times instilled with the glory of God. Their teaching and structure, however, were rooted in the shepherding movement. Its fruit was toxic. Wanting to belong and innocently believing that I was submitting to God, I accepted the criticisms and pressuring and submitted to a controlling leader. He was a wounded man who had assumed authority beyond the gifts God had given him. The leader and his elders directed what music my children should listen to, taught me to call the elders for prayer before consulting a doctor, tried to dictate when and where I

---

145 Numbers 17:1-13

might work, successfully curtailed at least one friendship and expected my attendance at every meeting. Wrenching free from their control was traumatic. My children and I were all wounded. Godly authority is never human domination. God's leaders never intimidate or expect submission to themselves and their agendas. They point others to Jesus. They recognize and respect family and parental authority, governmental authority and other God-ordained spheres of authority beyond their own. They teach, model and encourage healthy, mutual submission to one another and the word of God in holy love.

The significance of Aaron's rod as a symbol of God's choice and a type of Jesus's priesthood, is not to be trifled with. God chooses whom he chooses. Then God supports and protects the men and women of his choice. And when God calls a man or woman into his service, they might start out looking unfit, like a dead stick, but he can equip them to do his work overnight. God's work is accomplished by his Holy Spirit, by his servant's capacity to listen, love and obey him, not by his servant's natural qualifications.

Aaron's rod also foreshadows the authority of God upon Jesus as our great high priest. Priests do not serve themselves, they serve God and others by functioning as mediators between God and his people.

> *[Jesus] is able to save to the uttermost those who draw near to God through him, since he always lives to make intercession for them. Hebrews 7:25 ESV*

As believers following in Jesus's footsteps and obeying his words, Aaron's rod also prophetically pictures us. We are God's own holy and royal priesthood. Being a priest before God, nurturing the good fruit of the Holy Spirit and interceding for others is serious business.

> *But you are a chosen people, a royal priesthood, a holy nation,*
> *a people for God's own possession, to proclaim the virtues of*
> *Him who called you out of darkness into His marvelous light.*
> 1 Peter 2:9

God's supernatural intervention to bring Aaron's rod to life illustrates our birth in Jesus Christ and the powerful authority of God's life over all dormancy and death. All authority is from him.

> *For there is no authority except that which is from God.*
> Romans 13:1

Everything about the budding, flowering, fruit bearing rod pictures God's life-giving power. Jesus died, came back to life and lives forever. He gives new life to all who believe on his name.

THE STONE TABLETS

These were the very tablets God had commanded Moses to chisel out of rock and carry up to the top of Mount Sinai.[146] There, upon the mountain, the Lord told Moses,

> *Write down these words, for in accordance with these words I*
> *have made a covenant with you and with Israel." He wrote on*
> *the tablets the words of the covenant—the Ten Commandments.*
> Exodus 34: 27-28

Jesus Christ fulfilled every word that Moses chiseled in stone and placed within the ark. He brought life to God's words. In holy love, he embodied the full intent behind God's moral code. He was no legalist. In

---

146 See Appendix, entry on The Stone Tablets

fulfilling God's law, he transformed our understanding of it. He changed it from a list of dos and don'ts into a window revealing God's plan for a loving community. He made impossible standards possible by his dependance on the Holy Spirit. And then he died, to give the Holy Spirit to you and me.

Jesus was the antithesis of lawlessness. He honored his mother and father and he accepted and submitted to the laws of Caesar. Yet he also drew lines between illegitimate, spurious authority and legitimate God given authority. In obedience to his Father in Heaven he recognized true authority and established the primacy of God's law of love. Not once did he compromise God's order or his own complete, untarnished, constant holy love for his Father in heaven and for others. He did this by the same grace through faith that is available to us today. Doing only what he saw his Father doing, Jesus fulfilled every detail the prophets had foretold of his life and atoning death. He knew it, and quite plainly said,

> *Do not think that I have come to abolish the Law or the Prophets. I have not come to abolish them, but to about fulfill them. Matthew 5:17*

John, Jesus's beloved disciple, said the same thing.

> *And the Word became flesh and dwelt among us,*
>   *and we beheld His glory,*
> *the glory as of the only begotten of the Father,*
>   *full of grace and truth. John 1: 14*

For two thousand years, God's words, engraved upon those two stone tablets hidden within the ark, had taught Abraham's children God's high standards for healthy happy life on earth. These commandments from God also taught the Israelites that try as they might, no one could live up to them perfectly. Until Jesus. How did he do it? By surrendering to the Holy Spirit. The same Holy Spirit that indwells believers today had engraved every word, with every ramification and shade of meaning, upon his totally human heart. When I pause again to ask him, "How did you do it?" A voice in my heart answers, "It wasn't easy." And I remember Luke's description of Jesus's agony in Gethsemane. His sweat came like drops of blood falling to the ground[147] as he asked the Father, "Not My will, but yours be done" and bent his entire body and soul into agreement with the Holy Spirit.

---

147 Luke 22:44

I can't say it often enough, we can't keep God's law. It's impossible for us. But, by the power of the Holy Spirit, Jesus did it. In yielding to the Holy Spirit, Jesus completely fulfilled the intent of the law that is summed up in God's command to love him and others. When we believe in Jesus and yield to the Holy Spirit, God changes the stone-hard tablets of our hearts and fulfills his word.

I will give you a new heart and put a new spirit within you; I will remove your heart of stone [that is hard, unforgiving, legalistic and unable to accept God's love] and give you a heart of flesh [that is tender, open, forgiving and able to give and receive love]. Ezekiel 36:26

Oh Lord, write your law upon our hearts. Give us the joy of obedience that Jesus personified. Deliver us from pride. Give us tender hearts. Forgive every bit of hardness and self-justification that refuses to love others as you have loved us. Do the impossible in us. By faith may we live in union with you. Help us follow you. Bring your words to life in us.

The reality of union with God through Christ Jesus is astounding. By grace through faith, Jesus lives in us. As soon we say "Yes" to the Holy Spirit, he awakens us to God's heart of love. He helps us forgive with Jesus's mercy. He gives us Jesus's compassion. Not just for our own dear friends and family, but for God's family. In the ultimate test of love, the Holy Spirit helps us forgive and love our enemies, those who hurt us and cause pain. Our heavenly Father longs to give each one of us all the love that he designed us to contain, the very same love that fills the Godhead and sustains the world.

Lord, help us receive your law of love. Deliver us from fear, unbelief, and pride. Keep on tenderizing our defensive hardness and teach us your love. Strengthen us to oppose evil and deception; support us to stand steadfast in our trust of you. Thank you for giving the death-blow to our inborn rebelliousness at the cross. Help us surrender any lingering threads of willful fleshly pride to your love. Straighten our motives into agreement with your own righteousness. Establish us in you. Give us beauty and truth for ugliness and lies, hope for despair, peace for every anxiety and joy for our sorrows.

How can we not praise God for his goodness and mercy? And to think—all of these riches from God were hidden in the symbolism of the tabernacle in the wilderness.

The entire earth-history-purpose of God, as so clearly expressed in the book of Deuteronomy, where Moses recorded all the practical details of God's commands and ordinances, is to establish a community, a kingdom of love. God is after a people who will love and honor him as their Creator, a family who will learn to live together in ways that honor one another. He wants sons and daughters who will share his loving, truthful ways with people who live in violence, poverty, fear, contentions and the compulsions of unfulfilled desire. He wants sons and daughters who will follow the Holy Spirit as he works to oppose and overcome depression, indifference, anxiety, pride, greed, lust, cruelty, irresponsibility, entitlement, and deception. He wants a Bride who will be a helpmeet and partner for his only begotten Son.

God continues to work to that end. And, as in the past, his work often continues to be hidden. The ark was hidden behind a veil, the stone tablets were once concealed in the ark and the glory of God in Jesus was hidden from Herod, the high priests and the Pharisees. Throughout history God has veiled many powerful movements of his Holy Spirit from unbelieving eyes.

In recent decades, millions of men, women and children around the globe have come to know Jesus Christ as their Lord and Savior—but it's not reported on the world news. God is Spirit, and God's work must be spiritually discerned. Solomon wrote,

It is the glory of God to conceal a matter. Proverbs 25:2

Over fifty years ago I first read about God's hiddenness in a short quotation from Coventry Patmore. His words awakened a longing to know God's motivations for myself. In describing sanctity, Patmore wrote,

You may live in the same house with him and never find out. . . . He will give you an agreeable impression of his general inferiority to yourself. I once asked a person to tell me the real difference. The reply was that the saint does everything that any decent person does, only somewhat better and with a totally different motive.[148]

God's simplicity and grace, shining in Jesus's servanthood, hidden from worldly eyes, often seen in the ordinary, commonplace and menial, is true sanctity. Authentic holiness may be hidden, but its humility can't be faked. Though naturally appealing, its true source must be spiritually discerned. The Holy Spirit rules the motives, minds and emotions of God's children. They bow to Jesus. They know that he alone is worthy. They've learned that all attempts to live life by our own human intellects and drives, by applying our own thinking and feeling to God's word will eventually fall apart, lifeless, before the face of Jesus. Without the Holy Spirit given by Jesus, human misunderstandings of God's word have led

---

[148] This quotation from Coventry Patmore is most likely from the *Rod, the Root and the Flower*. It's now in the public domain and can be found on many webpage sites of well-known quotations. I read it first in *On Beginning from Within* © 1943, 1955, 1964 by Douglas V. Steere, Harper and Row

to legalism, to church schisms, spiritual abuse, extreme cruelties and violence and all kinds of error.[149] As Paul reminded us,

> *The natural man does not accept the things that come from the Spirit of God. For they are foolishness to him, and he cannot understand them, because they are spiritually discerned.*
> *1 Corinthians 2: 14*

Unfortunately, the natural man can be zealously religious. A friend who read this pointed out that "basically, the carnal nature is at enmity with the incredibly gracious, generous and non-discriminatory love of God. Satan works to steer faith into extremes so he can divert God's people into doing his own dirty work of hatred, division, strife and pride. He hides sin behind a religious mask. That is why considering the whole counsel of Scripture is so vitally important to balance out and restrain super-spirituality." [150]

God judges our carnality, the misuse and excesses of flesh and soul that would control us and us and others. He celebrates our natural humanity and says that our bodies our good. Reflecting on Jesus's example, as God in human flesh, he accepted his body, took care of it and ruled over himself. He slept when he was tired and ate when he was hungry. He liked a good meal and good wine. He knew how to fry

---

[149] The errors of culturally compromised Christians and Christian legalism have contributed to the Holocaust, witch-burnings, the Inquisition, the Crusades, the torture and forced conversions of Jews and others as well as to the extermination of Indians, cruel punishments for children, the abuse of labor, women and non-Christians, slavery, refusing medical treatment and pain-killers in childbirth and more. Without humility, grace and compassion, religious legalism brings out the worst in people because it seems to justify their sinful treatment of other human beings made in God's image. Jesus clearly said, *Not everyone who says to Me, "Lord, Lord,' will enter the kingdom of heaven, but only he who does the will of My Father in heaven. Many will say to Me on that day, 'Lord, Lord, did we not prophesy in Your name, and in Your name drive out demons and perform many miracles?'" Then I will tell them plainly, "I never knew you; depart from Me, you workers of lawlessness!" Matthew 7:21-23*

[150] Kathryn Riss, email, November 2021.

fish and wash people's dirty feet. He was a man's man—a carpenter capable of walking many, many miles. Yet he clearly had affectionate friendships with women, friendships of honor and respect that were built to last without shame through all eternity. He must have appreciated fragrant oils, or he would have stopped the women who anointed him with nard. He is our mediator. He does not use us or misuse us to satisfy his own needs. Those who know him best are generally filled with great joy and peace. In union with him, the living law, the living word of God comes alive in God's children with holy love—for God, themselves and others.

The emulsified mix of our humanness and God's mercy, righteousness and justice is possible in Jesus alone. Without Jesus's fresh and caring liveliness as the living Word, our own understanding of grace, love and mercy can easily turn to looseness and excess, to the cheap grace of sentiment, with its unprincipled lack of restraint and its people-pleasing compromise. Or, on the other side, our understanding of God's laws can turn to sour, condemning, pride-filled, binding legalism. When Jesus told the woman caught in adultery, *"Now go and sin no more,"*[151] she knew, from the powerful authority of his love, that Jesus wasn't condemning her. He wasn't pitying her either. And he wasn't compromising God's standards. He was cleansing and freeing her, standing her on her feet for a future of responsible righteousness and relationship with God and others.

Jesus reconciles us to God. The impossible-to-keep-perfectly ten commandments that were concealed under the mercy seat in the ark judge us by our failures. Because of Jesus's blood on the mercy seat, God forgives us for every failure. In the power of the Holy Spirit we can, by faith, access Jesus's capacity to keep God's law of love—not in our own strength, but by trusting him.

---

151   John 8:11

God's mercy, kindness and justice living *in us and through us* become his mercy, kindness and justice *to* us. We need that *in* us for others and *to* us for ourselves. Circumstances that challenge believers to live out the qualities of love can be divine set-ups to drive us to Jesus.

> *Love is patient, love is kind. It does not envy, it does not boast, it is not proud. It is not rude, it is not self-seeking, it is not easily angered, it keeps no account of wrongs. Love takes no pleasure in evil, but rejoices in the truth. It bears all things, believes all things, hopes all things, endures all things. 1 Corinthians 13:4-7*

At several times in my life I've been stunned into shock by confrontations with bullying behavior and demands. I recall one occasion when I withdrew, not knowing how to respond to an attack based on lies. I didn't know God's heart. The initial attack fit the biblical description of wickedness and evil. God doesn't agree with that. But I didn't know my attacker's heart or motives. I only knew our history and what happened. Would God's command to love my enemies mean to go the second mile and meet unfair, ungodly demands? Or would God's directions to discern and flee from evil lead to refusing all agreement with lies, intimidation and slander? I didn't know which of my responses might bring healing and stability, which might feed ongoing demands and entitlement, or if making the wrong choice might enable my attacker to make dangerous life-threatening choices. It was a conundrum. I knew the contention was not Godly and the battle was not mine or any person's. It was between God and Satan.

Only the Holy Spirit, who searches the hearts of all people, knows the depths of anyone's heart. In Jesus alone can mercy and justice be met—and that only by the power of the Holy Spirit. Love endures long, but at times we don't know if it's love for our enemies or love for God that is "enduring-long." Rather than get self-righteous, self-protective and defensive, we can get serious with God, repent of lovelessness and ask God to give us a First Corinthians 13 heart of love. That's how believers live, always needing God's discernment and strength to lovingly stand up and speak truth to destructive lies, like Jesus stood up to the Pharisees. And always needing and depending on God's forgiveness, humility, wisdom, love, mercy and justice—for ourselves and others.

If God released all the power of love and truth inherent in his word, we'd cry out for mercy. If God released all the power of judgment that's inherent in his word without his longsuffering lovingkindness, we'd cry out for mercy too. It would terrorize all who were not right with him. We'd be judged by his very holiness. One day that will happen. Every idol will fall.

When the Philistines took the ark from Israel

> God struck down some of the people of Beth-shemesh because they looked inside the ark of the LORD. He struck down seventy men, and the people mourned because the LORD had struck them with a great slaughter. 1 Samuel 6:19

Satan knows the holy power of a life lived in God's word.[152] That's why he didn't want Jesus to fulfill it. He tried to stop him. That's what Jesus's temptations in the wilderness were all about. Satan tried to persuade Jesus to disobey God's word (symbolized by the stone tablets), and misuse his authority (Aaron's rod), and to make bread (manna) to feed his physical hunger. Satan wanted to steal the contents of the ark from Jesus. But they were safe in the ark of his person.

---

[152] Reinhard Bonnke's life is one of the strongest examples of a life lived in God's word I can think of. To get a taste of the power, check out this video of Reinhard Bonnke's, *The Last Words* at https://www.youtube.com/watch?v=8ddhHJn9Lz8

Immediately after the Holy Spirit baptized Jesus with power, Jesus was led into the wilderness where Satan tempted him to deny God's word. Jesus quoted God's word to refuse and refute each of Satan's temptations. Defeated, Satan left Jesus. Immediately, the Holy Spirit led Jesus into his public ministry. In the authority of the Holy Spirit, Jesus revealed God's powerful love to those with eyes to see and ears to hear.

If we want to abide in Jesus and in union with him learn to see what our Father in Heaven is doing so that we can follow the Holy Spirit's plans, we too must overcome every temptation to doubt or deny God's word. As we yield to the Holy Spirit, live in Jesus and trust in God's word, it comes alive in us with authority, faith and love. The Holy will use us to reveal Jesus and convey God's good news that Jesus did not come to condemn the world but to save it.

> *In the past, God spoke to our forefathers through the prophets at many times and in various ways, but in these last days has spoken to us by His Son, whom he appointed heir of all things and through whom he made the universe. The Son is the radiance of God's glory and the exact representation of his being. Hebrews 1: 1-3a NIV*

> *For God so loved the world that He gave His one and only Son, that everyone who believes in him shall not perish but have eternal life. For God did not send His Son into the world to condemn the world, but to save the world through him. John 3:16-17*

THE TABERNACLE

THE MERCY SEAT

And I will meet with you there above the mercy seat, between the two cherubim that are over the Ark of the Testimony; I will commune with you about all that I command you regarding the Israelites. Exodus 25:22

JESUS IS GOD'S MERCY TO US

Jesus is our mercy seat. In Greek, the word for mercy seat is *hilasterion*. It's translated into English as *propitiation*, but the actual meaning is *mercy seat*. The mercy seat, sprinkled and consecrated with blood, covered the ark that held the stone tablets with the law, the manna, and Aarons's rod that budded. God told Moses,

> *And you are to construct a mercy seat of pure gold, two and a half cubits long and a cubit and a half wide. Make two cherubim of hammered gold at the ends of the mercy seat, one cherub on one end and one on the other, all made from one piece of gold. And the cherubim are to have wings that spread upward, overshadowing the mercy seat. The cherubim are to face each other, looking toward the mercy seat. Set the mercy seat atop the ark, and put the Testimony that I will give you into the ark. And I will meet with you there above the mercy seat, between the two cherubim that are over the ark of the Testimony; I will speak with you about all that I command you regarding the Israelites. Exodus 25: 17-22*

Historically, the mercy seat was the literal seat of sovereign power from which God ruled. It was his only earthly throne. Scripture after scripture testify that he is enthroned above the cherubim.[153]

> *The LORD reigns; let the nations tremble! He is enthroned above the cherubim; Psalm 99:1*

As we surrender before Jesus Christ at the mercy seat, we recognize him as Lord. In mercy, he takes us into union with himself and gives us his total love for our Father. At the cross, Jesus was savior; it's where he took our sin. At the mercy seat, Jesus rules. The mercy seat represents his legal transaction with God on our behalf. It is a prophetic symbol of his fully established, completed atonement for sin. Holiness rules there. At the mercy seat, God's justice is satisfied and reconciled with his merciful loving kindness.

> *Mercy and truth have met together; Righteousness and peace have kissed. Psalm 85:10 NKJV*

---

[153] See also, 1 Samuel 4:4; 2 Samul 6:1-2; 2 Kings 19:14-16, 19; Psalm 80:1-2

Hanging on the cross, when Jesus cried out "It is finished!" God's legal requirement, the death penalty for sin, was fully satisfied, settled and fulfilled. His death met God's governmental requirements.[154] His sacrifice as the Passover lamb who took away the sins of the world opened the way for sinners to regain the intimate unsullied relationship of dependence upon God that Adam willfully lost by asserting his human independence. Scripture says that before the beginning of Jesus's ministry, before his baptism,

> *John [the Baptist] saw Jesus coming toward him, and said, "Behold! The Lamb of God who takes away the sin of the world! John 1:29 NKJV*

It is no coincidence that God's mercy seat is between the cherubim or that it foreshadows the dwelling place of God's mercy within our own hearts. When God

> *drove the man out. . . of the garden of Eden He stationed the cherubim, and the flaming sword which turned every direction, to guard the way to the tree of life. Genesis 3:24 (adapted)*

Jesus is the way to the tree of life. When we abide in him, the flaming cherubim no longer block our return to communion with our Father in heaven. They lift open their golden wings to allow us into his presence. The glory that once filled the tabernacle and caused Moses's face to shine, shines upon us.

---

154 The concept of propitiation, how Jesus's death conciliated God's judgment with His mercy, is illustrated in *The Lion, the Witch and the Wardrobe*, a fantasy by C. S. Lewis based on biblical themes and principles. In Lewis's story, Aslan, a Christ figure, dies to free Edmond from the claims of an evil witch. Lewis's story makes propitiation real and understandable.

> *Do you not know that you yourselves are God's temple, and that God's Spirit dwells in you? If anyone destroys God's temple, God will destroy him; for God's temple is holy, and you are that temple. 1 Corinthians 3:16-17*

Amazingly, with God's Spirit in us, as we come before his mercy seat, he places his mercy seat within us. Mercy is an attribute of his kingdom, and as Jesus said,

> *"The kingdom of God [the place of his rule] does not come with observation; nor will they say, 'See here!' or 'See there!' For indeed, the kingdom of God is within you."*
> *Luke 17:20b-21 NKJV*

Like the song, "I love to tell the story . . . of Jesus and his love." I never tire of it. The truth of our redemption is always new. Wonder and gratitude for the glorious mystery of forgiveness and union with God through Jesus Christ never wear out.

    I keep repeating myself, not only because this book began as a tool for teaching and good teachers repeat themselves, but also because it's impossible to fully grasp the amazing grace of Jesus's love. He willingly gave his life for us and agreed with the Father's plan to be our substitute. When we identify with his death and accept that his blood atones for our sins, we exchange our sin nature for his holy nature and rise to new lives in Christ Jesus. At the cross, Jesus took the death-penalty for every thought, word and deed that once separated us from our holy Father. On our confession of faith in Jesus's death for us, God accepts his Son's sacrifice on our behalf and forgives us for falling short of his perfect love. As soon as we identify with Jesus's death and receive his resurrection-life, we enter into new lives of holy love. We can draw near to God as his own dearly beloved children, as sons and daughters of his very own Spirit, with every right to approach our heavenly Father's throne.

Our salvation is a two-way transaction with God. If we're willing, God gives us grace to receive Jesus's loving sacrifice for us. It takes our recognition of need, our repentance from sin, our faith-confession [155] and our acceptance of the blood of Jesus before God's legal requirements for justice are satisfied. As soon as we do our part, he freely, gladly and justly releases his mercy. We receive Jesus, the Holy Spirit and the riches of his glory by faith. Hallelujah! Yes! I love to tell the story.

> *For by grace you have been saved through faith; and that not of yourselves, it is the gift of God; Ephesians 2:8 NASB*

By faith in Jesus, mercy and justice are reconciled. [156] All because Jesus took the penalty of death for our sins.

> *For all have sinned and fall short of the glory of God, and are justified freely by His grace through the redemption that is in Christ Jesus. God presented him as the atoning sacrifice through faith in His blood . . . so as to be just and to justify the one who has faith in Jesus.* [157] *Romans 3:23-26*

---

155 See Appendix entry on Faith

156 The realm of faith challenges the 21st century world view of immanence. Our minds need rewiring to accept spiritual realities as actually real. The realm of faith can be powerful, whether invoked by a witchdoctor, a Harry Potter devotee or an adherent of occult religions. If you doubt me, I suggest checking out Larry Dossey's research *In Be Careful What You Pray*, Harper Collins, 1997. Dossey surveys both scientific evidence for faith and the effects of curses, sorcery, and prayer in world religions.

157 God's mercy is prefigured here in the exodus from Egypt. On the night the death angel took the first born of all the Egyptians, the Israelites were instructed to kill a lamb and place its blood on the lintels of their doors. God said, *When I see the blood, I will pass over you.* Exodus 12:13

If you've read this far without taking your questions to God or talking with him about any uneasy ping or two troubling your conscience, or if a corner of your heart is still hardened about a person or situation, now is a good time to get down to business with God. If you want more of his love, it's time to ask for it. If there's an old wound from darkness or a hidden place in your heart you've guarded from yourself and the Lord, now is the time to invite his probing mercy and his healing and delivering love. Now is the time to experience more of his grace, mercy and truth. It's never too late to find out for yourself what propitiation means to you. Stop reading and start talking to God. Talk with him all about it. Ask him for his faith. Ask him for his Holy Spirit. Take however long you need—not to delay, but to receive his answers and his help to become wholehearted in your response to him. He is the propitiation for all sin.

Are you ready to read on? If so, here, once again, in summary, is how the ark of the covenant illustrates propitiation. The animals sacrificed and offered for sin on the brazen altar foreshadowed Jesus's death—his broken body and shed blood on the cross in atonement for human sin. Once each year, on the Day of Atonement, the priest carried the sacrificial blood from the brazen altar into the holy of holies and presented it to God by sprinkling it once on the mercy seat and seven times on the ground. This sacrificial blood covered every transgression of the law. By faith, it appeased, placated, satisfied, and made peace between us and God.

After his death, Jesus carried his blood into the throne room of heaven and offered it to his Father.

> *He did not enter by means of the blood of goats and calves; but he entered the Most Holy Place once for all by His own blood, thus obtaining eternal redemption. Hebrews 9:12 NIV*

Jesus's offering ended the need for blood sacrifice that began when God killed an animal to cover Adam's naked body. God confirmed the need for blood sacrifice on the eve of the first Passover when he instructed the Israelites put the lamb's blood on the lintels of the doorposts of their homes as a protection from death. God said,

> *When I see the blood, I will pass over you. Exodus 12:13 NKJV*

When Jesus offered his sinless life on the cross, he established everlasting peace between God and all who accept Jesus's sacrifice on their behalf. When we, by faith, apply the blood of Jesus to our hearts, God's mercifully covers our nakedness, the automatic exposure of our sin before his holiness. In mercy, he delivers us from death.

Out of every place on earth where God might have placed his throne, his place of earthly governmental authority, he chose to rule from directly above the mercy seat in a tiny cubicle, inside a little tent, among the children of Israel. Our Creator, the Lord of all the universe and more, identified most closely with the place one earth that he had directed to prefigure the mercy flowing out to mankind from the blood sacrifice of Jesus, on the cross when his only begotten Son called out,

> *"Father forgive them, for they know not what they do!"*
> Luke 23:34 ESV

No wonder that the mercy seat is of acacia wood covered with gold—Jesus's humanness and ours, covered over with the glory of God.

Writing about the mercy seat as the place God chose for his throne, the place of his manifest presence, I sense the Holy Spirit wordlessly warning me, reminding me that many of us raised in western civilization will naturally tend to see the path from the outer court to worship in the glory of the mercy seat as a step-by-step pilgrimage. This book even suggests that. Our thinking is linear. But God is not exclusively linear. He is multi-dimensional, creative, emotional and relational. Our thinking, speaking and writing are limited by sequential, time-bound language. But God chooses to speak to us through dreams, visions, parables, poetry, metaphors, symbols, visual art, music, types and shadows. The progressive revelation of his redemptive plan may be sequential through historical time, but our personal journeys to find the straight-way and narrow gate into his heart may outwardly seem to move through time in rather erratic patterns. We may be spiritually mature in one area of our character and struggle in another. We can be well-balanced and gifted in one place and desperately need the counsel of brothers and sisters in Christ to fill in our blind spots, prop us up and encourage us other areas. Growing up in Christ, journeying from being an unbeliever outside of the community of faith to being a mature disciple who is joined to brothers and sisters in profitable love, isn't always a straight path. At times, when the Lord is healing old wounds or teaching new truth, we can logically and objectively, feel detoured. We might feel lost, like we're backtracking and crisscrossing our own path many times. But constants remain. We do not travel alone. The Lord will go ahead of us. He is with us. His love will never fail us. And every place in our journey toward knowing God is reached by faith.

Although God-events, in history as well as in our own hearts and souls, may seem to hop and skip around from mountain top to mountain top. The truth is that

> *In him and through faith in him we may enter God's presence with boldness and confidence. Ephesians 3:12*

There is not any prescribed cookie-cutter method or step by step climb to reach any exclusive, elite, higher, esoteric position with God. The only way up (to be closer to Jesus) is by bowing down, into greater humility and servanthood. God's presence is not assured for people like me who write about it. His Spirit might quickly visit a new believer with an intimacy or glory that eludes others who have logged in years of seeking and long hours of prayer. At times, especially during revivals and awakenings, men and women who are living in wretched sin may see life-changing revelations of God as he sovereignly pulls them out of darkness, cleans them up and establishes them in new lives under his holy light. But those who plug away, growing slowly year in and year out, always wanting more of Jesus, also experience the living truth of Peter's words that

> *His divine power has given us everything we need for life and godliness through the knowledge of Him who called us by His own glory and excellence. Through these He has given us His precious and magnificent promises, so that through them you may become partakers of the divine nature, now that you have escaped the corruption in the world caused by evil desires. [One step at a time,] make every effort to add to your faith virtue; and to virtue, knowledge; and to knowledge, self-control; and to self-control, perseverance; and to perseverance, godliness; and to godliness, brotherly kindness; and to brotherly kindness, love. For if you possess these qualities and continue to grow in them, they will keep you from being ineffective and unproductive in your knowledge of our Lord Jesus Christ.*
> *2 Peter 1:3-8*

To be fruitful in the knowledge of our Lord takes our cooperation. We must follow the Holy Spirit's lead to clean up our act, our mind, our heart. We keep clean and keep our relationship with Jesus alive by faith in his promises. Getting close to God is for those who simply receive his mercy, accept him in faith and obey his word. They make every effort to add to their faith the character of the fruit of the spirit that grows in love. It is these, the child-like,[158] trusting, humble, broken ones, forgiven and cleansed by the blood of Jesus who do exploits in his name. [159]

RECOGNIZING AND RECEIVING GOD'S MERCY

God is merciful. By amazing grace, we all experience his merciful loving-kindness long before we may know anything about it or recognize it for what it is. The sunrise and sunset are signs of God's mercy. When we describe God by saying "God *is* love" not "God *has* love" or "God is loving", we are saying that *God is merciful loving-kindness.*[160]

---

[158] About forty years ago, during his years of itinerant preaching, I heard Judson Cornwall speak of looking out over a congregation he'd never visited and asking the Lord, "Who is closest to you? Who loves you the most?" The Lord immediately pointed out a little girl about eight years old. Surprised, he asked, "How could that be?" The Lord answered, "She believes. She lives and does everything she knows about me." Most likely, that child intuitively understood God's mercy long before she understood the word *mercy*.

[159] I was challenged and changed by reading the autobiography of Reinhard Bonnke, *Living a Life of Fire* by Reinhard Bonnke, © by Harvester Services, 2010. He trusted God and obeyed. His love changed men and nations.

[160] The other day at a prayer meeting I heard someone say, "God is love, but love is not God." A good reminder.

It's who he is. But, for some of us, mercy is hard to recognize.[161] It's abstract, metaphysical, an attribute of God that's not a recognized reality in our lives.

When I was a girl, Jesus lived in my heart, but my mind was unconverted. My thinking and feelings weren't integrated. My spiritual experience was inconsistent with my culture-bound soul. My brain did not recognize or understand God's mercy to me.[162]

It is difficult for our western minds to understand that God's unity is complete. All God is and all he does—his being and doing—are a unified

---

161 Those of us who grew up with legalism, abuse or neglect may struggle to see and accept God's grace and merciful loving-kindness. A learned hardness can settle into our hearts; our thinking gets in the way. Mine did. I grew up with a legalistic god who rewarded deserving children who justified their existence by pleasing the adults in their lives. Favor was earned and rule-breaking, like being late without a very good reason was not acceptable. No exceptions—that is, no mercy.

Our culture also hinders understanding God's mercy. Education in a materialistic, relativistic post-Christian era derides the truth of an all-moral, all-powerful, all merciful loving Creator-Father-God. His truth is dismissed as mythical, dreamlike or irrelevant. Without God's high standards, the need for mercy evaporates. Our consciences are seared by consumeristic values and repeated media exposure to more violence, sin, turmoil and pain than our nervous systems are built to handle. It's natural to ask, "How could a merciful God allow such tragedy, fraud and pain?" Such honest questions are not easily unanswered by Christian leaders who focus on psychology, church growth strategy or denominational dogma. It takes brokenness and getting out of God's way to preach and teach his word with Holy Spirit power. It takes faith and love to trust God through the hard unanswerable questions about human tragedy. Only the Holy Spirit can bring real life into Bible truths about God's laws with mercy and loving kindness. Lord, give us teachers with love strong enough and prayer lively enough to bring your word to life. Legalists who are untouched by God's powerful love as well as moralists and well-meaning believers who accept the letter of the law without the power of the Holy Spirit and God's mercy are poor examples of the unswervingly high standards of God's holy, righteous ways, of the depths of his merciful lovingkindness and of Jesus's ability to help us meet his Father's standards. Father, thank you for the exceptions. Thank you, Father, for the courageous saints who call sin for what it is—not with condemnation or the cheap grace of compromise, but with compassionate love and truth that imparts hope to the hopeless and power to set sin's prisoners free from meaninglessness and darkly confusing compulsions. Lord, raise up more men and women to bring your holiness and tender healing mercies to a hard-hearted world.

162 It's an imperfect illustration, but I once read about an agnostic scientist who believed all truth was relative, denied the reality of faith and asserted that feelings, intuitions, imaginations and spiritual experiences were all chemical. But he loved his wife and children and could not live out his materialistic atheism at home. The principles and values of love that he allowed in his spirit, the feelings he felt when his children climbed into his lap, and the values he practiced and taught with his family were inconsistent with his principles and values as a scientist. He honestly acknowledged his dilemma and compartmentalized his inconsistencies. That was his world.

whole that can't be divided or taken apart. God does not compartmentalize anything. In perfect integrity, he is what he does and he does what he is. All he does is to his glory and is his glory. In a similar way, God is love and mercy in every act—even in judgments. I began to pick up this truth in the late 1970's by ideas in *What the Bible Teaches about Mercy* by Rex B. Andrews. He writes,[163]

> *"All the paths of the LORD are MERCY and truth to such as keep His covenant and His testimonies." Psalm 25:10 NKJV*

> *"Without it [mercy] there simply IS NO WORD OF GOD TO MAN. . . . Without the word mercy-lovingkindness the Bible is a dead book, . . . [with] no revelation of God at all. . . . Take the word mercy-lovingkindness out of the Bible and there is no Bible, no salvation, no Savior, no kingdom of God, no eternal life—nothing. . . . [mercy is] . . . the outworking of the true love of God."*

> *"MERCY is God's supply system for every need everywhere. Mercy is that kindness, compassion and tenderness which is a passion to suffer with, or participate in, another's ill or evils in order to relieve, heal and restore. It accepts another freely and gladly AS he is and supplies the needed good of life to build up and to bring to peace and keep in peace. It is to take another into one's heart JUST AS HE IS and cherish and nourish him there. Mercy takes another's sins and evils and faults as its own, and frees the other by bearing them to God. . . ."*

---

[163] I've retained Andrew's capitalization and typography to capture the feeling of his helpful thoughts about mercy.

That's objective truth. I love it and never tire of rereading Andrew's words. In my subjective experiences, mercy is a quiet, warm place of faith that settles within my heart when I'm connectively yielded to God. All our self-magnifying, self-justifying, self-protective, defensive, posturing attempts to take control will drive mercy away. But a humble acceptance and rest in God's mercy will drive away our inbred sins of self. Maybe that's because mercy is a manifestation or expression of Jesus's life within us. In this place of mercy, his compassion rules. We extend to others what God has given to us. While it can be grace-filled to take a strong stand against wickedness, we need the Holy Spirit to uphold God's standards without judging or condemning those who fall short. This battle between God's righteousness and mercy and human hatred of judgmentalism and compromising tolerance of sin permeates our culture in cliches like "hate the sin and love the sinner", "there for the grace of God go I" and "people who live in glass houses shouldn't throw stones." There's an experiential knowing in the human soul that God alone is judge. The closer believers get to God, the swifter his judgments. If I overstep my bounds and judge others, and I have, God judges me. Sometimes slowly, often instantly, by withdrawing the sense of his presence, the sweetness of experiencing his mercy. Jesus's words automatically come true:

> *Do not judge, or you will be judged. For with the same judgment you pronounce, you will be judged; and with the measure you use, it will be measured to you. Matthew 7:1-2*

His judgments aren't always harsh. They're to teach us, sometimes humorously. Back in the 1980's, I judged a local pastor and Bible school teacher whose wife for some obscure reason gave him a home permanent. His hair turned red from the solution. I questioned his faith and felt repelled by his auburn locks. At that time, I had never color rinsed my hair or wanted to, but not long after that, I felt curiously compelled to try a washable rinse of color highlights on my graying head. You got it. My hair turned many shades brighter red than his ever did. It took weeks to wash out and fade away. It was nothing like the color advertised. Needless to say, I was humbled. I repented of judging the teacher and asked God's forgiveness. I don't think my judgment influenced the man one bit, but judging my brother had changed my relationship with God. He felt the twist in my heart and didn't like it.

As Andrews puts it,

> *"Mercy is lived-unto-God, and unto him alone. For it flows forth from him and returns to him. Man's judgment has nothing whatever to do with the matter.... We do it in the heart first of all and last of all. We do it to others, yes, but we seek nothing in return—only to give..."*

THAT is God!

The Hebrew word for mercy, *hhesed,* is frequently translated into English as grace, but it actually means mercy and loving-kindness. Andrews highlights the mercy of Jesus in his amplified version of John 1:14.

> *"And the word was made flesh, and dwelt among us, (and we beheld his glory, the glory as of the only begotten of the Father,) full of HHESED [mercy and loving-kindness] and truth." And verses 16 and 17, "And of his fullness have all we received, and HHESED [mercy and loving-kindness] upon HHESED [mercy and loving-kindness]. For the law was given by Moses, but HHESED [mercy and loving-kindness] and truth came (became) by Jesus Christ."*

If we would follow JESUS, who embodies God's mercy, then we too will become men and women of mercy.[164]

> *Because of His great love for us, God, who is rich in mercy, made us alive with Christ, even when we were dead in our trespasses . . . Ephesians 2:4-5*

In Mercy

> *God so loved the world that He gave His one and only Son, that everyone who believes in him shall not perish but have eternal life. For God did not send His Son into the world to condemn the world, but to save the world through him. John 3: 16-17*

That is mercy—to be alive with Jesus, to be part of his beloved bride—to be the joy that was set before him when he endured the agony of the Cross. What mercy it will be to stand beside Jesus when he presents us to his Father and God welcomes us into his family home. It calls up the third stanza of Charles Wesley's hymn, "And Can it Be?"[165]

> *He left his Father's throne above,*
> *So free, so infinite his grace;*
> *Emptied himself of all but love,*
> *And bled for Adam's helpless race:*
> *'Tis mercy all, immense and free;*
> *For, O my God, it found out me.*
> *'Tis mercy all, immense and free;*
> *For, O my God, it found out me.*

---

[164] The quotations are all from *What the Bible Teaches about Mercy* by Rex B. Andrews, ©1985 by Zion Faith Homes, Zion, Illinois. Used by permission. A few used copies are available on amazon.com or contact Zion Faith Homes, Zion, Illinois http://www.zionfaithhomes.com

[165] Charles Wesley's hymn, "And Can it Be?", written in 1738, reflects Wesley's heartfelt awe at his conversion. Some sources say it's based on Romans 5:8, others Psalm 145

Most of Jesus's followers (myself included) live far short of all the love and grace, all the mercy and loving kindness and all the presence and power of God that is available to us. It's Jesus familiar parable of the of the sower and the seed.[166] Some seeds of God's word fall on the path where it's trampled and birds steal it; other seed falls on rocky soil and withers without moisture, some seed falls into the thorns and is choked out. Most of the time, we are so distracted by the challenges to faith, the world's cares and distractions and the devil's temptations to unbelief, that we don't think about what we're missing. We've barely tapped the glorious grace and mercy of his love. God wants

> ... the eyes of our hearts to be enlightened so that we may know the hope of His calling, the riches of His glorious inheritance in the saints, and the surpassing greatness of His power to us who believe. Ephesians 1: 18-19a (adpt)

God wants us to live in the holy of holies. Lord, help us enter in! The prophetic picture of that little room in a little tent in the Sinai desert hasn't yet been fully fulfilled in his church. The holy of holies foreshadows the glory of heaven come to live on earth in a people who are emptied of self and seek God as their all in all. When Jesus comes in his glory realm, heaven touches earth; God releases the signs and wonders that followed His Son. If the tabernacle typology is true, and I believe it is, God wants to speak with many of us face to face just as he once spoke with Moses and just as Moses and Jesus spoke with one another on the Mount of Transfiguration.

That said, caution is needed. Counterfeit revelations can lead us away from Biblical truth. Without knowledge of God's word and corrective

---

166 See Matthew 13: 1-23, Mark 4: 1-20 and Luke 8:4-15. Although this parable is often used to illustrate receiving God's word for salvation, it also illustrates the challenges, temptations, distractions faced by carnal and immature believers.

truth from the sound teaching of mature Christians, false "revelations" can lead to error and encourage mental and emotional imbalance. Deceptive dreams, visions, voices and "angelic visitations" have been used to spawn and uphold cults and occult churches. Although prophesy is to be sought after and heeded, it also must be "weighed carefully." There is safety in a humble Bible based, Jesus centered, body of believers.

> *Two or three prophets should speak, and the others should weigh carefully what is said. And if a revelation comes to someone who is seated, the first speaker should stop. For you can all prophesy in turn so that everyone may be instructed and encouraged. 1 Corinthians 14: 29-31.*

Wise readers will weigh the words of this book. They will ask God for discernment and seek his truth—even as they anticipate meeting with God.

A WAVE OF WORSHIP:
Final Thoughts and Looking Forward

Let's turn our thoughts to Jesus. Let us intently seek God for the humility needed to worship him in the fullness of his glory. When he comes, when his Holy Spirit moves in our midst, everything dissolves but his purposeful love.

He is all that matters. Jesus is truth. He is guileless reality. All that is inconsistent with his love is subterfuge. Jesus is life; he is light. All that contradicts his nature is darkness. He is freedom; he is love, with no shadow of fear, indifference or hate. He is faith without doubt and all goodness—as God alone is good. Seeking him, searching to know him, is our earth-time opportunity, our only worthy goal. He is worthy. How long is it since we've pondered Revelation Chapter 5?

> *Then I saw a scroll in the right hand of the One seated on the throne. It had writing on both sides and was sealed with seven seals. And I saw a mighty angel proclaiming in a loud voice, "Who is worthy to break the seals and open the scroll?"*
>
> *But no one in heaven or on earth or under the earth was able to open the scroll or look inside it. And I began to weep bitterly, because no one was found worthy to open the scroll or look inside it.*

THE TABERNACLE

Then one of the elders said to me, "Do not weep! Behold, the Lion of the tribe of Judah, the Root of David, has triumphed to open the scroll and its seven seals."

Then I saw a Lamb who appeared to have been slain, standing in the center of the throne, encircled by the four living creatures and the elders. The Lamb had seven horns and seven eyes, which represent the seven Spirits of God sent out into all the earth. And He came and took the scroll from the right hand of the One seated on the throne.

When He had taken the scroll, the four living creatures and the twenty-four elders fell down before the Lamb. Each one had a harp, and they were holding golden bowls full of incense, which are the prayers of the saints. And they sang a new song:

"Worthy are You to take the scroll and open its seals, because You were slain,
and by Your blood You purchased for God those from every tribe and tongue and people and nation.

*You have made them to be a kingdom and priests to serve our
God, and they will reign upon the earth."*

*Then I looked, and I heard the voices of many angels and living
creatures and elders encircling the throne, and their number was
number was myriads of myriads and thousands of thousands.
In a loud voice they were saying:*

*"Worthy is the Lamb who was slain, to receive
   power and riches
and wisdom and strength and honor and glory
   and blessing!"*

*And I heard every creature in heaven, and on earth, and under
the earth, and in the sea, and all that is in them, saying:*

*"To him who sits on the throne and to the Lamb be praise and
honor and glory and power forever and ever!"*

*And the four living creatures said, "Amen," and the elders fell
down and worshiped. Revelation 5*

Stop! Listen! All of heaven is worshipping Jesus. He is worthy. Can we join in Yes! Do we join the heavenly choirs? Hmm—I can't answer for you. Maybe you do. I can only answer for myself—at times, I do. I'm caught up in worship until all else fades. At other times, I fall short. In either case, I know I'm incapable of giving Jesus all the honor and glory and blessing and praise that he deserves.

We know these things intellectually. Oh, Lord. Get your truth into our hearts. Fill us with a longing to worship you as you deserve. Help us to cry out to see your face, to hear your voice.

THE TABERNACLE

The Holy Spirit speaks often and in many ways we've mentioned—through others, through our own thoughts and feelings, in dreams and visions and always through God's word. But once you hear the sweetness, love and strength of Jesus's own voice, you'll never forget it. He doesn't speak often. I remember when he once spoke to me. I had been at a Christian conference in a south Atlanta suburb, where we had praised and praised and worshipped and worshipped until God's glory came. Jesus was with us. Now the conference was over and I was driving home to Northern Illinois. I'd left Georgia before daybreak and hit the Indiana/Illinois tollway system on the southern outskirts of Chicago in evening rush hour traffic.

My gas tanks registered low—the auto's and my own physical tank. Cars were zooming at seventy plus miles an hour in all lanes and I was cruising along with the flow in the outer lane. No way did I have the courage to cross all four lanes of traffic and pull off the highway for gas. I recall the panic. I don't remember if I prayed or not, but suddenly my anxiety melted. I sensed Jesus was in the car with me before he matter-of-factly spoke eight practical words. "You have enough gas to get to Elgin." I heard so much love, so much sweetness, so much humility and truth in his voice that it was impossible to mistrust his loving word. I could not stop for gas. God had spoken.

Once through the city, I did make a much needed stop at the O'Hare Oasis to go to the washroom, but no way could I buy gas for the car. Jesus had said that I had enough. That settled it. When I got stuck in the slowest lane of long lines of cars waiting to exit for a concert outside of the Allstate Arena (then called the Rosemont Horizon), I would have let the motor die from lack of fuel rather than mistrust Jesus's word.

On reaching Elgin today, the exits from Inter-state 90 to Rte. 31 lead into huge busy multi-lane concrete complexity. Back then, it was a quiet, laidback, grassy, tree surrounded country corner on the northern outskirts of town. I don't recall a stoplight. Almost straight ahead of the exit ramp was a small tree shaded gas station. I pulled in, filled up the tank and turned toward my home, about eighteen miles north. Looking back, I've often wondered if Jesus's words. "You have enough gas to get to Elgin" were prophetic.

The infilling of God's glory I'd received at the conference and the loving power of God that filled my car on the drive from Valpo to Elgin had filled my spiritual tank with enough gas (or oil if you'd prefer) to keep me on course with God through a decade of change. Then, about ten years later, the Holy Spirit woke me up one Sunday morning with a strong, almost compelling desire to visit an Elgin church where Jesus's name was being honored. It became my church home. Today, thirty-two years later, Elgin brothers and sisters in Christ continue to honor Jesus's name. They are crying out to join the worship of heaven, to hear God's voice and see his face together. Together, we are trusting God to grow us up into a mature, corporate habitation for the Holy Spirit, a place of God's presence. Brothers and sisters there have prayed for this book. Is this all coincidence? I don't think so. Looking back over a lifetime of mountain tops and valleys with the Lord, it falls into place that Jesus's words, when he does speak, are never coincidental. A powerful, purposeful love fills Jesus's voice with more meaning that we can take in. He wants to speak to all of us and establish his direction for our lives, individually and as families and churches.

Moses's solitary experiences hearing God on the mountain top and in the holy of holies were the experiences of one isolated individual. Although God wanted closer relationship with the people, the people feared God and did not want to draw closer to him. God still wants closer relationships with us, individually and corporately.

Today, the Lord wants many to experience his glory. I believe that he eagerly waits, he longs for entire families, churches, and communities to experience all that was prefigured by his presence in the Holy of Holies. Over the centuries, he has given foretastes of Jesus's heavenly glory to believers in many well documented revivals. He does not change. It is his joy to give his children eternal life. He wants to fill us with the Holy Spirit and to transform our hearts and lives with the powerful love that motivated Jesus. The Holy Spirit waits to bring multitudes of us to our knees in humble adoration of Jesus. I'm not thinking of a physical rapture. I believe that our Father, Jesus, and the Holy Spirit are of one mind about calling earthly choirs to join in heaven's worship and give God the highest praise, the fullest sacrifice that any of us can offer—ourselves. I pray that in this coming generation unprecedented numbers of Adam's sons and daughters will step out of the slave mentality, the clouds of control darkening our world, and will step into the freedom of God's beloved children. I pray that our own longing prayers and cries might surge, swell and grow to the tipping point until they spill over onto earth to draw multitudes into holiness and adoration of Jesus.

That's part of my "take-home" from the glory of the holy of holies. The tabernacle encourages me to believe that God has more for us than salvation, sanctification, communion and prayer. What? How could that be? More? Our cups are already full and running over with more than enough to praise and thank our Father throughout eternity. Yet based on my tabernacle study and Jesus's words, I believe there's more. There's got to be. Listen carefully to all Jesus prayed for us as he talked to Our Father on the night before he died. He prayed,

> *I do not pray for these alone, but also for those who will believe in Me through their word; that they all may be one, as You Father, are in Me, and I in You; that they also may be one in Us, that the world may believe that You sent Me. And the glory*

which You gave Me I have given them, that they may be one just as We are one: I in them, and You in Me; that the world may know that You have sent Me, and have loved them as You have loved Me. John 17:20-23

Got it? One! One with the very God whose word exploded into a big bang that allows us to live and breathe and worship him on earth today. According to Jesus's words and tabernacle prophecy, our union with him and our worship in the holy of holies can be far more than most of us know. Through every hardship and challenge, in union with Jesus, by the power of the Holy Spirit, we are called to personify praise and worship to God, to carry the living word, to be manna for others, and to use God's priestly rod of authority as Jesus did. He wants us to speak God's truth to every man. He wants us to see what our Father is doing and do it. He wants his Holy Spirit to reach out through us to heal the sick, give sight to the blind, food to the hungry, hope to the hopeless and bring courage to those who face the future with fear.

Jesus is the first born of many. We are among the many; he is our way. Today is our time to yield to God's love and complete our little earthly slivers of his eternal plans.

GOD'S TIMETABLE

Today's our time? Yes! Today is our time. Why do I say "Today is *our* time"? Isn't every person's time their own right time for their part in God's plan? Well, yes, but times differ. Our part in God's plan today is different that it would have been in Moses's time, Daniel's time, St. Francis's, Martin Luther's, John Wesley's. D.L. Moody's or John Wimber's time. To understand our place in God's timetable in relationship to the tabernacle, I want to take is a somewhat superficial but dense, textbook-fact-based tour through Christian history in western civilization.[167] Stick with it; it opened my eyes to what God is doing today.

During the first three hundred years after Jesus's death, the church was guided by Spirit filled leaders. It was known for fervent faith, continued growth and strong opposition to heresies. It withstood persecution, misunderstanding, rejection and martyrdom in a pagan world.

A turning point came with the conversion of the Roman emperor Constantine in 312. After his father's death, Constantine fought to establish sovereignty over Rome against the emperor Maxentius, whose superior army threatened to annihilate Constantine's troops. Constantine saw a vision of a cross in the sky, with the words "in this sign conquer." After his victory, Constantine dedicated his life to serving God, legalized Christianity in the Roman Empire in 313, and was baptized on his deathbed (as was the custom) in 337.

During the next three hundred years, 300-600 AD, the church found greater social acceptance, while faith and fervor waned. Strong believers in the apostolic tradition, pioneers like St. Augustine, John Chrysostom, St. Patrick and St. Benedict continued to build the kingdom of God. Church leaders came together to oppose heresy and agree on doctrine, creeds and scripture. The church, as an organized social/political institution rather than a relationship-based organism, began to grow strong and powerful.

Despite pockets of holiness under Godly men like Bernard of Clairvaux and St. Francis, most conversions were political not personal, required by the ruler of the land. Faith was mixed with pagan traditions; cults of

---

167 God has always had His remnant of saints, individuals and communities who are united to Jesus and live in the truth of God's love in Jesus Christ. Also, historically, God has repeatedly revived His church by personal visitations that awaken believers and unbelievers alike from indifference, sleepy apathy and sinfulness. In revivals, God sovereignly awakens his church to new life, holiness and zeal. This overview is not about God's remnant or revivals, it is based on generalizations about sweepingly vast paradigm shifts in faith that effect large numbers of believers.

saints (especially Mary) multiplied; relics and shrines drew multitudes of the gullible and put money into the pockets of the unscrupulous—both in the church and out of it.

Around 800 AD, Charlemagne brought Europe together under the Holy Roman Empire. For the next thousand years, popes, emperors and rulers jockeyed for power. Bishops, cardinals and priests were appointed from the aristocracy with authority over large land holdings and their tenants. Universities such as Oxford were founded (1096), great cathedrals like Notre Dame (1163) and Cologne (1248) were built. But, despite many true saints, the institutional church kept God's word from the mostly illiterate people and did little to encourage common people to know and love their Creator or Savior except through the agency of ordained priests.

This began to change dramatically with the dawning of the Protestant Reformation. In England, Oxford don John Wycliffe translated the entire Bible into English in 1382, making it available to ordinary people in their native language for the first time. For this and his denunciations of Roman Catholic corruption, he was denounced as a heretic and imprisoned. The Czech theologian and reformer Jan Hus, who based his teachings on scripture, was burned at the stake as a heretic in 1415. At this point, if you ask me, God had had enough. He intervened in history, and his successive interventions have followed the pattern of worship established in the tabernacle Moses built in the wilderness.

With the invention of the printing press in 1440 and the publication of the Gutenberg Bible in 1455, the Holy Scriptures, which had formerly been the purview of priests and bishops alone, became widely available. Change intensified between 1500 and 1650 with the Protestant Reformation. The truth behind brazen altar's sacrificial function as the place of atonement for sin, while well known to many Catholic saints, began to be restored to the church at large. Martin Luther was a devout priest, but all his self-denial and penitence could not free his soul from guilt. When God illuminated the scripture to him, Luther declared that

> *For by grace you are saved through faith, and this not of yourselves; it is the gift of God. Ephesians 2:8 BLB.*

On the basis of his new-found faith, Luther rejected many unbiblical religious practices and advocated for major reforms in the church. This exploded into public debate when he posted his 95 theses on the door of Wittenberg church on October 31, 1517.

Because the new printing presses could quickly print copies of Luther's theses, his ideas about the truth of justification and salvation by faith in the sacrifice of Jesus spread rapidly across Europe. Luther's insistence on personal salvation and relationship with God was a vital component of a huge paradigm shift that influenced all levels of society. The law of works, which fostered buying indulgences and blind obedience to church leaders, began to crumble. The biblical truth about the priesthood of all believers began to be restored.

I'm not a church historian, (I've scrambled through history books, encyclopedias and Wikipedia articles and asked for confirmation and correction from those who know more than I do to write this section) but looking back over the last five hundred years of church history, it is increasingly clear that God's desire to bring heaven to earth through the pattern of tabernacle worship has never changed. When he met Moses on the mountain top in about 1500 BC, God began to teach the Israelites his ways through symbolic prototypes of the heavenly tabernacle. My own journey through the tabernacle showed me how God fulfilled the Old Testament types in Jesus and continues to fulfill them in individual believers. Looking at the broader picture of historical movements, however, something else appears to be going on. Around 1500 AD, God began to move in history to initiate paradigm shifts in large numbers of believers that suggest the fulfillment of the tabernacle's prophetic symbolism in the church at large.

In *The Lost Art of Intercession*, James Goll succinctly sums up how history has followed God's pattern of tabernacle worship. [168]

The Brazen Altar—Where Sinful Man Comes to God in Need of Salvation[169]
A. The Protestant Reformation (Repentance and Forgiveness . . .)
  1. Restoration of the Altar of Sacrifice
  2. Restoration of the sacrifice of the blood
  3. Restoration of justification by faith

Once saved by faith, God's people needed cleaning up. Restoration of the laver was not far behind. (Again I'm speaking not of individuals or unique communities, but of Holy Spirit's widespread influence, of light bright enough to bring cultural change on a larger, more popular social scale.)

Between the mid 17th and the late 18th centuries, as western civilization embraced reason and rationalism, the church became alive in a counter movement of renewal and revival that historians refer to as "The Great Awakening." Under Spirit-led men like Count Zinzendorf and the Moravian community in Germany, Jonathon Edwards in the American colonies, George Whitfield in England and the colonies, as well as John and Charles Wesley's Methodism and George Fox's teaching on the inner light to Quakers, vast numbers of men and women bowed under the conviction of the Holy Spirit and cried out to God in repentance for their sins. During the eighteen-hundreds awakening followed awakening. Revival broke forth in places as unlikely as Kentucky

---

[168] James Goll, *The Lost Art of Intercession*, Destiny Image, 2007, ©James Goll
[169] Goll, *The Lost Art of Intercession*, 38-39.

and the Hebrides. Conversions and holiness followed the preaching of Charles Finney in the young United States. God revived his church in Germany and the British Isles. The Welsh Revival spread around the globe, sparking Godly fire in places as far away from Wales as Korea and California.

Each move of the Holy Spirit brought conviction of sin, deep and abiding love for God, enduring commitment to holy living and increased understanding of Jesus's love for others. Men and women who came to know Jesus during the First Great Awakening in England led the battle to abolish the slave trade, worked toward prison reform, started schools and opposed social injustice.[170] Moved by the Holy Spirit, the missionary movement began and grew.

The Second Great Awakening in the States stirred the conscience of believers to fight for the abolition of slavery and for women's rights. The Holy Spirit invigorated Jesus's church toward greater personal holiness and love which in turn inspired increased missionary zeal in the western nations. Men and women gave their lives to carry the message of Jesus's liberation from sin and death to the non-Christian world. Followers of Jesus became catalysts for spreading the good news of Jesus and for demonstrating his compassion by establishing schools, orphanages, hospitals and many other good works of mercy around the globe.[171]

Goll compares this widespread move toward personal salvation, holiness and the spread of Judeo-Christian morality and values into larger society to the laver, the second piece of furniture in the tabernacle.

---

[170] Once again, I recommend Eric Metaxas's book, *Amazing Grace*, on how Wilberforce and his friends changed the moral climate of England. See Footnote 3.

[171] I disagree with relativists who denounce all Christian missionary efforts as control that imposes "white man's ways" on other cultural groups. Yes, there have been unfortunate missionary abuses, grievous ones, but Christians have laid their lives on the line to feed the hungry and care for the sick. Christian missionaries have built schools, orphanages and hospitals; they have opposed selling infant girls into Hindu cult prostitution; they have died to bring the love of Jesus to cannibals in Africa and South America. All cultural traditions are not equally worthy of honor and preservation.

B. The Holiness Movement (Cleansing and Sanctification...[172]
   1. Restoration of the Laver
   2. Restoration of the washing of the hands
   3. Restoration of cleansing and sanctification

Following the tabernacle's pattern, it's predictable that the next move of God in history would bring large numbers in the Body of Christ into the inner court. According to Goll, that's what happened. Following a season of church growth, consolidation, great biblical scholarship and increasing global missionary work, the Holy Spirit once again moved to disrupt the status quo of a getting-comfortable church.

In 1901, a small group of seeking believers were baptized in the Holy Spirit. Like the believers at Pentecost, they too began speaking in tongues. Soon, others in other places

> ... were filled with the Holy Spirit and began to speak in other tongues as the Spirit enabled them. Acts 2:4

Despite misunderstanding and opposition from many organized churches, the Holy Spirit's fire spread rapidly at a grass roots level. More and more believers began to move in the Holy Spirit's gifts.

Once again, God's hand became evident. Large segments of Jesus's church had embraced an external form of godliness without internal holiness or God's power. Their churches were settling into legalism. A new teaching called dispensationalism supported a powerless faith. Dispensationalists teach that God moves differently in different historical seasons and that the gifts of the Holy Spirit ended with Jesus's twelve apostles. When I went to a dispensationalist church in the 1940's, I heard that the Holy Spirit's gifts were only for the apostles and first century believers. They were not for us today.

---

172 Goll, *The Lost Art of Intercession*, 39.

Countering this teaching, news about the restoration of the baptism of the Holy Spirit with his manifestations of signs and wonders spread like wildfire. Seeking believers hungered for the Holy Spirit's gifts of healing, miracles, faith, and words of prophecy, wisdom and knowledge. Within less than fifteen years, Pentecostal believers were sharing the good news across North America and around the world. The Holy Spirit had returned his gifts and his power to Jesus's gospel. Thousands came to know Jesus as healing revivals began to spring up through the ministries of anointed men and women like Marie Woodworth-Etter, Oral Roberts, Kathryn Kuhlman, A. A. Allen and others. Argentina was transformed by revival. [173]

Sixty years later, the Holy Spirit moved again in a renewal of activity known as the Charismatic movement. This second outpouring of the Holy Spirit surprised believers in all denominations with new life and power. The Holy Spirit broke through denominational barriers to bring fellowship and unity in Jesus to believers in Catholic, Lutheran, Episcopal, Presbyterian and other main line churches. God continued restoring all the gifts he had given to the early church. Goll summarizes these prophetic links between the tabernacle's inner court and these twentieth century moves of the Holy Spirit as follows:

II. *The Inner Court—The Holy Place (for Priests Only)*
[Remember that the Reformation restored the priesthood of all believers]

    A. *The Pentecostal Outpouring (Illumination and Anointing . . .)*
        1. *Restoration of the golden lampstand* [More of the Holy Spirit]
        2. *Restoration of the lighting and burning of the seven golden candlesticks*
        3. *Restoration of the power and gifts of the Spirit*

---

[173] https://www.thearda.com/timeline/movements/movement_42.asp

B. The Charismatic Outpouring (the Full Portion of God's Bread...)
  1. Restoration of the table of shewbread
  2. Restoration of the 12 loaves of bread; representing the 12 tribes of Israel
  3. Restoration of fellowship across the Body of Christ [174]

Those of us like myself who were blessed to draw closer to Jesus's love in the Charismatic movement of the 1970's will remember the warm friendship, fellowship and unity we enjoyed in praying for one another. Jesus's love brought the joy of unity across the Body of Christ. At the time, I began attending Catholic Charismatic prayer meetings, I was an also an active member of a mainline, liberal protestant congregation. But when the local Catholic priest asked our charismatic prayer group to lay hands on him and pray that he'd receive the baptism of the Holy Spirit, nobody asked if I was Catholic. I joined my Lutheran and Catholic brothers and sisters in the circle of love that prayed for him that day. I was warmly invited to teach a chapter in a Roman Catholic Life in the Spirit Seminar. The fellowship and unity were wonderful.

But, in reading the outline above, did you notice the lampstand and table of showbread were prominent but the altar of incense was missing? It wasn't part of Goll's outline linking the Pentecostal and Charismatic movements to the inner cour.? According to Goll, the Holy Spirit did not restore the altar of incense to large numbers of believers until the 1990's. In *The Lost Art of Intercession* James Goll prophetically wrote,

The time of the incense has come!

James Goll could write those words with authority. The Holy Spirit had used his obedience and prayer to help restore the altar of incense to large numbers of believers. In 1993, few (if any) communities on the

---

174 Goll, *The Lost Art of Intercession*, 39.

globe sustained 24/7 meetings for prayer and worship. At that time, following the Holy Spirit's direction, James and his wife, Michal Ann, led a small group of prophetic intercessors to visit Herrnhut, Germany. In an unusual visitation of powerful, supernatural energy and direction, the Holy Ghost prayed through this group for the release of 24/7 houses of prayer and worship.[175] Within a few years, Houses of Prayer began to spring up in many nations. If you enter *24/7 Prayer* into your computer search engine today, you'll find more houses of prayer than you might want to count. Goll identifies the prayer movement of the last thirty years with the altar of incense.

 C. The Prayer Movement . . .
  1. *Restoration of the altar of incense*
  2. *Restoration of the fire continually burning on the altar*
  3. *Restoration of worship and prayer.* [176]

Goll's outline stops there, at the altar of incense, right before the veil into God's presence in the holy of holies. But Jesus didn't stop there and I don't want to stop there either! I've already noted God's longing for large numbers of believers to move into the holy of holies in worship. Tabernacle prophecy suggests the fulfillment of his desire, the largescale restoration of worship in the holy of holies. Together, many will experience more of God's manifest presence than has been customary in the past. We may shake and tremble with fear like the Israelites did before fire on the holy mountain, but this time we won't withdraw. I hope the time might be drawing near. It is a good sign that the number of prayer altars continues to multiply.

---

175 Goll, *The Lost Art of Intercession*, 21ff.
176 Goll, *The Lost Art of Intercession*, 39.

I don't know God's historical timetable, but it makes sense to anticipate a day when the incense of our prayers will fill the heavenly censers and God's tipping point will be reached. When that that kairos-moment arrives, the Holy Spirit will begin to draw more and more of believers into the holy of holies. I don't know exactly how it will happen, but the pattern of tabernacle worship suggests the way. Believers who have been faithful to identify with Jesus at the altar of the cross, cleanse themselves at the laver of his word, eat God's bread and stay in fellowship with one another in the light of his Holy Spirit and keep their watch before him at the golden altar of incense will be ready to meet with God when he appears. Thus, it makes sense to prepare ourselves and keep watch for his appearing.[177] If this prediction is right, then I'd continue Goll's outline like this:

D. The Worship Movement in the Holy of Holies
   In the maturity of bridal love for Jesus, large numbers of believers will receive
   Restoration of the ark and mercy seat
   Restoration of the full glory of God's presence
   Restoration of complete union with God—The fullness of Christ in us
   Restoration and consolidation of unity in the Body of Christ
   Mature functioning of every gift of the Holy Spirit
   Maturity of signs and wonders—an overflow of glory! (like Jesus)
   Fulfillment of Jesus's prayer in John 17:23
   and Paul's prayers in Ephesians 3 and 4

---

[177] Jesus tells his followers to keep watch for his coming in Luke 12:35-40. He says, "*Stay dressed for action! . . . for the Son of man is coming at an hour you do not expect.*" ESV

This worship movement in the holy of holies would answer Jesus's prayer:

> *May they also be in Us, so that the world may believe that You sent Me. I have given them the glory You gave Me, so that they may be one as We are one—I in them and You in Me—that they may be perfectly united, so that the world may know that You sent Me and have loved them just as You have loved Me. John 17: 21-23*

It would also answer Paul's prayer.

> *I ask that out of the riches of His glory . . . you may be filled with all the fullness of God. Ephesians 3:16-19*

> *Then we will no longer be infants, tossed about by the waves and carried around by every wind of teaching and by the clever cunning of men in their deceitful scheming. Instead, speaking the truth in love, we will in all things grow up into Christ himself, who is the head. Ephesians 4:14-16*

And, following the prophetic symbolism of the tabernacle, large numbers of believers will know the reality of Paul's experience when he wrote,

> *I have been crucified with Christ, and I no longer live, but Christ lives in me. The life I live in the body, I live by faith in the Son of God, who loved me and gave himself up for me. Galatians 2:20*

All believers die to themselves and live to Christ—to a degree. Countless forerunners have known union with Jesus. Names pop into my head like popping corn: John who was Jesus's Beloved Disciple, St. Paul, Brother Lawrence, Theresa of Avila, St. John of the Cross, St. Francis of Assisi, Amy Carmichael, A.B. Simpson, Frank Laubach,

Oswald Chambers, A.W. Tozer, Padre Pio and more Catholic saints than I can begin to list. Many of our great saints won converts to Jesus, built churches and founded lasting religious orders. Bands of followers and disciples gathered around them. But overall, these pockets of devotion and anointing were exceptions that did not change large segments of society.

These forerunners were not part of a widespread mature body of Christ living in union with God and one another. Many believers are currently learning to live in communion with God; many of have known brief, life-changing visitations from God, but very few of us live in the experience Martha Wing Robinson described when she wrote,

> *"In a moment we were gone and a greater One was there. Entire spirit, soul, and body were in a new and divine control. I walked out of the natural into the spiritual in the body as well as in the soul.... We felt that we had died and Christ had come to dwell where we had been. We knew only God and were hidden away in God in such a tremendous mystery—the very presence of God came upon us.... We found out it was a taste of something God is going to do in the last days."*[178]

Martha Wing Robinson described what happened to her as a "next generation experience." I am hoping that we are on the verge of it.

Are we, the body of Christ, ready? Do we want it? If so, we need to take the pattern of tabernacle worship seriously—not as a rigid formula, but as an invitation with a promise.

---

178 Gordon P. Gardiner, *Radiant Glory: The Life of Martha Wing Robinson*, Bread of Life, © Gordon P. Gardiner, 1962, p. 171

Whatever God is asking us to do, his simple, ancient pattern is profound and complete. Each day, we are given a fresh opportunity to

Stand at the crossroads and look.

Each day we are given an opportunity to

Ask for the ancient paths: "Where is the good way?"
Then walk in it, and you will find rest for your souls.
Jeremiah 6:16

It's not about rules and discipline, it's about loving God—about making dates to be together, about talking with him, listening to him and following his lead. It's about telling him when we mess up—as we might tell our husbands, wives or best friends. It's about confessing, repenting and receiving forgiveness when we fall from Godly standards and haven't trusted in his holy love enough to lean upon our Lord in every need. It's all about loving God and receiving his love in return.

Wanting more of Jesus's love, I've put together a one-page reminder to myself of God's pattern of tabernacle worship. These simple suggestions culled from the tabernacle are not rules or disciplines, they're opportunities to invite growth and transformation. They are doors that the Holy Spirit will open to welcome us into to closer relationship with our beloved Lord. As I read them, I don't beat myself up for my failures, I ask and trust the Holy Spirit to do in me what I can't do in and for myself. He will lead us all, one step at a time. The Holy Spirit does not set up a series of hoops for us to jump through. He guides us and reaches out a hand to help us. He wants to give us grace, faith and capacity for all the holy love that God is calling us to receive.

Caution! We must all let the Holy Spirit lead us. God is not into professionalism or performance. He does not set us up to fail. He deals with us one thing at a time. Seek Jesus and pray trustingly about what the Holy Spirit quickens to your heart and mind.

- *Willingness; teachableness; humility.*
  Leaving the camp (the world) and walking toward the tabernacle: Lord, Give us grace to leave our tents and walk toward your tabernacle, the place of your presence. *Lord, help us to humble ourselves, to willingly turn toward Jesus, to walk toward him, to leave all that falls short of your love.*

- *Gratitude, thanksgiving and praise.*
  The tents of Judah: Lord, fill us with praise. We'd be habitations of praise at all times and in all places. *We would praise you, for you are worthy of all praise. Lord, help us enter your courts with gratitude and praise. Help us realize that all we have, all we are and all we do is by your mercy. We are nothing in ourselves.*

- *Repentance, confession, and identification with Jesus.*
  The brazen altar: Lord, as we come before the brazen altar, we give ourselves to you as you gave yourself for us. *Lord, forgive us our sins. We invite you to take what we can't give. Help us to completely identify with Jesus's death and resurrection. Help us die to ourselves and receive the truth of Jesus's death for us and life in us. Help us to forgive others as you would forgive us. We want our new life in Jesus Christ to grow and mature.*

- *Ongoing cleansing, deliverance and refreshing in God's word.*
  The laver: Lord, makes us thirsty for the cleansing waters in the laver of your word. *Let your word, your living word in Jesus,*

speak to us. Help us align ourselves with it. Help us to get it into our hearts and live it—by your grace and power.

- *More Holy Spirit light.*
  The inner court and the lampstand: Lord, we would live in the inner court, where all we see is lit by the flame of your Holy Spirit. *Father, please fill us, and keep filling us, with the Holy Spirit's oil and light. Enlighten our eyes to see Jesus. Give us grace to follow in his meekness and holiness. Give us grace to see that without your light we are blind. We invite Jesus, who is light, into every darkened corner of our lives.*

- *Community and growth in God.*
  The inner court and the table of showbread: Lord, bring us into the fellowship and unity of your word with others. *Father, in the light of your Holy Spirit, connect us with your family. Feed us with the bread of your word. Join us with our brothers and sisters in Christ to answer Jesus's prayer for us that*

  > [We] may be one, as You, Father, are in Me, and I am in You. May they also be in Us, so that the world may believe that You sent Me. I have given them the glory You gave Me, so that they may be one as We are one—I in them and You in Me—that they may be perfectly united, so that the world may know that You sent Me and have loved them just as You have loved Me. John 17: 21-23

- *Holy Spirit prayer and worship.*
  The altar of incense: Holy Spirit, give us your prayer, praise and worship as we draw nearer to your throne of grace. *Dear Lord, fill our alone times with you. Help us to pray in the light of your*

Holy Spirit and in agreement with your word. Help us surrender to you in the beauty of your holiness, in the light of your presence, in the merciful loving kindness that holds the world together—in Jesus's love for us all. We would know Christ's boundless, abundant, wise, tender, strong and endless love as we seek for fuller union with him.

- *God's glory. His kingdom come, his will be done.*
  Bring us into the holy of holies. *Lord, fill us with yourself to fulfill your will in us. As we worship in your presence may we receive the desires and directions of your heart. Equip us to extend your love, truth, justice and mercy to a broken needy world. May we, like Jesus, be your tabernacle on earth!*

The goal of tabernacle worship is not personal holy-goose-bumps or devotional highs. The goal is to fulfill Jesus's prayer for his followers,

> *that all of them may be one, as You, Father, are in Me, and I am in You. May they also be in Us, so that the world may believe that You sent Me. John 17:21*

I can think of no better conclusion to this book on the tabernacle than the words Paul wrote to the Ephesians. He said that we are

> *. . . members of God's household, built on the foundation of the apostles and prophets, with Christ Jesus Himself as the cornerstone. In Him the whole building is fitted together and grows into a holy temple in the Lord. And in Him [in union with Jesus Christ] you too are being built together into a dwelling place for God in His Spirit. Ephesians 2:19b-22*

I ask that out of the riches of His glory He may strengthen you with power through His Spirit in your inner being, so that Christ may dwell in your hearts through faith. Then you, being rooted and grounded in love, will have power, together with all the saints, to comprehend the length and width and height and depth of the love of Christ, and to know this love that surpasses knowledge, that you may be filled with all the fullness of God.
Ephesians 3:16-19

In loving union with Jesus, our Father, the Holy Spirit and our brothers and sisters in Christ, may we all grow up to live the first and greatest commandments—to love the Lord our God with all our hearts, souls, minds and strength and to love others as ourselves. May we, individually and together become God's holy temple—filled with his glory, his alone.

AN AFTERWORD

After this manuscript was complete, while working on revisions and edits, I received a book in the mail. Opening it, I met Frances Metcalfe and *The Ladies of Gold* in three volumes of their writings compiled by James Maloney. The timing was a God-coincidence because, like Martha Wing Robinson, Frances and her companions were forerunners of the wave of worship prefigured by the holy of holies. She describes her experience of Jesus's love in words almost identical to Jeanne Guyon's and Martha Robinson's.

In face-to-face conversations with the Lord, Jesus also showed Frances that the full experience of his glory (which is barely touched on and hinted at in my journey) will one day be given to a large number of believers. In the fullness of God's time, the Holy Spirit will bring many believers into a mature and selfless union with Jesus and one another. May it be. I hope this study of the tabernacle has whet your appetite as it has mine. May we

> *Prepare the way for the Lord, make straight paths for him,*
> *Mark 1:3*

THE TABERNACLE

As the New Living Translation puts it.

Prepare the way for the LORD's coming! Clear the road for him!

Lord, baptize us in repentance for our sins. Lord, baptize us in your Holy Spirit and fire.

Wherever you lead us, we will follow.

APPENDIX

1 — Why is the Brazen Altar *That* Important?
2 — Inwardness
3 — Spirit Baptism
4 — Abiding
5 — The Stone Tablets
6 — Faith
7 — Worship

APPENDIX 1:
WHY IS THE BRAZEN ALTAR THAT IMPORTANT?

So why, here and now, in the 21st century, is the prophetic meaning of Jesus's blood sacrifice at the brazen altar all that important? I will do my best to explain.

God is love. His most essential command is to love him and each other. It takes humility and faith to love God and others. Proud people love their own thoughts. Humble people can surrender their thoughts and lives to God's wisdom. Seeking God's ways takes faith. God's kingdom and righteousness are all by faith, not by intellectual assent or acceptance, not by metaphysical reasoning, but by God-given faith. God himself is the source of our faith in him. He will give faith to all who sincerely ask. He wants us to live in the love, hope, joy, peace, faith and light of his very own life.

But life on earth is not always faith-filled, light and loving. It is tragic. The evils of unbelief, greed and poverty, violence and war, hunger, disease, deception, injustice, cruelty and death touch all of us. God never wanted it that way! He wants loving harmony, peace and justice. He wants to comfort us, strengthen us, sustain us and deliver us from all evil. He wants to save us from the darkness of eternal death. (See John 1: 1-12) But, God is also perfectly holy and totally just. We are not. At one time or another, every one of us has fallen short of God's law of love.

When Adam first disobeyed God, a seed of Satan's pride and the power of pride infiltrated the human race. Mercifully, God keeps his communication with pride-filled people distant and limited. If he got too close, his holiness would judge them prematurely and they'd die. So, God's Holy Spirit withdrew from Adam and his children have been stuck with human pride ever since. Pride has become so familiar that most of us don't even recognize it in ourselves.

But Jesus, who said, "Follow me, for I am meek and lowly, gentle and humble in heart" (Matthew 11:29, 30, adapted and amplified) was not proud. If we follow him, he will lead us out of pride. Jesus and the Holy Spirit will help us live in accord with God's laws.

God's law is not an optional idea scratched on ancient tablets of stone. It is not an irksome list of rules from old books that a punishing tyrant legalistically orders us to obey on the threat of undeserved consequences. His law is an expression of his great love for us. Failure to keep his command to love him and others sooner or later releases the natural consequences of sin upon us and our families. God's law is written into the very warp and woof of creation. It rules the universe. He established his law in the heavens and he gives it to us because he loves us and wants to teach us how to reconnect with divine life. In tune with God, we can live with ourselves and others safely, orderly, sanely, joyously, and peacefully. We can overcome the tragedies of life on earth with sanity and hope because we know that God's justice will prevail, if not in this world, then in the one to come.

Discarding God's laws of love leads to jealousy, dishonesty, contention, chaos, greed, hatred, anger, sorrow, angst and destruction. Refusing to love God and our fellow human beings has eternal consequences.

Only Jesus kept all of God's law. Only Jesus was or ever will be completely free of pride. Only Jesus is perfectly and consistently loving, merciful, just and true. Only Jesus is totally filled with the light of Godly life that our heavenly Father wants to give to us.

Because so many of this world's power brokers are without his life and separated from God, our search for his merciful loving kindness, justice and truth on earth can be disillusioning. In the face of injustice, sorrow and pain, something in us cries out, "It shouldn't be that way. Why the unfairness? Why the suffering innocents?" Although generations of compromise and unbelief have carried us forward into our time in history, mankind has no excuse for our blindness to God's existence and our refusal to learn and follow his ways.

> *For what may be known about God is plain . . . because God has made it plain . . . For since the creation of the world God's invisible qualities, His eternal power and divine nature, have been clearly seen, being understood from His workmanship, so that men are without excuse. Romans 1:19-10*

Rejecting God's law of love will have eternal consequences.

> *For God does not show favoritism. All who sin apart from the law will also perish apart from the law, and all who sin under the law will be judged by the law. For it is not the hearers of the law who are righteous before God, but it is the doers of the law who will be declared righteous.*

> *Indeed, when Gentiles, who do not have the law, do by nature what the law requires, they are a law to themselves, even though they do not have the law, since they show that the work of the law is written on their hearts, their consciences also bearing witness, and their thoughts either accusing or defending them. This will come to pass on that day when God will judge men's secrets through Christ Jesus, as proclaimed by my gospel. Romans 2:11-16*

God not only reveals his nature in creation, he is the source of our highest ideals of law, justice, mercy and fairness. His laws order the cosmos—from quarks to kangaroos, from honeybees and birds to a baby's burps. His most important law is to love him and to love our neighbor. But since love is grounded on free will, human history is a weaving of threads plied from two skeins. One skein is of dark fibers from the willful refusal to love God (threads of wars and famines, disease and destruction, violence, fear, greed, domination, cruelty and on and on).

The other threads are bright lines of light; they run through good times and bad—lines of kindness and compassion, freedom and courage, prosperity, opportunity, innovation, discovery, generosity, hospitality, charity and deeds of humble, self-sacrificial love.[179]

Jesus illustrated this in the parable of the wheat and the tares growing up together in the same field. The field is the world. The tares represent the reality of wickedness and evil in people. The wheat symbolizes the reality of godliness and loving people. Until the end of the age, the wheat and the tares will continue to grow in the same field. God continues to work through his servants to establish the integrity of his laws of love. Despite backwashes and darkness, men and women who truly live the

---

[179] For facts to support my claim, I once again strongly recommend *The Book that Made Your World: How the Bible Created the Soul of Western Civilization* by VishalMangalwadi, Thomas Nelson, 2011

Judeo-Christian values given us through Moses continue to salt the earth with Godly savor.

> *He has made everything beautiful in its time. He has also set eternity in the human heart; yet no one can fathom what God has done from beginning to end. Ecclesiastes 3:11 NIV*

The human sin of rejecting God is the foundational issue, the main problem. Adam and Eve's sin, their disobedience, brought sin into the world. Sin brought death—

> *For the wages of sin is death, but the gift of God is eternal life in Christ Jesus our Lord. Romans 6:23*

Each one of us will die because of our sinfulness. But every single person who believes in and follows Jesus Christ is a part of God's long-range plan to overcome sin and death.

Since the beginning of time, God has been working toward his end of time purposes through all who say "yes" to his love. At a specific time, about four thousand years ago, God chose a man named Abraham to teach his descendants, the Israelites, to believe him and learn his ways.

> *For I have chosen him, so that he will command his children and his household after him to keep the way of the LORD by doing what is right and just, in order that the LORD may bring upon Abraham what He has promised." Genesis 18:19*

Four hundred years later, God chose another man, Moses, to teach his ways to one branch of Abraham's descendants. God's instructions to Moses concerning the law and the tabernacle were quite specific because certain legalities had to be met. They provided a temporary way to bridge the gap between their human sin and God's perfect holy love.

As already said, God's holiness and justice require his absolute separation from all who fall short of his goodness. It's impossible for the complete holiness, absolute perfection, total love and incredible awesome sovereignty of the fullness of God's presence to co-exist with the minutest disharmony or disagreement with the intrinsic nature of his very being. Sin is impossible before his throne.[180] Sinners cannot draw near to God's holiness and live.

That is justice. Yet, with unfathomable, merciful, lovingkindness, our Creator longs to welcome us into his family. He does not want us to die. God is eager for our eternal life and our union with himself. To rescue beloved men and women from the immediate death due to guilty sinners and to resolve the impossible dilemma of making a choice between mercy and justice, God temporarily instituted animal sacrifice. He accepted the death of a sacrificed animal as a substitute to atone for human sin. Beginning with the tabernacle, the Israelites offered hundreds of thousands of animals to God in atonement for their sins, to propitiate God and secure his mercy. But that was not God's perfect or final plan. He does not delight in the sacrifice of animals.

> *For You do not delight in sacrifice, or I would bring it; You take no pleasure in burnt offerings. The sacrifices of God are a broken spirit; a broken and a contrite heart, O God, You will not despise. Psalm 51:16-17 (See also 1 Samuel 15:22, Isaiah 1:11, and Proverbs 23:1)*

---

[180] Only those who yield to God's majesty can survive his glorious presence. Our earthly lives are a probationary time, offering each of us an opportunity to reject God and continue in sin or to accept God's love and reject sin. If we reject God and hold on to sin, we die. If we accept him and turn from sin, God invites us into his family and we can begin to live in glorious reconciled union with our Creator. God is not cruel. He is just. If we reject his invitation, we die.

Appendix 1: Why Is The Brazen Altar that Important?

Eventually, according to the divine plan prefigured in the tabernacle, God sent his Son, Jesus, to die for us all. When Jesus died upon the cross in obedience to his Father God, everything changed.

Instead of an imperfect animal taking our place in a symbolic death to sin, Jesus, God's own Son, became the perfect sacrificial lamb of God. Only an innocent man, one without sin, one who never failed in love, could ever take our place of death. Jesus qualified. He alone was perfectly holy. He alone lived a sinless life; his very sinlessness broke the power of death that is the only justly valid punishment for sin. He redeemed us from death. As Fanny Crosby wrote, [181]

> *Redeemed, how I love to proclaim it!*
> *Redeemed by the blood of the Lamb;*
> *Redeemed through His infinite mercy,*
> *His child and forever I am.*

When Satan took the life of Jesus Christ, he overstepped his authority.

With Jesus's death every one of God's requirements to satisfy justice and release his merciful loving-kindness toward us was satisfied. We receive God's mercy when we accept Jesus's death for our sins. On confessing our sins and identifying with Jesus's death on our behalf, the Holy Spirit sets us free from the curse of death Satan has written across our earthly kingdoms and gives us eternal life in the kingdom of God, life that is not born from human flesh but of God's own eternal Spirit. As Jesus told Nicodemus,

> *Truly, truly, I tell you, no one can enter the kingdom of God*
> *unless he is born of water and the Spirit. Flesh is born of flesh,*

---

[181] "Redeemed, How I Love to Proclaim It!" words by Fanny J. Crosby, published in 1882. If you'd like to hear it, here's a link you might enjoy https://www.youtube.com/watch?v=07psmkNKAQg

but spirit is born of the Spirit. Do not be amazed that I said, 'You must be born again. John 3:5-7

Animal sacrifice at the brazen altar foreshadowed Jesus's death, his blood sacrifice on the cross. Can you see it? When we chose by faith to identify with his death and resurrection, the chasm, the unbridgeable breach between us and God is closed.

> *For the life of a creature is in the blood, and I have given it to you to make atonement for yourselves on the altar; it is the blood that makes atonement for one's life. Leviticus 17:11 NIV*

According to the Bible record, the tabernacle in the wilderness

> *... is an illustration for the present time, because the gifts and sacrifices being offered were unable to cleanse the conscience of the worshiper. . . . But when Christ came as high priest of the good things that have come, He went through the greater and more perfect tabernacle that is not made by hands and is not a part of this creation. He did not enter by the blood of goats and calves, but He entered the Most Holy Place once for all by His own blood, thus securing eternal redemption. Hebrews 9: 9, 11-12*

The writer of the book of Hebrews explains that animal sacrifice was imperfect. It offered temporary atonement and needed yearly repetition because it did not deal with our inborn sin nature. Jesus did! Our identification with his death on the cross provides for permanent deliverance from our inherited, universal, prideful tendency to reject God and choose our own ways. When we confess our sin and need and accept Jesus's death on our behalf, his blood atones for our sin. No wonder people never tire of singing "Amazing Grace!" In God's amazing grace, we are forgiven, we are saved from death's curse, and our sin nature, the chains that bound us, fall off.

> *According to the law, in fact, nearly everything must be purified with blood, and without the shedding of blood there is no forgiveness. Hebrews 9:22*

The instant our Father in heaven looks at us and sees that, by our faith, the blood of Jesus covers our sins, the Holy Spirit gladly comes into our hearts with his new life. We are born again not of the flesh but of the Spirit. This amazing expiation of our sins and reception of the Holy Spirt is what happens when we surrender to God before the cross that was foreshadowed by the brazen altar.

It's possible to know about God from outside the tabernacle court. Many church-goers (even pastors) think they are all right with God and belong to his family because they keep his rules and see themselves as "good" people. But there's a major difference between knowing about God and knowing him, between believing in Jesus and becoming his disciple by yielding to his life in us. I know about George Washington and about my great-grandfather, but I don't know them and never did. I'll say it again, to know God and be a welcomed into his family, to enter further into his courts, we must identify with Jesus's sacrifice upon the altar of the cross and continue in his love.

We can't clean up ourselves or bridge the distance between our failures and God's perfection alone. Good works won't get us into a loving family relationship with God or take us to heaven. That's particularly true if we do our good deeds to get points toward earning God's favor. That's what the Reformation was all about. Martin Luther taught a church that thought good deeds and money could buy favors from God that works and riches are not the coins of heaven. The light went on for Luther when he realized that

> *Because of His great love for us, God, who is rich in mercy, made us alive with Christ, even when we were dead in our trespasses. . . . For it is by grace you have been saved through faith, and this not from yourselves; it is the gift of God, not by works, so that no one can boast. For we are God's workmanship, created in Christ Jesus to do good works, which God prepared in advance as our way of life. Ephesians 2:4-5, 8-10*

That's why the brazen altar is important today. It prophesies the cross, where the Holy Spirit helps us see and confess how sin has separated us from God's love. At the cross, we acknowledge our need for Jesus's life; we accept his forgiveness; we welcome his Holy Spirit into our beings, and we begin to let the Holy Spirit change us from sinners to saints.

God's Spirit helps us surrender our self-will and self-focus to God's will. His Spirit begins to lead us into doing his good works and speaking his good words so that his kingdom will come and His will be done on earth as it is in heaven.[182] And it's not us! It's Christ in us by the power of the Holy Spirit. Because Jesus set us free from our sins, we can build a relationship with our heavenly Father and learn to live in consistent relationship with him. The Holy Spirit fills us with the compassion of Jesus. And that is what the tabernacle is all about. Following a straight line past the brazen altar will take us directly to the laver. From there we will move through the next veil into the holy place and then, by the grace and mercy of God our Father and the Lord Jesus Christ, we are offered the invitation to move through the final veil into the holy of holies and the glorious presence of their manifest majesty, uncompromising purity

---

182 Matthew 6:10

and powerful love. As we learn to look to Jesus and see his love, we want more of his perfection and beauty. We want to be where he is, do what he is doing and be like him as he was like his Father—our Creator, our Father, our God.

APPENDIX 2:
INWARDNESS

For years, I've kept this instruction from Martha Wing Robinson in a place where I can read it often. Reading it is inspiring encouragement. Perhaps it will help you too. I quote it as it was written.

Inwardness

When Jesus first sets vessels to love him, He wants them to see him all the time, every moment, and if they are very much in earnest, they live that way—moment by moment.

In the beginning of such experience, most of the time they pray, praise, wait on God, commune, and often, if at work, see Jesus in the soul.

If they grow in this experience and become vessels of God for His use, they begin to seek more for him, and He comes more to them, for He does to all who seek him from the heart.

Also, He begins to draw their thoughts all the time—every moment—to himself, causing them to find him within. This is the beginning of the inward or deeper life.

As soon as this change takes place, He then teaches, if He can make them to get it, either by teachers or by their light, how to "practice the presence of God" —that is, to keep the mind stayed on Jesus—each wandering thought, act, word or feeling being recalled (i.e, called back) by the will of the vessel in the love of God. God. Turn the mind back to God. Words come not appointed by him. Check such words at once, as soon as remembered. Look within and tell Jesus He rules, you will act, think, and speak as He would, and He will look after you to help you to be like that. God, etc. To so live for a time makes the inward change to abide in anyone who will go down to thus live; but if you keep to this lowliness, rest, and faith to be all the time in God, so then the voluntary act of dwelling in God, seeing God, thinking of God, and keeping is done altogether by the Holy Ghost, which is the true inwardness called for in every Christian.

APPENDIX 3:
SPIRIT BAPTISM

Jesus wants us to be baptized in the Holy Spirit. The word *baptize* means immerse. Jesus wants us to be immersed, as an empty vessel dropped into a pool of water will fill up on the inside and be surrounded with water on the outside. He wants us to be filled inside and surrounded on the outside with the Holy Spirit of God. Recalling that the light coming from the lampstand is a picture of the Holy Spirit, every bit of light shining on the inner court furniture and every bit of light entering the priest's eyes came from the lampstand. Similarly, Jesus wants our vision to depend on the light of his Spirit. In the lampstand, the flames that consumed flesh at the brazen altar (symbolic of the cross) now burn the pure oil of the Holy Spirit. Every bit of inner court symbolism prefigures God's desire for us to mature from salvation and cleansing (in the outer court) into mature dependence on the Holy Spirit (in the inner court). The Holy Spirit was so was so important to Jesus that he talked at length about him (the Holy Spirit). At his last Passover meal on the night before he died, he told his disciples,

> *If you love Me, you will keep My commandments. And I will ask the Father, and He will give you another Advocate[183] to be with you forever—the Spirit of truth. The world cannot receive him, because it neither sees him nor knows him. But you do know him, for He abides with you and will be in you.... the Advocate, the Holy Spirit, whom the Father will send in My name, will teach you all things and will remind you of everything I have told you. John 14:15-25*

The Holy Spirit was so vital and central to his thoughts that night that Jesus repeated himself with emphasis,

> *But I tell you the truth, it is for your benefit that I am going away. Unless I go away, the Advocate will not come to you; but if I go, I will send him to you. And when He comes, He will convict the world in regard to sin and righteousness and judgment: in regard to sin, because they do not believe in Me; in regard to righteousness, because I am going to the Father and you will no longer see Me; and in regard to judgment, because the prince of this world has been condemned.... when the Spirit of truth comes, He will guide you into all truth. For He will not speak on His own, but He will speak what He hears, and He will declare to you what is to come. He will glorify Me by taking from what is Mine and disclosing it to you. Everything that belongs to the Father is Mine. That is why I said that the Spirit will take from what is Mine and disclose it to you. John 16:7-15*

---

183 In Greek, *advocate* is *paraclete*, one who comes along side. Other translations include comforter, helper and counselor.

THE TABERNACLE

The Holy Spirit was so important to Jesus that after his death and resurrection, in his last words before he rose up into heaven, he told his disciples,

> *Do not leave Jerusalem. I'm going to send the gift the Father promised—you've heard Me discus it. Wait for it until you are clothed with power from on high. John baptized with water, but in a few days you will be baptized with the Holy Spirit."*
> *Acts 1: 4,5 and Luke 24:49 adapted*

They obeyed, and then,

> *When the day of Pentecost came, they were all together in one place. Suddenly a sound like a mighty rushing wind came from heaven and filled the whole house where they were sitting. They saw tongues like flames of fire that separated and came to rest on each of them. And they were all filled with the Holy Spirit and began to speak in other tongues as the Spirit enabled them.*
> *Acts 2:1-4*

The entire book of Acts tells what the Holy Spirit did next through Jesus's Spirit-filled, empowered disciples. The lampstand's fulfillment as a prophetic symbol of the Holy Spirit—first within Jesus and then within men and women, began to be realized. Ezekiel's reiteration of the promise of the laver and the lampstand was fulfilled.

> *I will also sprinkle clean water on you, and you will be clean. I will cleanse you from all your impurities and all your idols. I will give you a new heart and put a new spirit within you; I will remove your heart of stone and give you a heart of flesh. And I will put My Spirit within you and cause you to walk in My statutes and to carefully observe My ordinances.*
> *Ezekiel 36: 25-26*

And the way was paved for God's promise to us from the book of Joel to begin to come true. Its larger fulfillment began with the Pentecostal revival of the early 20th century.

> *And afterward, I will pour out My Spirit on all people. Your sons and daughters will prophesy, your old men will dream dreams, your young men will see visions. Even on My menservants and maidservants, I will pour out My Spirit in those days.*
> *Joel 2:28-29*

So, why wouldn't Christians want the promise of the Holy Spirit? I don't know. But in my lifetime, part of the controversy has centered around the gift of tongues.[184] For many, speaking in tongues, or unknown languages, is a sign of the Holy Spirit in a believer. When the Holy Spirit came at Pentecost, the one hundred twenty believers spoke in other tongues. Following that, the Holy Spirit repeatedly visited new believers with the gift of speaking in tongues. I recall that two or three years after I'd been filled with the Holy Spirit and spoke in tongues, my pastor, in a fairly liberal mainline denominational church, screamed at me, "That is NOT our tradition. I did not go to seminary to encourage people speaking in tongues."

This activity of the Holy Spirit was not welcome—nor was I. Was Jesus? Frankly, I don't know. God does. And the church belongs to Jesus, not to me. He alone knows human hearts and why we all react the way we do. But, according to the Scripture, Jesus himself, the Son of God at birth, was not empowered and released for ministry until after the Holy Spirit descended upon him at his baptism in the River Jordan.

Only the power of the Holy Spirit can empower us to obey God's commands to love him and others. God alone can share the goodness of

---

[184] For more information about the gift of tongues, see *They Speak with Other Tongues* by John Sherill and Brother Andrew, Chosen Books, 2018

Jesus through us. If speaking in tongues is a sign of the Holy Spirit, why would anyone reject the gift?

Paul wrote encouraging believers to receive the manifestation of the Spirit for the common good.

> *Now to each one the manifestation of the Spirit is given for the common good. To one there is given through the Spirit the message of wisdom, to another the message of knowledge by the same Spirit, to another faith by the same Spirit, to another gifts of healing by that one Spirit, to another the working of miracles, to another prophecy, to another distinguishing between spirits, to another speaking in various tongues, and to still another the interpretation of tongues. All these are the work of one and the same Spirit, who apportions them to each one as He determines.*
> 1 Corinthians 12: 7-11

That said, both Paul and Jesus emphasized that without love, without sensitivity to God's idea of the common good, the Holy Spirit's gifts were worthless. Every gift can be misused and counterfeited. Jesus does not know us by our gifts, but by our love. When the Holy Spirit gives gifts to us, he may not take them back, but whether we choose to use them for ourselves or for the glory of God is up to us. That may be one reason tongues are suspect.

God's gifts and His call are irrevocable. Romans 11:29

Some translations say, *God's gifts and call are without repentance.* That means God doesn't change his mind. He does not take away his gifts when Christians backslide or use them for selfish purposes. Many top-notch salesmen have God-given gifts of evangelism. The Holy Spirit's gifts can be used for our own glory and purposes or for God's. It is up to us. All that God asks of us is love and its fruit. And God's love gives us freedom to choose.

Jesus and the writers of the New Testament repeatedly remind us that Christians would be known by their character, by their moral goodness and love for one another, not by their gifts.

> *But the fruit of the Spirit is love, joy, peace, patience, kindness, goodness, faithfulness, gentleness, and self-control. Against such things there is no law. Galatians 5:22-23*

In the last six months, two clearly anointed high profile well-respected Christian leaders have made the news because of moral failure—one because of greed, another because of sexual immorality. Their ministries began in humility and conformity to God's word. Perhaps they became prideful because of their fame. When they began to compromise God's standards, he did not take away their gifts, both continued to teach God's word, but I wonder if Jesus knew them.

> *For of this you can be sure: No immoral, impure, or greedy person (that is, an idolater), has any inheritance in the kingdom of Christ and of God. Ephesians 5:6*
>
> *Not everyone who says to Me, 'Lord, Lord,' will enter the kingdom of heaven, but only he who does the will of My Father in heaven. Many will say to Me on that day, 'Lord, Lord, did we not prophesy in Your name, and in Your name drive out demons and perform many miracles?'*
>
> *Then I will tell them plainly, 'I never knew you; depart from Me, you workers of lawlessness! Matthew 7: 21-23*

Scriptures repeatedly warn us to test the spirits. How do we know when they need testing? How do we learn to discern the Holy Spirit of

God from false spirits, like the spirit guides and ascended masters of occult religions? How do we discern error not only in others but in our own hearts and minds? We begin by internalizing God's written word and doing our best to obey it. According to Scripture, testing spirits is very simple.

> *Beloved, do not believe every spirit, but test the spirits to see whether they are from God. For many false prophets have gone out into the world. By this you will know the Spirit of God: Every spirit that confesses that Jesus Christ has come in the flesh is from God, and every spirit that does not confess Jesus is not from God. This is the spirit of the antichrist, which you have heard is coming and which is already in the world at this time. 1 John 4:1-3*

Following God's word, simply ask the spirit where it comes from and who it serves. Ask it to confess that Jesus Christ has come to earth in the flesh. God's servant-messengers gladly confess that they serve Jesus Christ; demonic spirits will not confess serving Jesus as their Lord and Master. They cannot say that he came to earth in the flesh. Many pseudo-Christians believe in a christ-spirit, but refuse to acknowledge Jesus came in the flesh as God.

Discernment is a gift that grows with practice. It may take time to learn when the spirits need testing and to sort out the difference between demonic counterfeit voices and impressions and our own soulish intuitions, imaginations and opinions. But the Holy Spirit patiently teaches us by our own mistakes. I'm still learning. I made mistakes in my early drafts of this manuscript by misapplying a few scriptures and occasionally letting my imagination run with ideas not supported by God's word. Fortunately, the Holy Spirit cared enough about my desire to be faithful to his word to come alongside and help me. The comments and questions of kind friends sent me back to the Bible and other source material again and again to clarify, correct and refine. The writer of Hebrews offers a few clues when he writes that Jesus *"learned obedience."* I wish that writer had written more—he didn't fill in enough blanks for me before he went on to say,

> *We have much to say about this, but it is hard to explain, because you are dull of hearing. Although by this time you ought to be teachers, you need someone to reteach you the basic principles of God's word. You need milk, not solid food! For everyone who lives on milk is still an infant, inexperienced in the message of righteousness. But solid food is for the mature, who by constant use have trained their senses to distinguish good from evil. Hebrews 5: 11-14*

My take-home from this text was learning that we Christians must train our senses by constant use. We learn to discern.[185] Learning usually means making a few mistakes along the way. Let me give you an example. Believers raised in loving, God-fearing families or believers who come to God under strong conviction of sin and thorough repentance at salvation, are often so clean that the Holy Spirit will baptize them with himself and fill them with God's light quickly and easily, as soon as they ask. That wasn't my history. Despite my early experiences with God and youthful conversion to faith in Jesus, I was a mixed bag. My sincere faith in Jesus was riddled with worldly ideas, impurities and false teaching. I grew up in a culturally Christian home. My parents came to faith in Jesus later in life, and I came to faith in Jesus without any strong conviction

---

[185] For solid teaching on discernment, see *The Discerner* by James Goll, Whittaker House, 2017. Goll's teaching helps readers recognize, understand and evaluate easily overlooked impressions by referring them to the Word of God.

of sin and repentance. Perhaps that's why my own first experience in asking for more of the Holy Spirit was dark. I expected his light to fill me. It didn't. The Holy Spirit fills clean containers; I was an unclean vessel.

I was like a dimmer switch with a long slow turn before the light gradually increased. I don't recall all his early rays of light, but I sure remember when I became intentional about asking for more because I got a counterfeit. It's an embarrassing truth, but it's important enough to share. It was in the early 1970's, maybe '72 or '73. I'd begun to attend Friday night house meeting with the Community of Hope, a small, local Catholic charismatic group.

At the time, I knew Jesus lived in my heart. I knew he'd delivered me from death. I knew I was a child of God, but I lacked the love, peace, faith, hope and joy of my Catholic brothers and sisters in Christ, and I wanted it. Most of them testified to being "baptized in the Holy Spirit," and from time to time, in the meetings, many of them would speak, pray and sing in tongues. It seemed like the "more" of God and Jesus that I wanted.

Someone in the group gave me a book about the baptism in the Holy Spirit and speaking in tongues and suggested I read it. One morning, when all my children were in school and I was tidying up the house, I stopped for a moment, picked up the book and read the page with steps about how to ask the Lord for the Holy Spirit and the gift of tongues. I remember kneeling on the dark blue-green rug in the children's bedroom with the book before me and carefully praying through every step the author outlined. Wham-o! Instantly I began speaking in another language and was lifted into the most ecstatic experience of worship in my thirty-two or three-year-old life.

But I wasn't worshipping God or Jesus. I knew it clearly. I was worshipping the sun god, Ra. I knew that clearly too. It was weird. When the almost compelling ecstasy ended, I was shaken. I didn't know what

Appendix 3: Spirit Baptism

had happened to me. I didn't like it; it didn't feel clean and I became quite cautious about speaking in tongues. I didn't give up the idea completely, and guarding myself from false worship, I continued to seek God by attending meetings, reading my Bible and occasionally, cautiously, speaking in tongues. I never worshipped Ra again, and the first tongue didn't return, but the new tongues didn't do much for me. I'd no sense of drawing nearer to God or talking with him. One night, praying in this guarded way, I felt the Holy Spirit's peace with a thought in my heart that said, "Don't speak in that tongue any more, speak in this one." New words came, and I spoke them. My new tongue was like fresh water in a dirty pool. Somehow, I knew it was God's Holy Spirit.

God didn't explain my initial experience to me right away, but eventually, I got enough understanding to make sense of it. The insight came in pieces.

The first piece was learning that glossolalia, or speaking in tongues, is not an exclusively Christian experience. Tongues are a human phenomenon; they can come from our own spirit, from demonic spirits or from the Holy Spirit. It takes discernment to know if tongues or prophetic words are from God, from a human source or from a darker ungodly source.[186]

The second piece came when I learned that Pentecostal missionaries serving in nations where new converts were steeped in pagan occultism are not hasty to ask God to fill baby Christians with the Holy Spirit. Because the Holy Spirit will only indwell clean believers, it's essential for new converts to repent and get deliverance from pagan and occult spirits before asking God to baptize them with more of the Holy Spirit. We all need cleaning up at the laver (initially and daily) before moving into the inner court.

---

186 This is why Scripture tells us to judge prophecy and prophets. "Prophecies" that condemn, reject, boast or predict what humans selfishly desire can wound and lead believers astray. Every prophetic word is to be measured by the love of Jesus Christ and Scripture.

THE TABERNACLE

The third piece was filled in for me by a story told by a Pentecostal missionary pastor to illustrate the human spirit. Two women in a Pentecostal denomination would regularly contribute to their Sunday morning service, one with a message in tongues and the other with the interpretation. One Sunday, the woman who spoke in tongues stood up as usual and delivered a message in tongues to the congregation. But the other woman did not stand up to interpret the message. The pastor asked, "Is there any interpretation?" No one spoke. After an awkward time, the service went on. The message in tongues was left hanging, uninterpreted. After the meeting the tongues woman sought out the interpreter woman and said, "What was wrong? Why didn't you interpret the message?" The interpreter woman replied, "You were chewing out your husband in tongues about a disagreement you'd had this morning." Red faced, the tongues woman confessed they'd had a major disagreement before church and had come into the worship service without resolving it.

Now, how did putting these pieces together explain my first experiences of speaking in tongues? As a high school girl, I'd been fascinated by one of my dad's books called *The Great Pyramid Proof of God*. I poured over it. The information about the pyramid was fascinating, but something about my interest was off. I got interested in the Egyptian monotheism of Akhenaten's worship of the sun god, Ra. It glittered. I thought that was—what was the word in the 1950's?—"A big deal!" for a pharaoh to come up with monotheism on his own. I admired him. But all that glitters is not gold! Looking back, I realized that a sliver of admiration, a bit of spiritual deception about Ra had slipped under my skin and waited silently in my spirit, unknown, until I wanted to worship God. Then Ra popped up as if to say, "No. I've got some ground inside of you. I'll have you worship me." Yuck. I repented of false worship immediately and knew I'd been forgiven and set free from any spirit luring me, tempting to induce me to false worship.

I believe that the experimental guarded tongues I prayed in were most likely true glossolalia, but the source was from my own spirit, not the Holy Spirit. Sadly, that wasn't the last time I prayed in tongues that were not from God. I clearly remember when a dearly loved family member was being repeatedly hurt by another person. One evening, beside myself with anger, I poured out all my human emotion into a flood of tongues. I was so pridefully opinionated in my anger, so far from the love, forgiveness and mercy of God that I'm sure the Holy Spirit was not speaking through me that night!

When the Holy Spirit speaks through us in tongues, it is never to release our own wrath and anger, it is to praise God and/or to intercede according to his mind and to bring us into agreement with heavenly plans. The Holy Spirit will pray through us in tongues to strengthen our own spirits and to intercede to God's purposes. Our prayer and praise in tongues will glorify God and reveal Jesus. The gift of tongues from the Holy Spirit will always turn us to Jesus and bless others with something of his love.

Since my Catholic charismatic brothers and sisters in the 1970's all spoke in tongues, I initially saw tongues as "the" outward sign of the Holy Spirit's baptism. Looking back, I can see that the inward change in our lives was far greater and more profound than the outward sign of speaking in tongues. Perhaps the greatest sign of the Holy Spirit's increase in believers is their hunger for and understanding of God's word. Although my authentic Holy Spirit baptism was quiet, low-key and very slow to come, the inner change was real. I suddenly began to love God's word. I took my Bible everywhere. I read it often. It began to make sense to me.

Although some denominations assert that speaking in tongues is essential to Holy Spirit baptism, I don't find that exclusivity anywhere in the word of God. When Oswald Chambers asked for the baptism in the Holy Spirit, nothing happened, but Chambers later wrote that he received the Holy Spirit by faith. Before that hour, few if any listeners ever responded to the altar calls he gave when preaching and teaching. After that, the Holy Spirit moved on listeners to Chambers in such conviction and persuasive power that many came to know the Lord.

All this is important. We need the Holy Spirit and Jesus knew it. We need divine power. Since the 1940's occultism has increased in the United States. Anger is on the rise. Intellectuals tell us that western civilization is no longer Christian. Biblical literacy is at a low ebb. Increasing immorality predicts the downfall of our civilization.[187] Believers need all of the Holy Spirit's gifts and graces, all of his wisdom, teaching, guidance, comfort and power to keep our watch for the Lord.

We need the Holy Spirit's gift of discernment. As I write this, I wonder about the first time I spoke in tongues. What might have happened if I hadn't been born again? Would worshipping Ra have felt okay? Without the Holy Spirit, would I have known that something about my initial experience was off? I don't think so. Would I have cared? Most likely not. I thank God for the Holy Spirit's discernment. Whether I was consciously sensitive to him or not, he lived in my heart. Without his discernment, what might have happened next? I'll never know.

Counterfeits are a sign that an authentic thing exists. If a friend offered to give you a gold pin or a diamond, would you reject it as false because some deceptive imposter once passed off a piece of fake costume jewelry on you as real? I hope not. No one wants to be taken-in twice, but if we surrender to our fears, build defensive walls and refuse to risk the courage of forgiveness and the possibility of authentic love and truth, we sadly our ability to receive from God. It's sad when sincere believers reject Jesus's command to seek more of the Holy Spirit.

---

[187] See Kirk Durston's clear and easy to grasp summary of J.D. Unwin's research on patterns of human culture. Why Sexual Morality May be More Important than You Ever Thought. https://www.kirkdurston.com/blog/unwin

God wants to fill us with his Holy Spirit. He wants to illuminate our lives and fill temple of our hearts, with his light alone. His light is real. It's genuine, clear and penetrating. Jesus and the saints through all the ages have testified to the glory of God in human flesh. Lord, may we be like those one hundred and twenty who heard Jesus and went to the upper room and sought the Holy Spirit's light until he came.

Jesus still speaks to us through his word and today, telling us to

> *Ask, and it will be given to you; seek, and you will find; knock, and the door will be opened to you. For everyone who asks receives; he who seeks finds; and to him who knocks, the door will be opened.*
>
> *What father among you, if his son asks for a fish, will give him a snake instead? Or if he asks for an egg, will give him a scorpion? So if you who are evil know how to give good gifts to your children, how much more will your Father in heaven give the Holy Spirit to those who ask him!" Luke 11: 9-13*

APPENDIX 4:
ABIDING

Here's a bit of reflection on abiding in Jesus. Abiding can be very practical. It is no ivory tower, head in the clouds experience. Seeking to abide in communion with Jesus I often sense him urging me to wash the dishes sooner rather than later. Sometimes he directs my errands. One morning in intense heat, I needed to go to the post office, but felt no peace—no abiding in Jesus. In mid-afternoon, peace came, so I set out. Almost immediately, dark clouds covered the hot sun. A sudden summer storm blew up, and the temperature dropped quickly. I finished my errand in shade and comfort. As I pulled into my drive, the sun broke out again, the intense muggy heat returned. That's a little thing—but how loved I felt.

While the Holy Spirit generally guides me by peace, at times he indicates his will by withdrawing all awareness of his presence. I recently picked up a book I'd planned to read. The new information held me, but a few pages into it, my head began to ache; a few pages later, the headache was worse. I stopped reading and asked, "What's going on here?" His presence was gone. I closed the book and asked for forgiveness.

How do I know he's leading? I don't always. I make mistakes. But God has many ways of indicating his ways. He speaks to us most clearly and safely through the Bible. Recently, he's been talking with me through scriptures about not being afraid of change. He speaks to us by inner peace, answered prayers, counsel from others, circumstances, grace and an unusual (for us) willingness to step out and try the water. Often, he speaks to us through thoughts that settle into our souls over a long stretch of time and grow in strength or certainty. At times he speaks to us through words that come out of our own mouths. Once, years ago, I desperately wanted to go in one life-direction, but whenever a friend asked my plans, words indicating another direction (that later proved to be wise) came up from my heart and out of my mouth. The Lord also speaks to me through my writing and by a still small voice within. Many believers find guidance in their dreams. He speaks to all of us through our brothers and sisters in faith and anointed teaching and preaching.

Three times, I heard Jesus speak to me in person. Once, when I was ill, he stood at the foot of my bed and simply said, "Rest." Following the Holy Spirit, has led me into huge life changing choices, like changing jobs, getting therapy for inner healing, going back to school in my fifties, and caretaking my mother. At the age of sixty, by God's leading, I remarried my husband after thirty-years apart. At an age when many women might retire, still trying to follow God's lead, I began two unsuccessful publishing companies and followed his Holy Spirit as best I could when he led me out of publishing. Then, still trying to follow him, I self-published a couple unsuccessful books of my own and started a webpage. As the song declares, "Through it all, I've learned to trust in Jesus, I've learned to trust in God." I believe that many (not all) of my earthly failures are God's heavenly success stories—in influencing others and teaching me.

My list of God's leadings is all outer stuff—abiding is internal. Abiding takes "doing the work"—practicing the steps—not taking offense at misunderstanding or abuse, forgiving those who hurt us, asking for God's mercy and conviction on those who attack, deceive and betray us, letting go of resentments, repenting of all hardness of heart and getting up when we fall down. This is the big stuff.

When the Holy Spirit shows us a direction (or reveals a sin), whether it's a biggie or a sliver, acting on his input leads us to a moment that fulfills Jesus's prayer, "Thy kingdom come; Thy will be done on earth." Ignoring his direction —well, only he knows, the consequences can vary. Our "Yes" will bring eternal fruit. Lord teach us to abide in you.

> *The anointing which you have received from Him [the Holy Spirit] abides in you, and you do not need that anyone teach you; but as the same anointing teaches you concerning all things, and is true, and is not a lie, and just as it has taught you, you will abide in Him. 1 John 2: 27 NKJV*

APPENDIX 5:
THE STONE TABLETS

If you recall Exodus history, God gave his people four tablets of stone. The first two Moses received from God on Mount Sinai.

> *When the LORD had finished speaking with Moses on Mount Sinai, He gave him the two tablets of the Testimony, tablets of stone inscribed by the finger of God.*
> *Exodus 31:18*

You can find the whole fascinating story in Exodus 31. When Moses spent forty days on the mountain top with God, the people grew impatient. They asked Aaron to make them gods to go before them. So, Aaron collected all their golden earrings and molded a golden calf to worship. God was so angry with their idolatry that he wanted to destroy the people and make a great nation from Moses's family instead. But Moses interceded for the people and God relented. Then, when Moses came down from the mountain, tablets in hand, and

> *. . . approached the camp and saw the calf and the dancing, he burned with anger and threw the tablets out of his hands, shattering them at the base of the mountain.*
> *Exodus 32:19*

Moses smashed the first two tablets. He was angry because these former slaves refused to worship the all-powerful, invisible God who had set them free from slavery and delivered them from the idols of Egypt to worship him. They wanted to worship a tangible thing, a statue. They saw the golden calf, bowed down before it, and feasted around it. They chose the pleasure of stirred-up emotional worship rather than the humbling of God-given spiritual worship.

Have people changed? I think not. So many of us are still wanting false gods to grasp with our senses, we're still idolizing ourselves and our pleasures and lifting our own thoughts above God's revelation. We are like our first parents, Adam and Eve, who chose pleasure, independence and knowledge over loving obedience. Lord, we have sinned. We and our parents. Have mercy on us and turn us to you.

Our 21st century temptations have not changed. The human race still wants to seek and worship visible gods. Some of our gods are supported by scientific double-blind studies, others by popularity polls and review ratings or good media coverage. They are immanent gods of our own choice. These Israelites were so blind that despite the miracles in Egypt, the amazing parting of the Red Sea and the visible presence of God on the mountain top, they gave the golden calf credit for bringing them out of Egypt. They were stuck in a lifeless paradigm and choose to give credit to what they could see, touch and manipulate themselves. Their own thinking had blinded them to the invisible hand of God behind the miracles that had set them free from bondage.

How history repeats itself! Way back in the Garden of Eden, the woman saw the apple, something she could hold and taste. She wanted to know the pleasure of its taste. By her own free choice, her earthly desire overcame her love for God. Similarly, the lure of materialism tempts so many of us today.

Lord, help us. Moses wrote your word on a second set of tablets. Then you wrote your word on Jesus's heart, giving all mankind another chance. Now, today, write the truth of your loving law upon our hearts. Now today may our love for you overcome all other desires.

APPENDIX 6:
FAITH

Christians receive the Holy Spirit and God's love by faith. Satanists receive demonic directions by faith. Hitler had faith in the inner voice directing him. Misplaced faith eventually deceives and disappoints. Faith in God's truth fulfills. Both intellectual belief and presumption, often mistaken for faith, usually fail. It matters greatly whom or what we choose to believe. But even if we're believing the right thing, a belief that only gives mental assent to something is not the gift of faith from God. Maybe that's why Jesus put the warning about false prophets right after he admonished his disciples:

> *Enter through the narrow gate. For wide is the gate and broad is the way that leads to destruction, and many enter through it. But small is the gate and narrow the way that leads to life, and only a few find it. Beware of false prophets. They come to you in sheep's clothing, but inwardly they are ravenous wolves. Matthew 7:13-15*

Scientists who postulate the existence of multiple dimensions are catching onto a truth that believers have known by experience and the power of the Holy Spirit for centuries. The first Bible mention of an angel, a being from another dimension, is in Genesis 16. The angel of the Lord visited Hagar in the desert, Lot at Sodom, Abraham at Mt. Moriah and Jacob, as he dreamt of angels climbing up and down a ladder to heaven. They, and everyone visited by an angel, knows that there are more dimensions than our own. Current scientific verification of other dimensions might help doubters to open their minds to consider the possibility that heaven, the place of God's rule, might actually exist as a real spiritual realm or supra-dimension governed by faith. But believing in the possibility of a spiritual place isn't the same as faith to get there.

Christian experience, near-death experiences and scripture all point toward the reality of a realm beyond our own, a reality that exists either in another dimension or outside of all possible dimensions. Miracles from this realm, including the miracle of being born again by the Holy Spirit, are events that appear to supersede or break natural laws. They testify to the spiritual reality of this realm of faith.

Think about it. A faith realm, ruled by God, co-existing with our material world could never be proven, for then it wouldn't be faith. Modern science, which is often cited as the foundation for unbelief, strongly supports belief,[188] but all the proof and documentation in the world can't produce faith. Christian faith is a gift of God. This faith has power, it can move mountains. God doesn't want us trying to toss literal mountains around, so, it seems to me that he limits the gift of faith. Although he gives faith in proportion to our asking, he will give us no more than our characters can handle. But, when we agree with him, he will always give us enough faith to do everything that he wants us to do. Then, because he loves us so much, quite often he answers requests far beyond our faith level—for no other reason than our asking him. Aren't God's contradictions and mysteries delightful?

---

188 Once again, I strongly recommend reading *Is Atheism Dead* by Eric Metaxas. It's a well-documented easy-to-read summary of scientific, archeological and logical proofs that all point to God. Salem Books, 2021

APPENDIX 7:
WORSHIP

A brief journal of random thoughts on worship

In Genesis, when Abraham worshipped God, God drew near and made a covenant with him. In Exodus, God freed the Hebrew slaves so that they might worship him. In the New Testament Jesus told the Samaritan woman

> *But a time is coming and has now come when the true worshipers will worship the Father in spirit and in truth, for the Father is seeking such as these to worship him. God is Spirit, and His worshipers must worship him in spirit and in truth. John 4:23-24*

Human beings are born worshippers. As a child, I worshipped my parents. Mom and Dad took center stage in my life. Not in any profound, satisfying or transcendent spiritual sense, but I looked up to them, depended on them, and most of life was all about pleasing them and earning their favor. As I grew, other idols—other people, other interests and always an undercurrent of the worldly values of popularity, intelligence, success, money, beauty and fame vied to rule my affections. After coming to faith in Jesus I instinctively knew that only God is truly worthy of worship. Only as I worship him in Spirit and truth can I ever experience the transcendent joy of true holy adoration. This fuller capacity to worship God in Spirit and truth was given (or bought for us) by the blood of Jesus. He died to free us from shallow and false worship and captivity to idols. Our heavenly Father gives us the Holy Spirit, so that we might worship in Spirit and truth. The Holy Spirit saves us, cleanses us and lives in us to worship the Father and the Son. Worship flows from the grateful obedience of love; it is not a sideline. It's the main route to God himself, a journey that begins when we first turn to God in faith and continues as we learn to express our love in thanksgiving and praise.

True worship can be kindled by God's fire alone. Our emotions are not the fire of God's Holy Spirit; his fire burns up our emotions and purifies our human efforts to please him. We must never forget that the Holy Spirit's cleansing fire within our hearts is ours at the cost of Jesus' life, for

> ... *without the shedding of blood there is no forgiveness [of sin]. Hebrews 9:22*

Cain and Abel's story in Genesis 4 foreshadows this truth. God respected Abel's sacrifice of a lamb, symbolic of Jesus. But he did not respect Cain's offering of the fruit of the ground because it was produced by human effort from the ground that God had cursed.

The consistency of these ancient prophetic stories amazes me. They are, for me, more clear evidence of God's foreknowledge and historical plan. They anticipate and help explain God's willingness to sacrifice his only beloved Son. They reveal his purposeful, determined desire to prepare a bride for Jesus and to have a family, a holy people who will love him and receive his love in return. He longs for children who are filled with his own Holy Spirit. He wants a clean, healthy, humble, teachable, tenderhearted family, one free of all worldly illusion and hardness. God wants to Father a people who will center their lives around him and depend on him. He wants us to center our lives around him as I once, as a trusting child, centered my life around my mommy and daddy. God wants to guide us into strong, confident, vibrant maturity in Christ Jesus. He wants his family to carry and honor his name, to worship him with loving hearts and serve him by the power of his own indwelling Spirit.

He wants us to love our brothers and sisters in faith and to honor and serve one another as we join Jesus in union with our heavenly Father.

Only the Holy Spirit can bring this about. He alone reveals Jesus and the Father. He alone can bring us into the holiness we need to love God and live in the obedience of faith. He yearns for our surrender because he knows that without him we cannot and will not do anything of eternal worth. It humbles me to realize that the golden altar of incense looks ahead to John the Baptist's prediction that

> *He [Jesus] will baptize you with the Holy Spirit and fire.*
> *Matthew 3:11b NKJV*

Jesus was bluntly clear about this. When he told his disciples that he was going to die to send them (and us) the fire of the Holy Spirit, he was soberly intentional. He understood God's holiness, he knew his own longing for a holy bride. He understood his Father's longing for a holy family. In love with the Father and us, Jesus told His disciples,

> *But I tell you the truth, it is for your benefit that I am going away. Unless I go away, the Advocate [that is, the Holy Spirit] will not come to you; but if I go, I will send him to you. John 16:7*

Despite Jesus's words and their own prayers and faith in Jesus's predictions, his disciples were astounded when the Holy Spirit came as a rushing wind with visible flames of fire on the day of Pentecost.

> *They saw tongues like flames of fire that separated and came to rest on each of them. And they were all filled with the Holy Spirit . . . Acts 2:3-4a*

And the same dear Holy Spirit fills you and me today to lift us in worship to God in Spirit and in truth.

Appendix 7: Worship

Occasionally, the Holy Spirit may give young believers unusual supernatural revelations of God's love. His Spirit may draw them into ardent worship. But for most of us, getting clean, changing our old thought patterns and habits into Godly ones that agree with his word is a process. We learn to hear and heed the Holy Spirit. Keeping our focus on Jesus, we will follow the progression pictured by the tabernacle. It may take time, humbling, and repeated cleansings, breakings, confessions and repentance, but the Holy Spirit will be with us. He guides us and teaches us God's ways. He comforts us in sorrow and strengthens us in our weakness. He heals our wounds, washes away our filth, delivers us from our hang-ups, demolishes our strongholds and fills every cleansed area of our souls with holy life and love.

Initially, as young believers in the outer court, we may want God to meet our own needs. We don't think of his desires for our worship. But as a wise and loving Father, he most often answers our prayers. As zealous, grateful, growing believers, we may get sidetracked and distracted from worship by the outer court activities, by doing things for God, by working for him rather than letting him work in and through us. Maturing believers (and age has nothing to do with spiritual maturity—I've met teens who are closer to the Lord than I've been) don't seek answers for themselves but are so in love with God and Jesus that they long to worship him. They seek to pray God's prayers and live to please him alone. Lord, live in us and help us live in you.

> *For none of us lives to himself, and no one dies to himself. For if we live, we live to the Lord; and if we die, we die to the Lord. Therefore, whether we live or die, we are the Lord's. Romans 13:8-9 NKJV*

Maranatha!

Come, Lord, it's time,
Your glory we'd sing.
Come, touch your fire
to the offerings we bring.

Touch us with love
to burn all our chaff.
Come, Lord, it's time,
Your glory we'd sing.

Your glory we'd see,
Your glory we'd be.
Come, Lord, it's time
for you to touch me.

Come, Lamb of God,
come quickly, it's time.
Revive us according
to holy design.

Come, Lord, come here.
Come, Lord, it's time.
Prepare us to meet You.
It's time, Lord, it's time.

ABOUT THE AUTHOR

Borrowing from Jacob, I can say that my years seem few and many of them hard. My path has taken many turns. Through it all, I've learned that God loves me. In every challenge, I've found sustaining grace. Each day is another opportunity to receive God's mercy and learn to love.

If you want to know more, you'll find many stories from my life in this book. For still more, check out my website, givenwordnow.com

This book doesn't stand or fall on my writing skill or my journey, education, interests, connections or endorsements. It is valuable only if the Holy Spirit chooses to breathe life on a few of its words and speak to you.

Made in the USA
Monee, IL
02 July 2022